THE HOUSE OF LORDS

THE HOUSE OF LORDS

Second Edition

DONALD SHELL

University of Bristol

New York   London   Toronto   Sydney   Tokyo   Singapore

First published 1992 by
Harvester Wheatsheaf
Campus 400, Maylands Avenue
Hemel Hempstead
Hertfordshire, HP2 7EZ
A division of
Simon & Schuster International Group

Typeset in 10 pt Baskerville
by Photoprint, Torquay

Printed and bound in Great Britain by
Antony Rowe Ltd, Chippenham, Wiltshire

British Library Cataloguing in Publication Data

Shell, Donald
    The House of Lords. – 2nd ed.
    I. Title
    328.41

    ISBN 0–7450–1201–9
    ISBN 0–7450–1202–7 pbk

    2 3 4 5   96 95

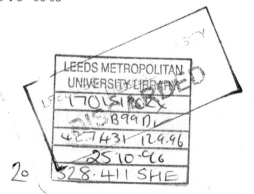

Contents

Contents

Tables and Figure

Preface

The House of Lords is a paradox. Predictions of its decay and collapse have been made frequently for over a hundred years, yet it not only survives, but appears to be in rather rude good health. Popular mythology has viewed the House as troublesome to Labour but co-operative to the Conservatives. Yet during the mid 1980s the House was widely described as more effective than the Commons in obliging the Thatcher Government to adjust and modify its legislation. As long ago as 1911 the preamble to the Parliament Act clearly embodied the widely held expectation that the House would soon be subject to comprehensive reform, indeed replacement. But the eighty years since have seen no such change. Late twentieth-century Britain retains a 'House of Lords' which is still, as far as nominal membership is concerned, composed predominantly of hereditary members.

Schemes for reform of the House have regularly been brought forward, but no substantial agreement about an alternative House has yet been attained. In default of this, the present House remains. Yet it is by no means an unchanged House. Throughout the past thirty years, ever since the 1958 Life Peerages Act, the activity of the House has steadily increased. Procedural adaptation and innovation have occurred. The party balance has shifted, and the character of the active membership has altered. This book seeks to describe, analyse and evaluate these facts. Who are the active members? How pronounced is the role of party within the House? What influence does the House have within the whole business of government? What changes have taken place within the House, and what further changes are contemplated? Such questions as these are the focus of this book. The possible reform of the House, or the implications of its removal, are not entirely overlooked, but these matters are considered incidentally rather than as the major theme.

This is neither a historical nor a comparative study. The introductory chapter briefly considers the 'bicameral' (or two-chamber) principle and glances back at the development of the British Parliament. But this is really only to set the scene, as it were. The reader who wants to know more about the history of Parliament, or the comparative study of parliaments or second chambers, must be directed elsewhere.

Not since Professor Peter Bromhead's book *The House of Lords and Contemporary Politics* appeared in 1958 has a work similar in scope to this been published. Janet Morgan's *The House of Lords and the Labour Government 1964–70* provided an excellent discussion of the attempt to reform the House in 1968–9, and ably set this in the context of an analysis of the work of the House in that period. But the period since then has seen no publication of a systematic study of the House. Undergraduates studying British politics, as well as all who teach the subject at various levels, will, I hope, benefit from this book. Those who work in and around Westminster, in Parliament, government or journalism – and want to develop a clearer understanding of the House of Lords – will also, I trust, find this work of some value.

The main sources for this book are listed on pp. 266–7. Comparatively few scholars have conducted research on the contemporary House of Lords, but those sources have been culled in the preparation of this work. I have over a number of years tried to keep a close eye on the House, and have frequently researched various aspects of its activities, and this study does of course draw on that work. I am indebted to many peers who over the years have given time to answer my questions and have furthered my understanding of the House. Several clerks have also been kind and generous in sharing with me their knowledge and insight concerning the House, as have a number of academic colleagues, particularly fellow members of the Study of Parliament Group. Particular mention must be made of David Beamish, now Establishment Officer in the House of Lords, and Gavin Drewry, now Professor of Public Administration at the University of London, both of whom read and commented on the manuscript for the first edition of this book. Their help has been of great value, both in prompting attention to matters overlooked and in enabling me to avoid errors. I am also grateful for comments on the first edition received from Dr Tony Barker, Dr Robert Borthwick, Professor Stephen Cretney and Dr Philippa Tudor.

For the second edition of this book, revision has been made in general up to June 1991. This has involved alterations to every chapter, though some much more extensively than others. In many different ways – some trivial, others important – the role of the House does change from Parliament to Parliament. The revised edition reflects the significant changes since 1987, among which – so it is argued here – has been the apparent hardening of the Government's attitude to the House since 1987.

Donald Shell
Bristol
August 1991

1

The House of Lords and Constitutional Development

Parliaments are frequently classified according to the number of chambers they possess. Those with a single chamber are termed unicameral, and those with two chambers bicameral. Most countries which have recognisable legislatures have unicameral bodies. But if attention is focused on liberal democracies, most are bicameral, and the minority with one-chamber legislatures are without exception comparatively small in population. They include a number whose switch from bicameralism to unicameralism has been made in the post-war era – for example New Zealand in 1950, Denmark in 1953, and Sweden in 1973, none of which has a population above ten million. We may generalise by saying that all large liberal democratic countries continue to have bicameral legislatures and that elsewhere bicameralism remains by no means uncommon, especially in liberal democracies. Why is this?

Bicameralism

The underlying justifications for bicameralism have changed as prevailing ideas about legitimate forms of government have altered. In the pre-democratic period parliamentary assemblies were generally two-chamber because this reflected the view that some sort of separate representation for aristocrats, or 'elders', or people of property, must be provided. As the acceptability of such notions of distinct class-based representation diminished, so the language in which second chambers were justified tended to alter. Instead of recognising the desirability of providing distinct representation for aristocracy and property, the need for a body to provide some restraint upon directly elected popular chambers came to be

1

emphasised. J.S. Mill spoke of the corrupting influence of undivided power. Others argued that a second chamber was desirable in order to impose delay upon what a first chamber might rashly decide. For some this became a defence of second chambers grounded in the principles of democracy itself, as entailing the overriding importance of a popular will. In 1918 the Bryce Commission justified the retention by the House of Lords of a power to delay legislation so as 'to enable the opinion of the nation to be adequately expressed'. Second chambers were considered desirable to limit potential excesses of first chambers and to ensure that they did not run too far ahead of public opinion.

But the argument for delay was never securely based. As democratic values became more widely accepted, it was an argument which lost credibility. A directly elected first chamber was always likely to be more sensitive to public opinion, and a more faithful interpreter of that opinion, than a second chamber constituted by appointment, heredity, or even indirect election. In more recent years the justification for second chambers based on a delaying power has tended to give way to a justification based on the need to revise legislation after it has been dealt with by the first chamber. The greater complexity of legislation is frequently cited in support of this view. The need for a different kind of body to have a 'second look' at legislation, quite distinct from the examination given to it by the first chamber, is stressed. To do this properly, or at least to ensure that whatever alterations proposed by the second chamber are taken seriously by the first, it may be necessary to retain a power to delay. But it is less a delay intended to enable public opinion to be expressed than a delay intended to oblige genuine attention to be given by the Government and Lower House to changes proposed by the second chamber.

If one theme in contemporary discussion about second chambers is the need for bodies capable of revising legislation, another is their value in providing 'checks and balances' within a constitution. This is not so much a matter of delaying controversial legislation passed by a first chamber as of providing a means by which a first chamber acting alone can be prevented from carrying through changes which are thought to have important constitutional implications. This may be particularly well illustrated in relation to federal systems, which provide an obvious rationale for second chambers. This rationale may be said to have been invented by the founding fathers of the

USA, even if it was by no means the only reason why a bicameral structure was preferred at the Philadelphia Convention. Almost without exception, wherever a federal system has been embodied, a bicameral national legislature has been established. Second chambers are a convenience in such situations: they can be composed in such a way as to provide a measure of reassurance to the constituent parts of a federation, and they can be given powers to fulfil the same purpose.

In practice, of course, they may scarcely fulfil this role. The German Bundesrat consists of members appointed by the Länder (or State) governments, and its functions are closely related to the federal structure in regard to which its formal powers are actually superior to those of the Bundestag. But in other matters its powers are very weak, and in political terms it has become a very marginal body. The Canadian Senate represents the provinces in a formal sense, but unevenly, with twenty-four members from both of the largest two provinces and six members from each of the five smallest. In its activity, however, the Canadian Senate does not defend provincial interests; but neither has it any clear political role: rather, it has become a very quiescent, if not moribund, body. By contrast, the US Senate, the composition of which is also linked to the federal structure, with two senators per state irrespective of population, has become in political terms the senior House within Congress. And in its operation the US Senate has been by no means restricted to the role of defendant of states' rights (see Table 1.1).

If the role of providing 'checks and balances' within a constitution is most easily illustrated within federal systems, it is not necessarily confined to such systems. Second chambers frequently have particular powers in respect of ensuring the continuity of constitutional arrangements. Significantly, when the Parliament Act of 1911, limiting the powers of the House of Lords, was passed, an exception was made for any bill to extend the life of a Parliament. On such a measure the House of Lords retains an absolute veto. This is intended to ensure that the House of Commons does not have the sole power to postpone a general election beyond a five-year interval. Such postponement was possible in wartime (from 1940 to 1945), but only because both Houses agreed on the matter.

Second chambers, therefore, have diverse roles. They may help to safeguard the interests, even the integrity, of units within a federation. They may be of value because of their work in revising

Table 1.1 Second Chambers in Seven Democracies

Country	Date of constitution	Federal	Directly elected president	Size of upper house	Method of appointment to upper house	Length of term of upper house
USA	1787	Yes	Yes	100	Direct election by simple majority	6 years (⅓ re-elected every 2 years)
France	1958	No	Yes	319	Indirect election by electoral college	9 years (⅓ re-elected every 3 years)
Germany	1949	Yes	No	41 (plus 4 non-voting)	Appointed by Land governments	4 years
Italy	1948	No	No	315 (plus ex officio)	Direct election PR	5 years
Canada	1867	Yes	No	104	Appointed by Governor-General	To retirement at 75
Australia	1901	Yes	No	64	Direct election by STV	6 years (½ re-elected every 3 years)
Ireland	1937	No	No	60	Elected from electoral colleges and co-opted	5 years

the details of legislation. They may be a means by which checks and balances within a constitution can be maintained. In a more general and less easily definable way, they may afford points of access to government which help to keep the executive in a modern state responsive to the interests and needs of different sections of the community. Any or all of these factors may seem important within a particular country, and as the needs of state and society develop, so the functions of second chambers will change.

Wherever they exist, second chambers have invariably been subject to attack from the political left. The historical legacy they carry in the popular mind as being bodies representing propertied or aristocratic classes is one reason for this. But more modern arguments for second chambers, focusing on their restraining and revising roles or their responsibilities as constitutional watchdogs, do not endear them to the radically minded. Their composition, too, usually ensures that they contain a high proportion of senior public figures. The average age of their members is invariably greater than that of first chambers, and age and radicalism rarely combine. Second chambers, if elected at all, are usually elected less frequently and by less direct methods than first chambers. Not surprisingly, the principle of bicameralism finds less general support on the left than on the right in politics.

Wherever a bicameral legislature exists, there is the possibility of conflict between the two chambers. That this can be damaging to the interests of a society is not to be doubted, but it need not be so. After all, conflict is inherent in the whole political enterprise. The real need is for institutions to be arranged in such a way as to ensure that processes for conciliation exist. A bicameral legislature may be part of such a process. The oft-quoted remark of Sièyes that if the second chamber disagreed with the first it was obnoxious and that if it agreed it was superfluous may have a certain logic about it, but in real political life agreement and disagreement are rarely so clear-cut. Rather, there tend to be both formal rules and informal understandings that shape the pattern of relations between two chambers. For example, the primacy of first chambers in regard to finance and taxation is general. Where a cabinet system of government exists, with the executive responsible to Parliament in the sense of being removable by Parliament, it is necessary clearly to establish that responsibility is to one chamber rather than to both. The Australian crisis of 1975 arose because this principle was not clear; the

Australian Senate used its power to withhold supply in such a way as to bring about the downfall of the Whitlam Government at a time when that Government still retained the confidence of the Lower House (see Butler, 1976). In the USA the President is not responsible to either House of Congress, and differences between the two Houses, as well as differences between Congress and President, are resolved according to rules stipulated in the Constitution and by various conventions. In the UK, as the notion of government responsible to Parliament developed in the eighteenth century, it became established, though not without difficulty, that it was to the Commons and not to the Lords that governments were responsible.

Any discussion of the reasons underlying bicameralism runs the risk of implying a degree of deliberate self-conscious intent in the design of constitutions. This would be false to the reality of constitution-making. The UK may be a rather extreme case in this regard, but all constitutions which have survived for any length of time show signs of adaptation. The consequences of this are that particular institutions operate in practice in such a way as to belie, to some extent, their original purpose. It may well be argued that the retention of second chambers has more to do with inertia and the force of tradition than with any clear or widely accepted rationale. Second chambers exist because they always have existed. Where a second chamber is present, it requires a considerable act of political will to abolish such a body. Even where entirely new constitutional arrangements are introduced, as in Germany after the war or France in 1958, the continuation of a bicameral structure of some kind may be due largely to the force of tradition and the sense of what is appropriate for a legislature, feelings and sentiments derived from the past.

Apart from reasons of constitutional principle which may offer some justification for second chambers, a practical point of considerable importance may be that such bodies do afford membership, status, and offices to individuals whose aspirations in this regard need to be satisfied. (Significantly, the way to abolition of the Kenyan Senate in 1966 was eased by securing seats for all incumbent senators in an expanded lower house.) In Britain the House of Lords undoubtedly has a value in providing a dignified home for rather senior political figures who might otherwise, through their continued occupancy of Commons seats, block the entrance of new blood.

If the reasons underlying the widespread continuation of bicameralism are varied, so are the ways in which second chambers are composed. Most are elected, but frequently election is indirect and may effectively amount to nomination. The German Bundesrat has forty-one voting members, who are members of the Länder (or State) Cabinets. Where election to a second chamber is direct, this is usually from larger units and for longer terms than is the case for the lower house. In the USA senators are elected for six-year terms, with partial re-election every two years. An implication of senior status is hard to resist, even if formally the powers of both chambers are equal. A significant minority of second chambers contain members appointed by the executive, and some are entirely composed in this way, though a formula may constrain the choice to ensure a degree of representation (as in the case of the Canadian Senate). Such a method of appointment almost inevitably carries with it the notion of award or honour, as for example with peerages in Britain. To do away with a second chamber may well involve the abolition of positions very highly valued by a minority, while being regarded with indifference by the vast majority. Britain alone retains heredity as a basis of membership. Why is this? For an answer we must look more specifically at the way the British Constitution has developed.

Development of the British Parliament

The British Parliament may reasonably claim to be the oldest continuing parliament in the world. Its origins lie in the Witans consulted by Saxon kings over a thousand years ago. Sometime in the fourteenth century two distinct houses emerged, with the representatives of the shires and boroughs becoming known as the Commons and beginning to meet separately from the magnates or great men of England, the Lords. Over the next two centuries the right of an individual to receive a writ of summons, as opposed to the right of the Monarch to choose whom he summoned, became established. Thus the basis for membership of the Upper House became more clearly defined. The emergence of various ranks within the peerage also took place (Powell and Wallis, 1968).

In the Tudor period there arose the classical theory of the English Constitution, a mixed form of government in which, following Aristotle, 'the King represented the monarchic element; the House of Lords the aristocratic; and the House of Commons the democratic' (Weston, 1965, p. 2). This provided a theoretical justification for the institutional arrangements which had emerged. It was a justification which outlived the seventeenth-century Puritan revolution. During that period, for eleven years, the Throne was vacant and the House of Lords did not meet. But the Cromwellian era was an interlude. In 1660 separate sittings of the Upper House resumed. A Restoration took place, the monarchy was brought back, and the classical theory of the Constitution became ascendant throughout the eighteenth century. Important changes had of course taken place, involving limitations on the power of the Monarch and alterations in the relationship between Lords and Commons. But these were accomplished through the modification of ancient institutions rather than through their abolition or replacement. For this reason no formal or written constitution ever became necessary. The House of Lords, like the monarchy and other institutions, gradually evolved. No authoritative document ever defined its role, though commentators propounded various doctrines to explain and justify the pattern of relationships which existed.

Because the House of Lords acquiesced in change – if with great reluctance at times – it survived, a point the truth of which has been demonstrated right down to the present day. For example, immediately after the Restoration the House of Lords attempted to involve itself in matters of finance. The Commons' privilege here had been implicit in the emergence of two separate Houses, but in response to the Lords' action, the Commons resolved in 1671 that 'in all aids given the King by the Commons the rate of tax ought not to be altered by the Lords', and in 1678, after a further attempt by the Lords to amend a financial bill, the Commons passed a stronger resolution stating that it alone possessed the right to grant aids and supplies and to determine the purposes for which they were used.

The eighteenth century saw confirmation of the idea that the King's Government was responsible to Parliament, but it was responsibility to the Lower House which became recognised as fundamental. This may seem strange, because most of the great offices of state were still held by members of the Lords. But it was the Commons which had insisted on a Bill of Rights in 1689 – establishing the authority of Parliament *vis-à-vis* the King – and it was the Commons which had successfully asserted its primacy over taxation matters and the control of supply, an area of ever-growing importance. But of the need for reform of the Lords, or argument for its abolition, very little was heard in the eighteenth century. Discussion of reform for the Commons could proceed apace, the more so as the century ebbed away, but that was in order to improve the quality of the democratic element within what was thought to be a perfectly balanced constitution, rather than in obedience to any doctrine of democratic supremacy. A further reason why no serious conflict between the two Houses emerged lay in the extent to which Commons membership was still controlled by peers through their powers of patronage.

In the event, the great Reform Act of 1832 not only brought an extension of the franchise but also, in effect, brought about the collapse of the theory of mixed government. During debates on the bill, Whig leaders declared that it would constitute a permanent settlement of what had become a great constitutional question. But as soon as the bill was passed – and this, be it noted, against the intentions of Monarch and Lords – the democratic element within the Constitution had been recognised as pre-eminent. From then on the House of Lords was talked of as a revising chamber, and schemes for its reform abounded. In 1836 James Mill called for the Lords' veto over legislation to become suspensive only, a proposal eventually adopted in 1911. In 1867 Bagehot first published his *English Constitution*, which firmly relegated the House of Lords to the status of a dignified rather than an efficient part of the Constitution; earlier (in the eighteenth century), the House of Lords, if not a 'directing chamber', had at least been 'a chamber of directors', but by the mid nineteenth century its value lay in the fact that it inspired reverence in the people and, while clearly subordinate to the Commons, could yet revise and possibly suspend bills (Bagehot, 1963, Ch. 3).

For fifty years after 1832 the 'two Houses lived together in general harmony, quarrelling about privilege rather than about policy' (Le May, 1979, p. 127). One reason for this lay in the continued influence of aristocratic families in the House of Commons, though this gradually diminished, more markedly after the second Reform Act of 1867. More significant was the rise of the modern notion of party. In the latter part of the century government became first and foremost party government, with power more heavily concentrated among the few who forced their way into the front ranks of the parties. Talk of the decline of Parliament began – and has continued ever since. Within the House of Lords, Conservative peers under the influence of the third Marquess of Salisbury developed the 'Referendal Theory'. According to this doctrine it could be right for the Lords to delay legislation about which the opinion of the nation was not clear until a 'higher authority than the House of Lords' (the phrase was Salisbury's) had spoken. The problem with this theory lay in the impossibility most of the time of deriving from an election result any clear view of what national opinion was on a specific issue. Nevertheless it was a doctrine which emboldened Conservative peers in their opposition to the measures promoted by Liberal governments. In particular the events of 1893 to 1895, with the Lords defeating home rule for Ireland and the Liberal Government being itself convincingly defeated at the polls, encouraged Conservative peers to see the Lords as once again a decisive factor in government.

The Pre-World War I Constitutional Crisis and Its Effects

When the election of 1906 gave the Liberals 400 seats in a Commons of 670 members, conflict with the Conservative-dominated Lords was inevitable. The new Government's reforming legislation was soon being mutilated or rejected by the Upper House. The Conservative leader, Balfour, declared in 1907 that the Lords had a duty to see that the laws of the country were not 'the hasty and ill-considered offspring of one passionate election'. In the same year the Commons approved a resolution emphasising that the will of the Lower House must prevail. The parties were set on a collision course. But what would be the best issue on which the Government should take a stand against the peers? And what constitutional adjustment should then take place? Opinion within Liberal Party circles was divided. Some argued for a suspensory veto, others for a plan which would have allowed 100 peers to join with MPs to vote together on disputed issues, a proposal which would have meant that the legislation of any non-Conservative government lacking a comfortable Commons majority would be at risk. While social reform was an obvious area of controversy, the spectre of Irish home rule haunted British politics throughout this period.

In 1909 the Lords rejected outright the Finance Bill embodying that year's budget proposals. This was a challenge the Government had to take up. Throughout 1910 the argument raged; two general elections were fought, with Liberals losing ground in the first but holding their position in the second. A constitutional conference between party leaders met for several months (Blewett, 1972). Eventually the Parliament Act of 1911 was passed, but only because Conservative peers knew that if they did not acquiesce, enough Liberals would be given peerages to swamp their majority. This major constitutional measure removed the Lords' right of veto, replacing it with a power to delay ordinary legislation for approximately two years; bills certified by the Speaker of the Commons as Money Bills could be held up for only one month. The Parliament Act dealt with the most urgent question, which was the power of the Lords, but its preamble made clear that it was intended only as an interim measure before the composition of the Upper House was fundamentally altered. Schemes for reform abounded, with peers themselves, in 1910, accepting by 175 votes to 17 a resolution endorsing the view that possession of a peerage should no longer automatically carry with it the right to sit and vote in the Lords. In 1917 a Commission was set up under Lord Bryce to consider both the powers and the composition of the Upper House.

Meanwhile the constitutional crisis, though ameliorated by the 1911 Act, was not exhausted. In 1912 the Government brought forward its home rule bill for Ireland; the Conservatives objected violently to this measure and it was rejected repeatedly by the Lords. The new Parliament Act procedure was invoked. Not until 1914 did the bill reach the Statute Book, only to be immediately suspended because of the arrival of war, by which time the Government had become convinced of the need to exclude Ulster. Between 1911 and 1914 the House of Lords rejected at second reading two other bills, one of which (the Welsh Church Act) was subsequently passed under the Parliament Act, while the other (the Plural Voting Bill) was dropped by the Government. Compromise between the two Houses was reached on a further bill, the Temperance (Scotland) Bill, after it had been reintroduced in 1913 following the Lords' refusal to pass it in the form accepted by the Commons. As these examples illustrate, notwithstanding their defeat over the Parliament Act, Conservative peers were still quite prepared to make vigorous use of the remaining powers of the House.

War brought an interlude, and by the time normal peacetime policies had started up again the Conservative Party was once again dominant within government. The Bryce Commission, which consisted of thirty-two of the leading political figures of the day, produced its report in 1918 (Cd 9038). As to powers, its members agreed that the 1911 Parliament Act did not provide a suitable permanent solution. Instead it recommended arrangements by which members of both Houses would meet jointly to resolve differences, having also carefully considered but rejected proposals for referenda in such circumstances. As to composition, it proposed an Upper House partly elected by MPs and partly chosen by a joint committee of both Houses in such a way as to ensure that some hereditary peers remained as members. But on this some members of the Bryce Commission dissented.

Most subsequent references to the Bryce Commission have been to its definition of the functions of the Lords, which remains worth citing despite the passage of the years. Four functions for a second chamber received general endorsement: first, the examination and revision of bills brought from the Commons; second, the initiation of bills of a non-controversial character, which may have an easier passage through the Commons if they have been fully discussed and put into a well-considered shape before being submitted to it; third, the interposition of so much delay (and no more) in the passing of a bill into law as may be needed to enable the opinion of the nation to be adequately expressed upon it (this would be especially desirable on bills affecting the Constitution); and fourth, the full and free discussion of large and important questions, especially when the Commons is otherwise occupied, and possibly with the advantage that in a second chamber such discussions can take place without the constraint that the fate of the Government might depend on the outcome of any divisions which may take place.

Subsequent discussion of the functions of the Upper House has invariably endorsed three of the four above points (for example, the Labour Government White Paper in 1968 did so), but controversy has surrounded the delaying function. It has always seemed artificial to entrust to an unelected chamber the task of deciding when delay should be imposed in order to enable public opinion to be expressed on a matter. Inevitably any exercise of this function would be selective, and it never seemed likely – at least until the 1980s – that Conservative governments would run any serious risk of having delay imposed on measures they considered important. At the same time the possibility of leaving the second chamber totally without powers of any kind has seemed inappropriate to most Labour, as well as Conservative, governments.

After the Bryce Commission report, a general expectation that reform of the House would take place continued. Government proposals, not unlike those of the Bryce Commission itself, were put forward in 1922 and again in 1927. On both occasions the proposals received substantial parliamentary debate and general endorsement. But no detailed progress on reform was made, the basic reason being that the motivation for any change lay too transparently in the Conservatives' desire to enhance the legitimacy of the Lords so as to enable it to block the sort of legislation which a majority Labour Government might introduce. Only twice in the whole interwar period, however, did Labour take the reins of office, but neither in 1924 nor again between 1929 and 1931 did it have a Commons majority. The legislation passed by the Commons could not therefore be of a kind to arouse strong objections from other parties or from the Lords. In 1931 one government bill was rejected at second reading by the Lords (a measure to raise the school-leaving age), but shortly afterwards the Government collapsed. Proposals for reform of the Lords continued, but governments clearly thought they had more important matters to engage their attention.

By the time Labour first came to power with a clear overall majority (of 152, no fewer) in 1945, memories of the bitter pre-1914 disputes had faded, replaced by immediate recollections of co-operation between leading politicians during the Second World War. Labour in office preferred to concentrate on its nationalisation measures, and the establishment of the welfare state, rather than divert attention to the Lords. For their part Conservative peers refrained from voting down government bills because they accepted guidance formulated by their leader, the fifth Marquess of Salisbury, to the effect that it was wrong for the House to reject measures which had received clear endorsement by the electorate. Even the iron and steel nationalisation bill, the introduction of which was delayed by the Government because of its more contentious character, was accepted by peers without division at second reading, though the Lords did successfully press the Government to agree to delay implementation of the bill until after the 1950 election.

Uncertain as to whether the House of Lords might become more obstructive as the prospect of an election loomed closer, the Government introduced a bill to amend the 1911 Parliament Act by reducing the power of delay from two years to one. During the passage of this bill in 1948, all-party discussions took place about the possibility of reform in the composition of the Upper House. These made some progress before breaking down over irreconcilable differences on the power the Lords should retain, though the gap between the two parties on this was ostensibly a mere three months. The Parliament Act of 1949 was therefore passed under the provisions of the 1911 Act – the first time these had been used since the First World War. In general, however, the actions of Conservative peers from 1945 to 1951 showed clearly that they had now accepted the subordinate status of the Lords: the Upper House did not contest power with the Commons in the way it had done early in the century.

The outcome of the all-party discussions in 1948 revealed a considerable consensus. The final paragraph of the party leaders' agreed statement is worth quoting: 'The representatives of all three Parties were united in their desire to see the House of Lords continue to play its proper part in the Legislature; and in particular to exercise the valuable functions of revising Bills sent up by the Commons, and initiating discussion on public affairs. It was regarded as essential, moreover, that there should be available to the country a legislative body composed of men of mature judgement and experience gained in many spheres of public life . . .' (Cmd 7380, 1948). The differences over powers were nevertheless held to be fundamental, preventing the carrying forward in detail of proposals for reform. The same document did indicate a number of agreed principles regarding reform of composition. These included: the view that modification of the existing House of Lords was preferable to the creation of a new body – say one based on election; that no party should have a permanent majority; that heredity alone should not confer a right of membership; that women should be included; that some remuneration should be payable to members; that peers, not members of the second chamber, should be eligible for membership of the Commons; and that some provision for disqualification from membership should be made for those who neglect or become unable to fulfil their duties as members.

Though no comprehensive reform could take place, it had long been obvious that some piecemeal changes were desirable. Indeed, four of the proposals quoted above made by the 1948 conference were taken up in various ways during the lifetime of Conservative governments from 1951 to 1964. The payment of expenses and the introduction of leave-of-absence arrangements were minor changes, though the former undoubtedly had an important impact on the work of the Lords through enabling some members who were otherwise unable to attend to do so. The admission of women and the ability of hereditary peers to remain eligible for Commons membership were further changes made in this period. Most significant, though, was the institution of life peerages.

Life Peerages

The principle of awarding life peerages had been considered frequently in the past. From the early nineteenth century onwards an increased proportion of new peerages went to distinguished public servants who did not possess the large estates considered necessary to support a peerage. In some cases estates were awarded by a grateful government – to Wellington and Nelson, for example; in others substantial pensions were paid, so that at least the recipient of a peerage could live in an appropriate style. But what of the heirs of such men? Would they become landless, even penniless, peers? To guard against such distasteful possibilities, life peerages, supported perhaps by state pensions, were advocated, most commonly for victorious generals, but then especially for senior judges. And in the latter case an additional argument lay in the need adequately to staff the House of Lords for its judicial work, an activity which peers were loath to see removed. But the argument against life peerages was also strongly made, centring on the view that the independence of the Upper House could no longer be guaranteed if such peerages were conferred.

For twenty years in the middle of the last century the Lords resisted active attempts by successive governments to introduce life peers (see Bromhead, 1958, pp. 245–6). Eventually, in 1876, in the context of other judicial reforms, provision was made for two judges to be appointed as Lords of Appeal in Ordinary, with life peerages conferred upon appointment. Compromise in relation to a precisely defined group had proved possible. But further attempts to extend the life peerage principle over the next eighty years were frustrated, initially by a fear that such a principle would weaken the independence of the Upper House, but latterly out of a reluctance to allow piecemeal rather than fundamental reform of the Lords to take place.

Because the Labour Party believed that a comprehensive reform of the House ought to take place, it was always ambivalent about the creation of any new peerages. In 1938 there were still only 15 Labour peers, compared with 80 Liberals and 400 Conservatives (Laski, 1938). Attlee, however, took a decidedly practical view and ennobled 44 Labour supporters between 1945 and 1951. Labour representation in the House of Lords became adequate, but never generous. Back in Opposition, Labour numbers began to decline, and Conservative prime ministers were reluctant to give hereditary awards to their opponents. In any case, with new hereditary creations running on average at almost ten per year, the House of Lords was growing in size by more than fifty per decade. Unless the flow of new creations were increased, the proportion of peers by succession would grow, a trend which had nothing to recommend it.

A simple bill to award life peerages provided a means of escape from the trap. Prior to its introduction the Government undertook some discussions with Labour leaders about possible reforms, but in the end acted on its own in bringing forward the Life Peerages Bill. During debate in both Houses Labour leaders made clear their suspicion that the Government's main intention was to enhance the prestige of the Lords, while retaining the hereditary principle. The Government, for its part, carefully avoided making any commitment which might constrain in any way a future prime minister's freedom to choose people as he wished. On second reading, R.A. Butler said in the Commons that life peerages would be given to distinguished people whose membership would strengthen the second chamber and ensure that it adequately and accurately reflected the life of the nation. This could well have been said of previous hereditary awards. An incidental innovation was the proposal that life peerages could be conferred on women as well as men. In the Lords' at committee stage 'gentlemen's club' arguments flowed for a short while, but the men present voted by 134 to 30 in support of female eligibility to join their House – or club.

To begin with, life peers were appointed with the implication that they would be working members of the Upper House, and their names would be announced separately from the regular honours lists. Soon, however, the New Year and Queen's Birthday honours lists included life peers, and when the Labour Party came to office in 1964, Mr Wilson announced that he would not recommend any further hereditary peerages.

The Life Peerages Act permitted the substantial reinforcement of the Labour benches in the Lords. Less foreseeable was the subsequent growth in the cross-benchers. The total number of new peerages created was much greater, and since 1958 the activity of the House of Lords has gradually and continuously increased. All these points are taken up in the following chapters. Meanwhile, mention should be made of two other minor changes which took place at about the same time.

During the 1957–8 debates on the Life Peerages Bill, the Labour leader, Mr Gaitskell, emphasised the difficulty in finding Labour supporters able to spend time working without pay in the Lords. A reading of Gaitskell's diary underlines the point (Gaitskell, 1983, pp. 416, 564). The day of the penniless peer had arrived; but some of those least well-off financially were among those whose participation the Lords most required. Their presence was necessary to keep the opposition front bench from total collapse. An allowance was therefore introduced in 1957 to enable peers to claim out-of-pocket expenses incurred in attending the House of Lords. This allowance steadily increased over the following years and the definition of expenses which may legitimately be claimed widened, for example, to include secretarial costs (see Appendix A for details).

The second minor change also derived from the peculiarities of the Upper House's composition. This was the introduction of leave of absence for peers who did not wish to attend the House of which they were members. The fact that the royal writ of summons commanded the attendance of a peer at the House of Lords 'waiving all excuses' was an embarrassment to some who were near-permanent absentees. But a further and more serious embarrass-ment arose when peers who generally were absent suddenly appeared in quite large numbers to vote on some controversial issue. The sixty peers by succession who came to vote against the abolition of the death penalty in 1956, after four years of silent membership, gave new credence to the old cry of 'backwoodsman'. Soon afterwards a Lords select committee was set up 'to consider the powers of the House in relation to the attendance of its members'. In agreement with its proposals (HL 60, 1957–8) standing orders were amended to enable peers to apply for leave of absence.

This arrangement does give a decent indemnity to the permanent absentee, but it is very doubtful whether it has had any other effect. The term 'backwoodsman' has no clearly defined meaning. It can be brought into use after any large turnout by those who wish to bring discredit on a particular vote or on the House of Lords itself. It popularly describes Conservative peers by succession who, from deep in the shires, answer a bugle call from their Chief Whip to appear for crucial divisions to swell Conservative numbers. But the very rare attenders are in fact the frail and elderly, or very busy people with heavy and genuine commitments away from Westminster. They are not predominantly hereditary peers, nor Conservatives. They include law lords and bishops and many others who owe their first allegiance to their professional duties (see Table 2.6, p. 50 and Ch. 4, p. 105).

The Peerage Act 1963

Proposals to allow individuals to renounce peerages which they inherit had frequently been made over the past hundred years, most recently as amendments to the Life Peerages Bill. None had succeeded. Some MPs who had become disqualified for continued membership of the Commons through inheriting a peerage had left the Lower House with considerable reluctance. In 1960 a 35-year-old MP, Anthony Wedgwood Benn, who had been elected as member for Bristol South-East in 1950, inherited a peerage. As a popular, young and very able member of the Parliamentary Labour Party he had an understandable ambition to remain in the Commons. When he succeeded to his peerage the Commons Committee for Privileges ruled that he was disqualified from membership of the Lower House, and a by-election for his seat was declared. Benn stood as a candidate and gained an increased majority, but then found himself unseated by an election court, which declared his Conservative opponent (who had fewer than half as many votes) elected. For the next two years the member who sat in the Commons for Bristol South-East was the man soundly defeated at this by-election!

A joint select committee of both Houses was set up to consider the matters raised by this constitutional imbroglio (HL 23, HC 38,

1962–3). Its recommendations were embodied in the 1963 Peerage Act, which permitted peers by succession to renounce their peerages for life. Mr Benn naturally took the earliest opportunity to do this, and was once more elected MP for Bristol South-East at a by-election precipitated by the immediate resignation of the Conservative member once the Peerage Act was given Royal assent.

Ironically, the consequences of this legislation were much more far-reaching for the Conservative Party than for Labour. It enabled the Conservative succession to pass from Macmillan to Lord Home in October 1963, and brought another leading Conservative, Lord Hailsham – also a contender for the party leadership – back into the Commons as well. The Peerage Act laid down that all peers by succession could renounce their peerages; those who had already inherited, and newly succeeding peers, had twelve months to decide what to do – unless they were MPs, in which case a decision had to be given within a month. Peerages so renounced could be taken up again by the next heir upon the death of the 'disclaimer'.

Opportunity was taken in the same legislation to reduce some anomalies in regard to membership of the House of Lords. Most notable was the admission of women who had succeeded to peerages, excluded up to 1963 despite the entry of women as life peers. This represented the removal of a very minor but totally unjustified element of sex discrimination. Only eighteen women were involved. A second change brought into the Lords all thirty-one holders of Scottish peerages in place of the previous arrangement under which this group elected sixteen of their number for each Parliament. This, it should be noted, involved the abandonment of a practice, the extension of which had been advocated frequently in the past, as a way of reducing the number of hereditary peers who had a right to sit in the House of Lords. The Labour Opposition tolerated these minor extensions of the hereditary membership of the Lords because of its eagerness to establish the right to disclaim peerages.

A final effect of the 1963 Peerage Act was to regularise somewhat the position of peers of Ireland. The Union with Ireland Act in 1800 abolished the Irish House of Lords, but gave to the holders of Irish peerages the right to elect twenty-eight of their number to sit in the United Kingdom House of Lords. However, a consequence of the 1920 Government of Ireland Act had been the abolition of the machinery by which such elections took place. Despite pressure from Irish peers, no further elections were held. Existing elected peers continued to sit in the Lords, but the last of these died in 1961. Some Irish peers also held other peerages which entitled them to seats, but about seventy were not only excluded from the Lords but were unable to vote in elections to the Commons and, though entitled to sit as MPs for any mainland constituency, not eligible to do so for a seat in Ulster. The 1963 Act relieved them of these disabilities, but failed to make it quite clear that an Irish peerage conferred no right to a seat in the Lords. In 1966 the House of Lords agreed to a report from its Committee for Privileges which rejected a petition to allow seats to holders of Irish peerages (HL 53, 1966–7).

These were relatively minor rationalisations. As far as the 1963 Peerage Act was concerned, most attention focused on the provisions which allowed for renunciation. How many hereditary peers would forsake the Lords? Would there be a hundred, or even more? Was it likely that 'the shot in the arm given by the Life Peerages Act of 1958 would now be counterbalanced by the loss of good blood back to the Commons', as Crick suggested? (Crick, 1964, p. 140). Such expectations were not fulfilled. Disclaiming never caught on. Initially 4 of the 750 or so peers by succession renounced their peerages. Between 1964 and 1977 another eleven did so, an average of less than one a year out of fifteen to twenty-five who succeeded to peerages each year. Since 1977 no disclaiming at all has taken place, and indeed three heirs have taken up the peerages renounced by their fathers and become active in the House (see Appendix B). This is not at all the outcome expected when the Peerage Act was first passed. It illustrates in a small way the changed attitude to the House of Lords over the last twenty or so years.

The 1960s: The House of Lords Reinvigorated

From the atrophy of the 1950s the House of Lords gradually reasserted itself. Labour became a much more vigorous opposition in the early 1960s, reinvigorated by the arrival of new life peers fresh from the Commons; some bills – notably the London Government Bill – were fought with a tenacity hitherto unknown in the Upper House. Almost as many divisions took place on this one bill as had been held in the entire previous Parliament. As the 1960s progressed, a marked change in the ethos of the Lords became apparent (Vincent, 1966). Instead of a large majority supporting the death penalty, as in 1956, the Lords voted in 1965 by a majority of 100 for abolition. In the late 1960s peers took a leading part in enacting the so-called permissive-society legislation on divorce, abortion and homosexuality.

But even if the character of the House of Lords had changed and Labour's strength increased, a huge party imbalance remained. With Labour back in office after 1964, the Lords inflicted numerous defeats on the Government. The Conservatives forced many more divisions than they had when last in Opposition, and these they almost invariably won. Sometimes the Government decided to compromise after defeat, but more usually it sought and obtained the deletion of Lords' amendments back in the Commons and the subsequent acquiescence of peers.

For the Conservative leadership a major concern remained the 'exercise of some control so that we don't defeat the Government too often', as Lord St Aldwyn, Tory Chief Whip, put the matter in a radio interview in May 1970. It was growing restiveness among Conservative peers which erupted in an ill-advised and pointless confrontation with the Government on the Southern Rhodesia Sanctions Order in June 1968. The order was defeated – the first time the House of Lords had used its veto power over a Statutory Instrument (see Chapter 8) – but only by a narrow margin (193 votes to 184). It was a hollow victory, the main result of which was government anger and opposition embarrassment (Morgan, 1975).

An immediate consequence was the breaking off by the Government of all-party talks on the reform of the Upper House which had been initiated in 1967 – for the 1960s had become a decade of institutional reform. Labour in office, with tacit support from the Conservatives under Mr Heath, sought to modernise Britain by the simple expedient of structural reform – in the civil service, in local government, in the education system and, of course, in Parliament itself, including the House of Lords. Before they were abruptly terminated, these all-party talks on the Lords had attained a considerable measure of agreement, and this became the basis of the White Paper entitled *House of Lords Reform* (Cmnd 3799, 1968).

These proposals were a rational attempt at evolutionary reform. The Lords would have continued as recognisably the same body, but eventually all hereditary members would have been removed, and an entirely nominated Upper House would have emerged.

Crucial to the reform was the introduction of a so-called two-writ scheme, under which some members of the House of Lords would be entitled to vote but others only to attend and speak. Non-voting members initially were to have included all existing peers by succession, but on their decease their heirs, while inheriting their peerages, would not inherit any right to membership of the Upper House. Created peers who attended fewer than one-third of the sittings or were over retirement age (stipulated as 72) would also be non-voting members. Those entitled to vote would therefore be the more regularly attending life peers below the age of 72, but including a reduced number of bishops and law lords. All told, the voting Lords would have been about 230 strong, with the government of the day being the largest party, though without an overall majority.

The White Paper discussed the functions of the Lords, though only briefly. The retention of some power was deemed fitting, and this was fixed at an ability to delay legislation for six months 'from the point of disagreement between the two Houses' – a period not likely to be very different in practice from the twelve-month delay measured from the date of a Commons second reading, established in 1949. However, in addition to the function of revising bills brought from the Commons, initiating less controversial bills and providing a forum for debate, the White Paper made particular mention of the Lords' role in considering subordinate legislation, dealing with private bills, and 'the scrutiny of the activities of the executive'. An appendix to the White Paper spoke of an enhanced role for a reformed House of Lords in such activities, and held out the prospect – enticing to some of the more active peers – of participation in a range of joint select committees of the two Houses. Reform for the second chamber was clearly being envisaged as a means to make the Upper House a more effective part of Parliament – not simply to arrest its decline (as had been done with the 1958 Life Peerages Act) but to reassert its significance.

The House of Lords voted by 251 to 56 in favour of the White Paper proposals, with the 43 Conservatives opposing being out-numbered more than two to one by Conservatives in support. In the Commons a vote on the proposals also produced a majority, though a much less convincing one.

The planned reform was embodied in the Parliament (No. 2) Bill. This achieved a Commons second reading, but soon got completely bogged down in committee (taken on the floor of the House because this was a constitutional measure). Many Labour MPs objected to the continuation of the second chamber, especially one still linked to the peerage and the honours system; they feared that, thus reformed, it would prove a more formidable body than the unreformed House of Lords. Conservative MPs were fearful of the loss of independence involved in the sacrifice of the hereditary basis of membership: some would have preferred an elected element, but no consensus existed about that. Two formidable back-benchers – Mr Foot and Mr Powell – though representing contrasting viewpoints, joined forces in obstructing the bill. Proceedings ground to a virtual halt and the bill was dropped. Nowhere had the proposals generated real enthusiasm. The front benches of both parties offered support, but only in a lukewarm manner. Those most disappointed with the failure of the scheme were probably active members of the House of Lords.

This débâcle did affect the mood of the Lords. Peers had overwhelmingly endorsed these proposals: they had fallen because MPs disliked them and because the Government was unwilling to persist with them. The unmodernised composition of the House was no longer the fault of the peers themselves. They were embarrassed by it but helpless to remedy it. Why, then, should the House take special care to avoid conflict with the Commons? MPs had treated the Lords shabbily, so why should not peers allow a little more awkwardness into the relationship between the Houses? Such arguments had a partial validity. They were heard almost immediately over the 1969 House of Commons (Redistribution of Seats) Bill, a measure which sought to delay the revision of parliamentary constituency boundaries and could thus be described as having strong constitutional overtones. The Lords showed every intention of using its legal powers to exhaustion on this bill, but the Government sidestepped conflict with the peers by the rather unscrupulous use of a procedural device in the Commons which allowed it to get its way without the need for legislation at all (on all this see Morgan, 1975).

Further conflict between the Houses was postponed as a result of the Conservative election victory in 1970. But further evidence of the more general reinvigoration of the House was provided by the markedly different relationship between the Heath Government and the Lords between 1970 and 1974 from that of previous Conservative governments. Labour peers were three times as numerous in

1970 as they had been in the early 1960s, and the number of cross-benchers had grown. No longer did the Conservatives have an overall majority. On twenty-six occasions the Government was defeated, and when this occurred ground was usually, though not invariably, given to the Lords. On the 1971 Immigration Bill, peers insisted (by 93 votes to 79) on an amendment providing reassurance for existing immigrants. On the 1972 National Health Service Bill, peers voted in favour of free contraception services, and only when the Commons asserted financial privilege (see Chapter 5) did they give way. The House of Lords was generally a good deal less submissive to the Heath Government than it had been to his Conservative predecessors.

The Labour Opposition flexed its new muscle in the House, exploiting the relative absence of procedural constraints to mount an onslaught on some of the Heath Government's more contentious bills. Notable was the attack on the Industrial Relations Bill, which took 27 days for committee and report stages, and upon which 138 divisions took place – figures unsurpassed before or since on any single measure. The Government won every one of these divisions, and made few concessions (Moran, 1977). But the strenuous efforts of Labour peers earned praise in quarters usually hostile to the House; Eric Heffer, spokesman for many on the Labour left, wrote of the 'magnificent fight' and the 'gallant efforts' of the Labour lords in his chronicle on this bill's enactment (Heffer, 1973, pp. 267–8). Neither Labour election manifesto of 1974 mentioned the House of Lords. But with Labour back in office again, the situation was soon to change drastically.

Labour in Conflict with the House

The period 1974–9 was exceptional within both Houses of Parliament. Two particular factors contributed to make it so. First, no longer did any special sanctions apparently attach to government defeat in the Commons. The constitutional myth that governments might have to resign if defeated on major matters had been exploded. Second, for all of this period the Government lacked a secure majority in the Commons, and for most of the time it lacked any overall majority. But whereas in the past governments with insecure majorities had refrained from bringing forward very controversial legislation, Labour showed no inhibitions about doing so between 1974 and 1976.

The Conservatives in Opposition pressed divisions on large numbers of hostile amendments to government bills, defeating the Government over 350 times in the division lobby (or in over 80 per cent of all divisions which took place). Sometimes the Government found itself unable to reverse the Lords' amendments back in the Commons – for example on the Housing Finance Bill of 1975 and the Dock Work Regulation Bill of 1976; the emasculation of these measures was the result of defection by Labour MPs as much as action by the House of Lords. Where the Lords' amendments were cancelled by the Commons, peers generally gave way without more ado. But the Opposition did decide to dig in its heels and quite deliberately use the power of the Lords on three carefully chosen matters.

The first of these involved the 1975 Trade Union and Labour Relations Bill, and concerned the provision of safeguards against possible abuse of the 'closed shop' principle among journalists. The Government's leading opponent in the Upper House was the formidable cross-bench peer Lord Goodman, behind whom, through much of this controversy, the Conservatives took shelter. The bill fell at the end of the 1974–5 session and was reintroduced in the following session, but eventually passed without the Parliament Act procedures running their full course, mainly because the Government changed its position and the Conservative Party got in a muddle (see Beloff, 1976). The second confrontation was over the bill nationalising aerospace and shipbuilding introduced in the 1975–6 session. Again the bill fell at the end of the session because the two Houses were still in dispute over amendments to delete ship-repairing. But here a technical procedural device became available because the bill was found by clerks to be 'hybrid' and therefore liable to an elaborate time-consuming parliamentary procedure (see Chapter 8). In the Commons the Government had the 'hybridity' rule set aside (though by only a single vote: 304–303). In the Lords no such easy way of escape from potentially lengthy select committee hearings was available, so Labour ministers reluctantly compromised and dropped ship-repairing from the bill.

The third exercise of power involved the outright rejection of a bill which would have brought Felixstowe Dock into public ownership, but because this was a private bill promoted by the British Dock and Harbour Board – albeit one with clear government support, and one which had already passed the Commons – the Government could do nothing to overcome the decision of the House (see pp. 211–15).

By 1977 the Government had lost its overall majority in the Commons; this meant that legislation which did not command support beyond Labour's own ranks could not pass through the Commons, let alone the Lords. Tension between the two Houses subsided. But by that time Labour had renewed its historic commitment to abolish the House outright, and to reform Parliament into an 'efficient single-chamber legislating body'. This provoked debate elsewhere about the future of the Lords. An official Conservative Party committee recommended a scheme of reform which ultimately would have removed hereditary peers, and created a two-thirds elected and one-third appointed House, with its powers slightly enhanced. The report, though emanating from a committee chaired by Lord Home of the Hirsel, had a lukewarm reception, even within the Conservative Party (see Chapter 9).

The Thatcher Years

During the first two years of the Thatcher premiership, however, there was considerable pressure within the Conservative Party for reform of the House of Lords (see, for example, party conference debates in 1980 and 1981). Attempting to secure agreement with Labour would be pointless (how different from 1968!), but the precedent of the 1958 Life Peerages Act – carried unilaterally by a Conservative Government – was cited.

Mrs Thatcher showed no interest in the question. Her priorities generally lay in directions other than institutional change. Talk of reform receded. In its place, attention began to focus on the enhanced influence of the Lords. After the 1983 election, which gave the Government such a huge Commons majority, it was even suggested that the Lords was more effective than the Lower House in obliging the Government to change its mind on particular questions. Party leaders in the Lords talked openly of the extra responsibilities placed on the Upper House by this parliamentary situation, as they did again in 1987 (see, for example, HL Debs, 25 June 1987, col. 21).

On the Labour side, the very weakness of the Party in Commons and country, especially at the time of the 1983 election, appeared to enhance the role of the Lords. The Labour peers were probably the most united and generally best-organised section of the Party in these years. The televising of the Lords emphasised how responsible and dignified they looked, perhaps confirming to some party activists the irrelevance of the House of Lords and the desirability of its abolition. But they were not irrelevant, as the Party (and country) had reason to realise when the Conservative Government began to face defeat on some quite major issues, such as its strategy for abolition of the GLC. On the Conservative side, Mrs Thatcher's growing ascendancy within the Party throughout the early 1980s, seen clearly in the Commons after the influx of new MPs at the 1983 election, was not so readily apparent in the Lords. The sheer continuity of the Upper House ensured that the Party there was less 'Thatcherite' and remained more tempered by the old paternalistic Tory tradition.

During Mrs Thatcher's second term, the House of Lords looked more confident of itself and of its role in the whole business of parliamentary government than it had for many years past. In October 1987 the Leader of the House, Viscount Whitelaw, made a speech to a fringe meeting at the Conservative Party Conference in which he forecast that the Government faced the prospect of serious defeats in the Upper House during the coming session; however, rather than warning his fellow peers not to press their opposition too far, he urged MPs and ministers not to push the House of Lords too hard (*The Independent*, 9 October 1987).

But during the 1987 Parliament the attitude of the Thatcher Government to the House of Lords appeared to harden. A new determination to overcome resistance in the Upper House became evident and, if this were not possible, to insist on the reversal of Lords' amendments in the Commons. When Lord Whitelaw resigned from the Government in January 1988 (because of ill-health) he was not replaced by a similar heavyweight. Indeed, for a time in 1988–9 the Government front bench in the Lords was devoid of any minister with previous experience of the Commons, a situation with no recent precedent. And Mrs Thatcher took good care as Prime Minister to keep the opposition benches in the Lords starved of new recruits. It seemed as if the Prime Minister had grown impatient with the Lords and wanted to ignore the place as much as possible. A note of contempt for the House became apparent in ministers' attitudes, as exemplified over the Government's insistence on overriding opposition from the Lords to its War Crimes Bill. With Labour in the late 1980s somewhat half-heartedly putting forward proposals for replacing the House, it seemed as if the Conservatives would be no more than half-hearted in its defence (see Chapter 9).

Though no fundamental reform had taken place, it is interesting to note how the House of Lords had quietly developed its activities, taking up where it could suggestions made in the 1968 White Paper. The establishment of the European Communities Committee in 1974 was a notable, but by no means isolated, example. Clearly the question of fundamental reform will inevitably return to the political agenda sooner or later, but meanwhile the activity of the House grows.

Between the House of Lords of today and its predecessor body of 600 years ago there is an unbroken institutional continuity, but along with this continuity there has also been great change. The House of Lords has become more meritocratic and rather less aristocratic. From being the senior part of Parliament it has become very much a junior part. More recently, from being an ill-attended body sustained by the enthusiasm of a few amateur, part-time or retired politicians, it has become much better attended and a partly professional House. From Parliament to Parliament significant, if subtle, changes are continuously evident. The institution may be the same body as existed centuries ago, yet it is also completely different. It is to the analysis of the House of Lords as it has become in the 1990s that the remainder of this book is largely devoted.

2

Membership of the House

At the commencement of each session of Parliament the Clerk of the Parliaments prepares a roll of 'Lords Spiritual and Temporal'. This is the authoritative list of all those eligible for membership of the House of Lords; it is tabled in the House and subsequently published. In November 1990 it contained the names of 1,197 individuals, holding between them 1,215 different peerages. The list included eleven peerages disclaimed for life, and eighteen individuals who were listed more than once, either because they held more than one peerage or because they were listed in respect of an office they held as well as in respect of their peerage. Some of those named on the roll were effectively full-time politicians, attending the House almost every sitting day and making it very much the centre of their working lives. Many others were part-time members, contributing selectively to the proceedings of the House while pursuing other careers or other activities. Some attended the House too infrequently even to be considered part-timers, while still others had nothing at all to do with the place. While it is the more active element within the House that is our major concern, it is necessary to commence our analysis by formally classifying all those who are entitled to seats. Table 2.1 does this.

Archbishops and Bishops

The 'Lords Spiritual' consist of twenty-six senior bishops of the Church of England. The Archbishops of Canterbury and York sit as of right, as do the occupants of the Sees of London, Durham and

Table 2.1　Composition of the House of Lords, May 1990

	Total	*Of whom women*	*Percentage of total membership*
Lords Spiritual			
Archbishops	2	– }	2.2
Bishops	24	– }	
Lords Temporal			
Royal dukes	5	–	0.4
Peers by succession	761	20	64.2
Hereditary created peers	17	–	1.4
Life peers created under			
Appellate Jurisdiction Act			
1876 as amended	19	–	1.6
Life peers created under			
Life Peerages Act 1958	358	53	30.2
	1,186	73	
Peers without writs	86	–	7.3
Peers with leave of absence	139	–	11.7

Winchester. Until 1847 all other diocesan bishops also had seats in the Lords, but since that date the creation of new Sees has not been accompanied by any extension of the right to seats in the House of Lords. The number of diocesan bishops with seats has therefore been fixed at twenty-one, plus the three senior diocesan bishops mentioned above. The twenty-one places are filled according to seniority as measured from the date of first appointment to a diocesan See. Apart from the Bishop of Sodor and Man (who has a seat in the House of Keys on the Isle of Man) and the Bishop of Gibraltar in Europe, an extra-territorial diocese created in 1970, all other diocesan bishops are eligible for membership of the Lords. When a bishop retires from his See (which he must now do by the age of 70) he loses his seat in the Lords, his place being taken by the most senior bishop not yet a member of the House of Lords. In recent years newly appointed diocesan bishops have had to wait between four and eight years before taking a seat in the Lords. Sometimes bishops are translated from one See to another – in which case, if already a member of the House of Lords, they are simply reintroduced in their new capacity.

The 'Lords Spiritual' are the only members of the House of Lords who do not remain for life. Several retiring archbishops have been created peers (including the most recent four), but in all other cases retirement entails departure from the Lords. Individual bishops do therefore tend to have a relatively short membership of the House of Lords: in 1990 only three of the twenty-six had been members for ten years or more. The bishop with longest membership in recent years was Dr Say, who entered the Lords in 1969 as Bishop of Rochester and retired from that See in 1988.

Royal Peers

The category of 'royal peers' is somewhat anomalous in that the few individuals involved could be included elsewhere in Table 2.1, but the effect of so doing would be in some degree misleading. The Duke of Edinburgh was created a Duke upon his marriage to Princess Elizabeth in 1947. He has taken his seat in the House of Lords, but has never spoken. Prince Charles was created Duke of Cornwall when Queen Elizabeth, his mother, succeeded to the Throne, but he did not enter the Lords until the age of 21. In 1986 his younger brother was created Duke of York upon marriage, and he entered the Lords in 1987. Both these royal princes were accorded full ceremonies of introduction because their peerages were regarded as new creations, though they took titles which had been held in the past by members of the Sovereign's immediate family. Prince Charles did make a maiden speech in 1974 in a debate on sport and leisure, introducing his remarks with a reference to the fact that no member of his family had spoken in the House of Lords for about a hundred years. He spoke again in 1975 on voluntary community service but has not done so since, to the time of writing.

The two other royal peers are the Duke of Gloucester and the Duke of Kent, both the second holders of peerages conferred on their fathers, the younger sons of King George V. The Duke of Kent has not spoken in the House, but the Duke of Gloucester, ten years after taking his seat, made a forthright speech on smoking and health in a debate in 1984, and spoke again in 1987 on professional liability, basing his remarks on his experience as an architect.

In the early nineteenth century royal peers spoke frequently, by no means eschewing matters of political controversy. Today members of the royal family must necessarily avoid any appearance of political partisanship, but this would not be difficult in respect of many debates which take place in the Lords. There is no reason why contributions from royal peers should not be made in a House characterised both for the breadth of subject matter debated and, in respect of some debates, the low or non-existent party political content.

Peers by Succession and Hereditary Created Peers

Peers by succession are all those who have inherited their peerages; hereditary created peers are the first holders of peerages which can be passed on to heirs. Taken together, these may be referred to as holders of hereditary peerages. All such peerages awarded this century have been United Kingdom peerages, but formerly Irish peerages were awarded (with imperial peerages being of Great Britain), and before the Act of Union in 1707 peerages of Scotland were also awarded. As already mentioned in Chapter 1, the arrangements by which peers of Ireland and of Scotland used to elect representatives to the Lords have now ceased. All holders of Scottish peerages are members of the House of Lords, but the possession of an Irish peerage no longer qualifies a person for membership. However, some holders of Irish peerages do sit in the House of Lords because they are qualified to do so by virtue of other peerages which they also hold. It is a source of confusion that some of these are known by their Irish title (so, for example, the Earl of Longford has sat in the Lords since 1945, when he was the recipient of a United Kingdom peerage as Baron Pakenham, but since 1962 he has been known by the Irish title which he inherited in that year). Many other individuals who do not themselves hold peerages use titles to indicate their blood relationship to a peer. Such titles are known as 'courtesy titles'; their use is not regulated by law, though from time to time the Sovereign has issued rules to govern, or at least to guide, their use. Thus the eldest son of a higher-ranking peer will generally use a courtesy title deriving from a lesser peerage held by his father.

Taking account only of those peerages which confer the right to a seat in the Lords, in November 1990 there were 22 dukes (the most senior rank), followed in order of precedence by marquesses (27), earls and countesses (156), viscounts (102), and the barons, baronesses and ladies (471). The last non-royal dukedom was created in 1874; several marquesses have been created in the twentieth century but none since the Second World War, while earldoms and viscountcies have been conferred up to the present time. When hereditary peerages were regularly awarded prior to 1964, former prime ministers, if they took a peerage, became earls, and former cabinet ministers usually became viscounts. Sometimes a person awarded one peerage would later be advanced to a higher peerage in recognition of further achievements.

The distinction between various ranks of peerage is of no importance with regard to the work of the House of Lords. Peers of higher rank have higher formal precedence, but this confers no privileges over lower-ranking peers in the proceedings of the Lords. However, as regards membership, the distinction between hereditary peerages and life peerages is important. It is worth noting that no new hereditary peerages were awarded after 1964, when Labour came to office, until Mrs Thatcher's second term as Prime Minister in 1983. This was a sufficiently long period under Conservative as well as Labour governments to have established an expectation that such awards would never again be made. However, in 1983 Mrs Thatcher recommended hereditary peerages at the rank of viscount for both her cabinet deputy, William Whitelaw, and the former Speaker of the Commons (and ex-Labour Cabinet Minister) George Thomas, who became Viscount Tonypandy. This was presumably intended as a mark of special distinction for these individuals, despite the fact that by this time two other former Speakers of the Commons and two other former prime ministers had all accepted life peerages. Neither of these two had eligible heirs, so their peerages will become extinct upon their deaths, but in 1984 an earldom was conferred upon former Prime Minister Harold Macmillan, Earl of Stockton. When he died in 1987 his peerage was inherited by his grandson.

It seems unlikely that many hereditary peerages will be awarded in the future. If the motive for making such awards is to mark out individuals of exceptional achievement from the ordinary run of life peers, then it would seem more sensible to confer life peerages at a higher rank than that of baron, though this has never been done and it is doubtful whether it could be done without further legislation.

The rules governing the succession of peerages are very complex and need not detain us here, though it is necessary briefly to explain their significance. When a hereditary peer dies he is succeeded by the nearest direct descendant of the original holder of the peerage. For the first holder of a peerage this can only be a member of his immediate family (son or grandson). For the holder of a peerage which was first conferred many generations ago, distant relatives may be eligible heirs.

An implication worth noting is that hereditary peerages most at risk of extinction are those which have been in existence for a single generation – because only direct descendants of the first holder are eligible heirs. Of the ninety hereditary peerages which became extinct between 1966 and 1990, forty-three had been held for a single generation only. Occasionally publicity has been given to calculations about when all hereditary peerages would become extinct (assuming no new creations took place). Such calculations, by extrapolating from the overall extinction rate in recent years, produce a misleading result because they do not allow for the lower extinction rate among the holders of older peerages.

A striking feature of Table 2.1 is the small number of hereditary peerages held by women. Depending on the terms in which a peerage was originally granted, some cannot be held by a female, while others cannot be transmitted through a female line of succession. But even where either or both of these possibilities exist, any male line of succession always takes precedence over a female line. In some cases, where the first holder of a hereditary peerage has had no male heirs, the letters patent for the peerage have deliberately been framed so as to allow for succession through a female line – for example, in the case of Earl Mountbatten of Burma: he was created a peer in 1946, had no male heirs, and his peerage was inherited by his daughter upon his assassination in 1979. Viscount Whitelaw likewise has no sons: his peerage will become extinct because the letters patent do not allow for it to be passed to his eldest daughter. This is in some ways a trivial point, yet it does represent the perpetuation of sex discrimination with regard to a male-dominated institution. The reply to a parliamentary question in early 1987 indicated that the Government had no plans to remove this discrimination (HL Debs, 5.2.87, cols. 326–8).

By Standing Order of the Upper House no peer may take his seat until the age of 21, an age unchanged when the age of majority generally was lowered to 18. Of the eighty-six peers shown in Table 2.1 as lacking a writ of summons, two were minors, the vast majority of the remainder being hereditary peers who would have little or no difficulty in establishing their claim to a writ but have simply not bothered, presumably because they have no interest in attending the Lords. Quite a number of these live overseas, and in some cases their links with the UK are very slight. Peers may also have their writ of summons withdrawn if they are undischarged bankrupts.

It is peers by succession who give the House of Lords its strong aristocratic inclination. But it is worth noting that comparatively few members hold ancient peerages: fewer than 100 survive from before the seventeenth-century civil war, and well over half of all peers by succession hold peerages first conferred within the last hundred years.

Law Lords

As is well known, the House of Lords, as well as being the second chamber of Parliament, is also the highest court of appeal in the land. Up to eleven judges may now hold office as Lords of Appeal in Ordinary. When they retire, unlike the bishops, they do not lose their seats in the Lords. Their peerages are for life, not for term only. The figure of nineteen in Table 2.1 includes all serving and retired peers who were awarded peerages upon appointment as Lords of Appeal in Ordinary.

A few peers who have held high judicial office, but have not been created peers under the Appellate Jurisdiction Act, are also entitled to sit judicially. These may include: senior Scottish judges accorded life peerages; the Lord Chief Justice of Northern Ireland; and some senior English judicial figures who have been awarded peerages as well as the Lord Chancellor and all former Lord Chancellors. The term 'law lords' is usually applied to this wider group, consisting of all peers entitled to sit judicially. Their contribution to the work of the House of Lords is discussed below (pp. 56–9).

Life Peerages

The final category in Table 2.1 is life peers created under the 1958 Life Peerages Act. Not only have the great bulk of all peerages

Table 2.2 The Creation of Life Peerages, 1/1/58–30/4/91

Prime Minister	Cons	Lab	Lib/SDP	Cross-bench	Total	Average per 12 months
Macmillan/Home	17	29	1	18	65	17
1958–64	(25)		(1)	(22)	(48)	
Wilson	11	78	6	46	141	25
1964–70						
Heath	23	5	3	15	46	13
1970–4						
Wilson/Callaghan	17	82	6	34	139	27
1974–9						
Thatcher	99	45	10	45	199	18
1979–90	(2)			(2)	(4)	
Major	6	5	1	1	13	
Total –	173	244	27	159	603	

Notes: a) Resignation honours have been attributed to outgoing prime ministers in 1964, 1970, 1974, 1979, 1990.
   b) Political affiliation is that taken by a peer upon first entering the House.
   c) Figures in parentheses give the number of hereditary peerages awarded (excluding advancements from one rank of peerage to a higher rank).
   d) Figures exclude Sir Ian Horobin, whose peerage was announced on 29.3.62, but who was subsequently granted permission to withdraw his acceptance. Figures include Mr John Davies, whose peerage was announced on 16.6.79, but who died on 4.7.79 before letters patent had been issued.

created since then been life rather than hereditary peerages, but the total number of peers created between 1958 and 1991 was slightly more than double the number created in the thirty years before 1958. The House of Lords has been transformed by the influx of life peers. Table 2.2 shows the varied propensities of different prime ministers to create peers. Mr Wilson was the most prolific; he recommended no fewer than 217 individuals for membership of the Lords during his eight years as Prime Minister, while Mrs Thatcher recommended 199 (excluding hereditary awards) during her eleven-and-a-half years. Before analysing the background of life peers, something needs to be said about the award of peerages.

The Award of Peerages

All peerages are conferred by the Sovereign, who acts on the advice of the Prime Minister. Usually the New Year's honours list and Queen's Birthday honours list are headed by the names of a small number of people to whom peerages are awarded. Occasionally a special honours list is announced; recent examples have been on the occasion of the Queen's Jubilee, and following success in the Falklands War.

Dissolution honours lists are always published at the time of a general election. If the election results in a change of government, then the outgoing Prime Minister customarily draws up a resignation honours list, which may replace his or her contribution to a dissolution honours list. Sometimes a dissolution honours list has been issued before an election, but more usually after. In 1987 a list containing nineteen names was issued on 30 July (following a June election), sixteen of whom had resigned, one had been defeated, one had been de-selected by his Party and one had retired at the previous election in 1983. It has become customary for a resignation list to be issued whenever a prime minister leaves office, for whatever reason. Mr Heath's resignation honours list in 1974 contained nine peerages, as did Mr Wilson's in 1976; Mr Callaghan's in 1979 contained ten names, while Mrs Thatcher's in 1990 contained seven.

From time to time lists of new peers quite separate from any of the above occasions have been issued, the stated intention of such lists being to increase the working strength of the House of Lords. Mrs Thatcher issued lists of so-called 'working peers' in April 1981, December 1982, April 1985, February 1987 and April 1990. By no means have all the peers on such lists subsequently become active members of the Lords, though Labour nominees have tended to be more assiduous than Conservative nominees. Many of those included on such lists have been men and women of considerable public distinction: the sort of people who might quite reasonably have received awards in the regular honours lists. But some have been relatively unknown and apparently undistinguished: for example, six of the fourteen names included in a list of Labour working peers issued in August 1967 could not be found in *Who's Who* at the time their peerage was announced, though subsequently some of these became highly regarded members of the House of

Lords. A life peerage is both the highest regular 'honour' awarded in
our society and the necessary qualification for membership of the
second chamber, which does nowadays need to recruit a number of
willing party workhorses in order to ensure that the work of the
Lords is adequately completed.

In the case of dissolution or resignation honours, as well as lists of
working peers, the actual choice of individuals who are not members
of the Prime Minister's Party is recognised as being made by the
other party leaders. When a dissolution honours list or a list of new
working peers is being prepared, the Prime Minister will indicate to
other party leaders how many names they may put forward, and the
choice of whom to suggest is left to them. In 1983 it was widely
reported in the press that Mr Foot wished to recommend over
twenty former Labour MPs for peerages, but Mrs Thatcher would
allow only eight. It was then further reported that when the Prime
Minister received Mr Foot's list of eight she sent it back to him for
reconsideration because it contained the names of some relatively
junior political figures and failed to include some former cabinet
ministers. Mr Foot insisted that he would recommend only
individuals who would become regular and reliable working peers.
His choice of names was accepted, but in the following New Year's
honours list two former Labour cabinet ministers, omitted from Mr
Foot's list, received peerages on Mrs Thatcher's recommendation.
In the next dissolution honours list in 1987, six Labour nominees –
all very senior parliamentarians – were put forward by Mr Kinnock.

In 1985 the Social Democratic Party was invited to make a single
nomination, and its leader chose a former MP who had been a
Deputy Speaker in the Commons, Lord Crawshaw of Aintree. He
died the following year, but in drawing up another list of working
peers in February 1987 Mrs Thatcher refused to invite a nomination
from either Alliance Party, much to the anger of Dr Owen, the SDP
leader; after the election, though, two Alliance Party members were
included in the dissolution honours list, and in the next list of
'working peers' one of the fourteen names was that of a Liberal
Democrat. The Liberal Party was disappointed by the refusal of
Conservative prime ministers from 1958 to 1964 to invite nominations from the Liberal leader. The omission of Enoch Powell from
the dissolution honours list in 1987 occasioned widespread and
conflicting press comment, though in a radio programme he stated
that he had not been offered a peerage of any kind (Hennessy, 1987).

In some cases individuals decline to accept peerages, though it is impossible to say how frequently such refusals are made. Janet Morgan lists eight who declined peerages between 1964 and 1970 (Morgan, 1975, p. 22).

Ever since the scandal associated with Lloyd George's almost open sale of honours just after the First World War, a political honours scrutiny committee has existed. Following the considerable controversy occasioned by Mr Wilson's resignation honours in 1976, this committee was reconstituted, and it was made known that if in future it objected to any candidate, it would convey its objections not only to the Prime Minister but, if this had no effect, to the Queen herself. According to newspaper reports, the name of Jeffery Archer was removed from Mrs Thatcher's resignation honours list following objections from this committee (*Observer*, 23 December 1990). The committee is responsible for ensuring that honours are not awarded in return for financial support, nor should honours be conferred on individuals about whom some public scandal is likely to arise. However, in 1983 the procedures by which the committee must satisfy itself that no honour is proposed in return for financial gifts to a political party were tightened up (*The Times*, 3 December 1983). Although this has not silenced criticism of the fact that individuals associated with companies which have made substantial financial donations to the Conservative Party have received honours, including peerages, the evidence about such links seems highly ambiguous (Radio 4: 'The Power of Patronage', broadcast 10 January 1991). No single honours list has caused such notoriety as Mr Wilson's list in 1976, which included the names of several individuals whose public service was hard to recognise (see Walker, 1987, Ch. 6; Roth, 1977, Ch. 2).

Analysis of Life Peerages

Any classification of new peers is somewhat arbitrary. Many have had varied careers with experience in several areas. For the purposes of Table 2.3 a person's major sphere of employment up to the time when the peerage was awarded has been recorded. Even in cases where a peerage has clearly been granted because of service given to a political party, and announced in a list of so-called 'working' peers, the person concerned has been classified according to whatever professional background he or she had.

Table 2.3   Professional Background of Life Peers Created 1958–91

Former MPs			204
	includes	Conservative	83
		Labour	109
		Liberal	9
		Others	3
Business			86
Trade unions and Co-operative movement			26
Universities			65
Local government			35
Civil and diplomatic service			19
Military			9
Other public service			50
Doctors			11
Lawyers			30
Editors/Journalists			15
Arts			8
Ministers of religion			8
Widows			9
Miscellaneous			26

Note: At some stage 215 had been MPs, but in 11 cases their subsequent career seemed more appropriate for their categorisation.

The House of Commons remains the greatest single source for the recruitment of new peers. The House of Lords is undoubtedly felt by many former MPs to be a pleasant place for semi-retirement from political life. There is still the proximity to the Commons, the sense of atmosphere found at Westminster, old friends to consort with, and the possibility of doing a little useful political work from a base in the Upper House. These advantages are available without constituency work to cope with, or the pressures of parliamentary life as they are encountered in the Commons, or indeed the strain of election campaigns. 'I knew I had been right to retire from the Commons, but did not want to be completely cut off from Westminster,' commented a former Labour cabinet minister in his memoirs (Stewart, 1980). Former MPs whose departure from the Commons was not of their own choosing – through election defeat or even failure to be re-selected – may still be relatively youthful and not without political ambition. But they may calculate that their chances of quickly getting back into active political life through finding and winning a Commons seat are relatively low, and in such circumstances be grateful for the opportunity to go to the Lords. Here they may well receive a warm welcome on their party front bench, and even hope to gain ministerial office if their party is subsequently returned to power. Exceptionally, a minister who loses his Commons seat in an election may even continue his ministerial career without interruption through the immediate award of a peerage, as happened to Lord Gray of Contin in 1983. In 1987 the Solicitor-General for Scotland, Peter Fraser, lost his seat; he continued to hold his ministerial post, though outside the House of Commons, but when he was promoted to Lord Advocate in 1989 he took a peerage.

About a third of the former MPs to receive peerages had attained cabinet rank within government, and most of the remainder had at some stage held ministerial office. A few former cabinet ministers never become peers: maybe because they don't want to, or maybe because their party leader declines to recommend them and the Prime Minister of the day is not disposed to intervene (examples since the 1960s include John Nott, Ray Gunter, William Rodgers and Shirley Williams). Only a minority of former junior ministers have been created peers after leaving the Commons. Of the forty-three Conservative MPs who retired in 1987, twelve had received peerages by 1991. Of Labour's forty-one retiring MPs, only five had received peerages by 1991.

Throughout the twentieth century the House of Lords has received recruits from among the most successful men of business, including manufacturing and heavy industry, retailing and the world of finance. In some cases the individuals concerned have remained very absorbed in their business activities and have not become much involved in the work of the Lords, at least until their retirement. Lord Kearton was created a peer in 1970 but did not make his maiden speech until 1982, after which he became quite active in the Upper House. Mrs Thatcher's creations included such men as Lord Weinstock (GEC) and Lord Sieff of Brimpton (Marks and Spencer), neither of whom took an active part in the House of Lords, at least initially. Typically the eminent businessman who becomes a peer while still highly committed to his business career sits on the cross-benches, and makes occasional contributions in debates on particular subjects. Some peers categorised here as businessmen were known as active supporters of a political party –

for example, the February 1987 list of 'working' peers included Sir Charles Johnston, a director of various engineering companies, who had been chairman of the National Union of Conservative Associations and then president for the year 1986–7; and Sir James Goold, a former president of the CBI in Scotland as well as chairman of the Scottish Conservative Party.

If the world of business has provided numerous recruits, especially to Conservative benches in the House of Lords, the trade-union movement has since 1958 been a reservoir from which the Labour Party has drawn. Before the Life Peerages Act the only trade-union leader to become a peer was Lord Citrine, who entered the Lords in 1946 after twenty years as General Secretary of the TUC. Neither of his two successors in that post became a peer, but after 1958 a steady stream of trade-union leaders entered the Lords, several on the recommendation of Conservative prime ministers. Almost all had been leaders of large unions, usually taking peerages after retirement. An exception was Lord Delacourt-Smith, who continued as General Secretary of the Post Office Engineering Union after becoming a peer in 1967, and even for a time combined his union post with office in the Labour Government. Not all trade-union peers become active members of the House of Lords, though all bar one have taken the Labour Whip: the exception, Lord Chapple, made a peer in 1985, chose to sit on the cross-benches. Trade-union representation in the Lords is also facilitated by peers who were formerly trade-union-sponsored MPs.

A large number of life peers have been drawn from universities, which were little represented before 1958. Some of these have been former vice-chancellors or heads of colleges, whose names became household words through their chairmanship of well-known commissions or committees of inquiry, such as Lord Wolfenden, Lord Fulton and Baroness Warnock. Other university peers have been well-known as supporters of a political party and their peerage has been awarded to enable them to voice such support in the Lords – for example Lords Balogh, Crowther-Hunt and Wedderburn of Charlton on the Labour side, and Lords Beloff, Butterworth and Bauer among Conservatives.

Almost all the life peers classified as 'local government' achieved their main distinction as elected councillors, generally in positions of leadership within their authorities. Several had also tried to win election to the House of Commons, but without success. Only two professional local-authority officers were given peerages: Lord Alexander of Potterhill in 1974, after many years as secretary of the Association of Education Committees, and Baroness Faithfull, a Conservative, in 1976; she had been director of Social Services for Oxford. The original purpose of the 1958 Life Peerages Act might have implied that expertise acquired through professional work within local government would have been of potential value to the Lords, but prime ministers seemed reluctant to draw on this reservoir of talent and experience, perhaps because so many peers – both hereditary as well as life peers – had experience of local government, though as elected councillors rather than as professional employees.

The group described as 'civil and diplomatic service' changed its character after 1958, but the change seems to have had more to do with the end of Empire than with the Life Peerages Act. Before the Act was passed many hereditary peerages were conferred upon colonial governors, ambassadors and other diplomats, but few on home civil servants. Since 1958 the disappearance of many of these great offices overseas has brought with it an attrition in peerages of this kind – and officers in the armed services have received fewer life peerages than their predecessors received hereditary peerages. On the other hand, peerages for home civil servants, formerly rare, have become relatively numerous. A peerage for the retiring head of the civil service has become customary, even when (as in 1982) the person concerned – Lord Bancroft – had been prematurely retired and reckoned to be outside prime ministerial favour. On the other hand, though every recent head of the diplomatic service had received a peerage upon retirement, no such award was made to Sir Michael Palliser, who retired in 1983 (a year after the Falklands conflict), which underlines the point that such awards cannot be viewed as automatic.

The category 'other public service' includes peers drawn from a variety of areas. For example: three former prime ministers of Ulster; some former chairmen of nationalised industries; and others whom it is hard to classify because of their varied experience. Lord Hunt led the successful Everest expedition in 1953, and after many years in the army served as Director of the Duke of Edinburgh's Award Scheme for ten years before becoming a peer in 1966. Surprisingly the first former senior police officer to receive a peerage was Sir Philip Knights in 1987, an omission the more worthy of mention because the House of Lords so frequently debates law and order questions; in 1991 a former metropolitan police commander, Jennifer Hilton, was included as a Labour nominee in a list of working peers. No former prison governors have become peers.

Representation of the professions among new peerages remained irregular even after 1958. A few lawyers in addition to law lords received peerages before and after 1958, as did former presidents of the older medical royal colleges. No leading psychiatrist or veterinary surgeon received a peerage between 1958 and 1991. Two Protestant ministers, the Methodist Donald Soper and George MacLeod of the Church of Scotland, joined the bishops and ennobled former archbishops, as did Lord Jakobovits, the Chief Rabbi, in 1988, but no Roman Catholic priests were recruited. A small number of people prominent in the arts received life peerages, including Lords Bernstein, Britten, Olivier and Miles. Prime ministers have been only moderately imaginative in their attempts to bring in voices from other corners of the nation's life. Mr Wilson's recommendation in 1970 of a thirty-four-year-old woman disabled in a riding accident, to assist in voicing the needs of the handicapped, deserves some credit on this score; she was Baroness Masham of Ilton, the youngest person ever to receive a life peerage. Enough women were given peerages – eighty-five all told to 1991 – to give the Upper House a female membership, among life baronesses alone, far exceeding that of the Commons. The practice of giving peerages to the widows of prominent politicians who, had they lived, could reasonably have expected peerages, appears to have been discontinued; the last such award was to Baroness Airey of Abingdon in 1979, shortly after her husband (Airey Neave) had been assassinated.

How much difference has the Life Peerages Act made to the House? Some broadening of the field of recruitment to the peerage has taken place, and undoubtedly many people – especially, but by no means exclusively, within the Labour Party – who would have refused hereditary peerages have been willing to accept life peerages. Furthermore, if all life peerages had been awarded as hereditary peerages, the Lords would have grown in size even more rapidly than it has, because well over a hundred more heirs would have become eligible to take seats in the House of Lords over the last thirty years. But the vast majority of life peers are the same kind of people as might have been offered hereditary peerages in the past.

Some are elder statesmen, others are eminent men and women ennobled for their achievements in various walks of life. Some are party nominees appointed in expectation of regular and reliable support for their party in the Lords.

The House of Lords in 1990

In the House of Lords as a whole the 760 or so peers by succession still dominate, even if in terms of the active House they are more or less balanced by the 360 or so life peers. Though taxation may have destroyed the opulence of earlier generations, peers by succession remain predominantly men of substance. Over half can be described as landowners, many of whom own vast estates. About a quarter of all those who own fine stately homes and large landholdings are members of the Lords (Roth, 1986). According to the *Sunday Times* (1991) forty-four of the two hundred richest people in Britain were members of the House of Lords, thirty-five of them peers by succession and nine created peers. There are very few tenant-farmers. There are more heads of Oxbridge colleges than comprehensive school teachers – or head-teachers, for that matter. Some three dozen life peers have had experience as manual workers, but most of these are separated by at least two decades from their last direct experience of factory or mine. Five times as many work in banking and finance as in engineering. When the Lords debated the Lloyd's Bill in 1982, over half the peers who took part in the second reading declared an interest as Lloyd's underwriters. A survey of peers' directorships in 1985 indicated that 355 peers held *in toto* 1,755 directorships; 201 of these were Conservative, 89 non-party, 33 Alliance parties, and 31 Labour. (By way of comparison, 180 MPs held cumulatively 435 directorships.) All kinds of companies were represented, but with a particular concentration in banking, insurance and finance; 136 peers were found to be directors of 'Square Mile' companies or partners in stockbrokers and jobbers (*Labour Research*, December 1985, vol. 74, no. 12; see also *Labour Research*, April 1986, vol. 75, no. 4). The same emphasis can be noted from Andrew Roth's figures for 1972. His book *Lord on the Board* gave information on the financial interests of all peers, and at the end of his work he listed peers with interests in various areas. This showed, for example, 678 peers with interests in property, 171

Table 2.4 Occupational Background of All Peers

Occupation	Number of hereditary peers	Number of life peers	Total as % of House
Landowner/farmer	463	60	44
Public service/administrator	109	238	30
Industrialist/service/ manufacturing/retail	155	109	23
Military (regular)	156	25	15
Political work	23	143	14
Banking/insurance	89	32	10
Judge/barrister/solicitor	45	75	10
Civil service/diplomatic	48	66	10
Journalist/author/publisher/printer	70	44	10
Teacher (university, school)	27	77	9
Arts/entertainment	39	36	4
Church	3	31	3
Advertising/public relations	20	6	2
Accountant/economist	15	10	2
Engineer	12	13	2
Other	178	91	22

Sources: This Table is adapted from one published in the *News of the World*, 15 March 1987, which in turn had been taken from N. Baldwin, PhD Thesis, Exeter University.

Note: Occupations have been used as the basis of analysis in this Table. Since some peers have more than one occupation, totals exceed the membership of the House of Lords.

with interests in insurance, 139 with interests in investment trusts and stockbroking, and 131 with interests in banking.

Table 2.4 summarises the occupational background of peers. It is based on the careful researches of Nicholas Baldwin, and relates the position as he found it in 1981. Again, the difficulties in categorising peers must be emphasised, but the overall balance in membership presented here is indicative of the character of the House of Lords. In terms of occupational class background, Baldwin summarised the position in 1981 as 86 per cent drawn from business or professional classes, 2 per cent from the working classes, and 13 per cent miscellaneous or not known.

Even more striking are figures regarding peers' education. In 1981 no fewer than 431 peers were old Etonians – over a third of the total membership of the House of Lords. Overwhelmingly these were peers by succession (over half of all peers by succession went to Eton), but as many as 10 per cent of life peers had also been to Eton, a slightly higher figure than the proportion of old Etonians in the Commons. Over 86 per cent of peers by succession and as many as 45 per cent of life peers had been educated at public schools – the latter being almost exactly the same proportion as for all MPs – though only 5 per cent of the total population attended such schools.

The House of Lords remains disproportionately composed of men, public-school-educated and financially well-to-do. This fact must be emphasised because it is sometimes claimed, half jokingly, that peers by succession, being in the House of Lords through the accident of birth (and death), are a cross-section of society. Any such claim is nonsense. However, it is also true that the device of succession does provide, by chance, a representation different from – and in some respects wider than – that which would be provided by nomination or election. The House of Lords, in the course of its business, hears little or nothing from people straight up from factory shop-floor or lorry-driving, or small-scale tenant-farming. But unexpected and unlikely contributions do occur, and are heard with gratitude. A debate on transport questions can be assisted by contributions from a London bus driver or a lorry driver; a debate on prisons must surely be enriched by someone who has recently served a gaol sentence; just as a debate on drug addiction is given more meaning through the contribution of a former heroin addict. Peers by succession are more likely than MPs in the contemporary world to include people with such experience, and these are in fact actual examples.

On one point at least, the succession system does produce welcome variety. Through the chance of birth and death, the House of Lords' membership includes a few dozen people in their twenties and thirties who have time to contribute to its business, and very few of these possess those special ambitions without which it is impossible to gain election to the Commons at an early age. In 1990, of the 815 peers who attended the House during the session, 45 were under 40 years old and all these were peers by succession, while of the 333 peers under 60 who attended the House, only 35 were life peers. The average age of all peers was 65, but the average age of life peers alone was 71. An entirely appointed House of Lords would almost certainly be a very elderly House indeed.

The Active House of Lords

In some senses the House of Lords defies definition. It consists of peers who belong to it, but some belong so loosely that they are scarcely members in any real sense. The Lords resembles many clubs or other organisations – even trade-union branches – in that it has a nucleus and a bigger membership. In 1989–90 7 peers attended 146 of the 147 sittings and 36 others attended 140 times or more; but at the other extreme 46 attended only once and over 350 not at all. At any single sitting most of those present are likely to be people who attend most of the sittings, but there will also be a few who have for some reason selected that sitting for a rare appearance.

Technically it may be correct to say that the House of Lords consists of all peers eligible to receive a writ of summons. But at any one time one should obviously subtract those not in receipt of the writ, and also those on leave of absence. Perhaps one should go further and deduct all who fail to attend in any given session, even if they have writs and are not on leave of absence (though non-attenders must positively ask not to be placed on leave of absence, otherwise they are automatically given leave). Peers who attend just once or twice cannot be excluded from an analysis, but they are members to a lesser degree than peers who attend over a hundred times a year.

Attendance is one yardstick for assessing the active House of Lords. But some members attend frequently without apparently contributing much to the work of the Lords; in the 1989–90 session, nineteen peers who attended over two-thirds of the sittings said nothing (nine of these were life peers). On the other hand, some peers attend seldom, but when they do come they make weighty speeches. For example Lord Lane, Lord Chief Justice, attended only twice in the 1989–90 session, both times making speeches on the Courts and Legal Services Bill, while the Archbishop of York attended only six times, but made five speeches.

In the following analysis we examine both attendance and interventions in debate as recorded by the Hansard Sessional Index. The total number of peers eligible to attend the House of Lords at

Table 2.5 Peers' Attendance and Interventions in Debates, 1989–90*

	Eligible for attendance	Attended once or more	Intervened in debates once or more
All created peers (including bishops and law lords)	423	381	286
Peers by succession	763	445	235
Total	1,186	826	521

Sources: Calculated from Hansard Index and information supplied by House of Lords Journal and Information Office.

Note: * Peers eligible for membership at end of session, i.e. excluding peers who died during the session, but including those who became eligible during the session.

the close of the 1989–90 session was 1,186. Of this total, 86 were without writs of summons and 139 were on leave of absence. If we exclude these we are left with a total of 961, of whom over 85 per cent attended once or more during the previous session, leaving 135 peers who did not attend, even though they were not on leave of absence. In the same session 521 peers spoke in debates, leaving 305 who attended at least once but never spoke on the floor of the House during that year.

The most striking feature of Table 2.5 is the contrast between created peers and peers by succession in terms of their relative likelihood to attend or to speak. Before the 1958 Life Peerages Act, most of the regular attenders had inherited their peerages and most were Conservative. By the late 1960s this was no longer true, and by the 1980s Conservative and hereditary dominance within the working House had been further eroded. It was the arrival in considerable numbers of relatively active life peers which brought about this change. Over 90 per cent of created peers attended, and over two-thirds spoke in debates in the House of Lords. By contrast, less than 60 per cent of peers by succession attended, and less than one-third spoke.

Table 2.6 gives a more detailed analysis of attendance in the same 1989–90 session. The 1968 White Paper defined regular attenders as those who were present on more than one-third of the sitting days, and also gave figures for those attending up to one in twenty sittings. Table 2.6 uses both these criteria, but also incorporates the more demanding criterion of attendance at over two-thirds of the sittings. The relative assiduity of life peers and the predominance of created peers among regular attenders is clear. The table also shows that while the Conservative Party was the largest group in the House of Lords, at every attendance frequency level Conservative peers were outnumbered by the other groups combined. Noticeable too is the high proportion of Labour peers who attended regularly compared with peers in other parties. Over half of all Labour peers attended over two-thirds of the sittings, and three-quarters at least one-third, while for the Conservative Party the corresponding figures were less than one-quarter and two-fifths.

Intervention in debates by peers is analysed in Table 2.7. No less than 80 per cent of all Labour peers who attended the Lords also spoke, whereas less than 60 per cent of Conservative peers who

Table 2.6 Attendance Frequency of Peers, 1989–90 Session*

			Number of attendances				
		Nil	Up to 5% (1–7)	Over 5% (8–48)	Over ⅓ (49–97)	Over ⅔ (98–147)	Total
Conservative	C	4	10	35	37	31	117
	S	48	68	97	53	65	331
Labour	C	7	6	9	26	54	102
	S	1	2	1	3	4	11
Lib/SDP	C	1	0	7	12	18	38
	S	6	5	8	8	7	34
Cross-bench	C	22	30	41	12	16	121
	S	263	52	35	17	20	387
Bishops		2	5	19	0	0	26
Law lords		6	1	9	2	1	19
All created	(C)	42	52	120	89	120	423
All succeeded	(S)	318	127	141	81	96	763
Total		360	179	261	170	216	1,186

Source: Author's calculations, based on information supplied by Party Whips and by House of Lords Information Office.

Note: C = created; S = succeeded.

* Excludes peers who died during the session.

Table 2.7   Interventions by Peers in Debates, 1989–90*

		Number of interventions			
		1–10	*11–50*	*Over 51*	*Total*
Conservative	C	56	22	13	91
	S	86	39	15	140
Labour	C	18	34	24	76
	S	3	4	2	9
Lib/SDP	C	8	16	6	30
	S	12	10	1	23
Cross-bench	C	41	15	1	57
	S	47	12	4	63
Bishops		17	1	0	18
Law lords		9	5	0	14
All created	(C)	149	93	44	286
All succeeded	(S)	148	65	22	235
Total		297	158	66	521*

Source: Number of interventions calculated from Hansard Index; interventions made on the same day on the same motion, question, or
stage of a bill have been counted as a single intervention.
Note: C = created; S = succeeded.
   * Excludes peers who died during the session.

attended spoke in the chamber. Though peers by succession formed
the majority of those who attended the Lords, they were outnumbered by created peers when contributions to debate are
considered, and among the most regular contributors – who
intervened over fifty times in the session – created peers outnumbered peers by succession by almost two to one. In this group of
the most frequent speakers, a majority were front-bench spokesmen,
whose role is further considered in the next chapter.

In examining the activity of the House of Lords, it is helpful to
conclude by considering specifically the work of particular groups of
peers. Two easily recognisable groups are the bishops and the law
lords, both already referred to in our analysis of membership. These
deserve particular attention because a second chamber designed on
corporate lines would consist of groups essentially similar to bishops
and law lords.

Bishops

The activity of the bishops in the House of Lords has changed a good deal during this century. Before the First World War they took an active part, not least in matters of sharp political controversy; but in the interwar period the activity of bishops in the Lords declined until by the Second World War most had become rare visitors, though there were a few individual exceptions (Bromhead, 1958, pp. 56–8). A sense of caution about voting on political issues was accentuated during the 1940s and 1950s, but reversed in the more lively atmosphere in the House following the introduction of life peers in 1958. In 1953 only one bishop voted against the Government on the Central African Federation, and in 1956 two voted when the Government's Suez policy was debated. But in 1968 no fewer than eighteen bishops voted (all with the Labour Government) in a sharply contested division on sanctions against Rhodesia. From time to time throughout the 1970s and 1980s bishops took a significant part in the business of the Lords, including politically controversial matters.

Bishops have been prominent when so-called issues of conscience have come before the Lords, notably in the late 1960s. The Divorce Reform Bill of 1969, which introduced the concept of breakdown of marriage as a ground for divorce, followed a considerable debate in which the Church had taken a leading part. When legislation to reform the law on homosexuality was introduced, Lord Dilhorne, a former Lord Chancellor, could not remember any bill on which the bishops had taken so much part. On abortion, in 1968, the bishops were divided, with the Archbishop of Canterbury, Dr Ramsey, supporting an amendment to remove the so-called social grounds for abortion from the bill, but some of his brother prelates helping eventually to defeat this amendment. On the death penalty question bishops were divided in 1948 (when only two voted) and again in 1956, but by 1965 all were abolitionists, and in 1969 no fewer than twenty bishops voted when the death penalty was finally abolished (following a four-year trial period of abolition). This was the largest voting turnout of bishops since twenty-four had voted in 1927 on the prayer book controversy.

Legislation on these issues of conscience has usually been introduced by private members, and passed on free votes. A good deal of government legislation also deals with matters where ethical, moral or social questions are raised, and the bishops have not infrequently taken a vigorous part on such bills too. Bishops voted regularly against immigration controls from the 1960s to the 1980s; for example, in 1981 eight bishops voted against the Conservative Government on the British Nationality Bill, and at committee stage several amendments were put down to retain the principle that any child born in the UK would be entitled to British citizenship, including one amendment in the name of the Archbishop of Canterbury and three other bishops which was lost by 134 votes to 92. During the final stages on the Health and Medicines Bill in November 1988, in two successive divisions seven and eight bishops voted against the Government's proposals for increasing charges for dental inspections and eye tests. In October 1990 eleven bishops voted against the Government during the final stage of the Human Fertilisation and Embryology Bill; they were resisting a Commons amendment which allowed abortion up to the point of birth in cases of serious foetal handicap.

On some government bills the bishops have effectively acted as spokesmen for the particular interest they represent, though this should not be thought of simply as a narrow Church of England interest. For example, in 1976 the Labour Government's Community Land Bill gave rise to great concern on the part of land-owning charities, the largest of many affected being the Church of England. In the Lords the Bishop of London (Dr Ellison) led the attack, eventually pressing his amendments, which were carried by large majorities against the Government on divisions in which bishops acted as 'tellers'. When the changes made were altered by the Commons, the bishop wanted the Lords to insist on its amendments, but the Conservative Opposition decided to concentrate its attack against the Government on another bill, and the bishops had to accept defeat. The Bishop of London, Dr Leonard, was very active on the 1988 Education Reform Bill, at one point moving – and, with the help in the division lobby of six other bishops, including the Archbishop of Canterbury, carrying – an amendment to make more restrictive the conditions under which schools could opt out of local-authority control (see below p. 172). During the passage of the Broadcasting Bill in 1990 the Central Religious Advisory Council for broadcasting came under severe attack from some peers but was stoutly defended by the chairman of the Council, the Bishop of Liverpool, and his predecessor, the Bishop of London (9 July 1990).

When, in 1985, the Conservative Government introduced a bill to remove restrictions on Sunday trading, its action provoked widespread opposition from the Churches. This bill was first introduced in the Lords, where the bishops led the attack, and though the Government got the bill through virtually unscathed, an unusually intense campaign had been unleashed in the country, which led to it being defeated outright at second reading in the Commons. In the Lords, bishops had forced a division at second reading (lost by 141 votes to 85), and in committee up to nineteen bishops voted at one time, but in the only government defeat on this bill (which concerned continued protection for shop-workers under employment law), no bishop voted.

In almost any area of legislation, an episcopal contribution may be forthcoming. Sometimes this will be a second-reading speech drawing attention to the social or moral questions which underlie much legislation. The Bishop of Durham, Dr Jenkins, gained some headlines for his claim, made during the debate on the 1985 Transport Bill, that the doctrine behind this measure looked dangerously like idolatry. He took no part in the later stages on that bill, and by the late 1980s had become a very rare attender at the House. In 1984 the Bishop of Rochester, Dr Say, spoke at the second reading of the Local Government (Interim Provisions) Bill, explaining that it was only with reluctance that the bishops joined debate on such a highly charged party political matter, but that they did so because the Churches in London were united in their opposition to the abolition of the GLC. Subsequently three bishops voted against the Government on this bill in a division which entailed the Thatcher Government's most serious defeat in the Lords (see Chapter 6).

Bishops do not appear to show any inhibition in voting against the Government, or even helping to bring about a government defeat. During a debate in 1971 on disestablishment of the Church, a peer suggested that bishops take care not to use their voting strength against the Government of the day, but he was immediately contradicted by the Archbishop of Canterbury and other bishops (HL Debs, 20 January 1971, vol. 520). In the 1980s tension between the Church of England and Mrs Thatcher's Conservative Government became very obvious, and bishops in the Lords found themselves voting against the Government much more frequently than in its support. But it must also be said that bishops were not on the whole either regular attenders or regular voters. In 1988–9 not a single bishop voted in 153 of the 189 divisions for which the Government placed a whip.

Bishops also take part in the non-legislative work of the House of Lords. The Archbishop of Canterbury has occasionally initiated a full day's debate, most recently on the fortieth anniversary of the United Nations in 1985. Other bishops, too, sometimes put down motions or ask questions, the latter possibly dealing with matters relating especially to their dioceses. Participation by bishops in debates on motions is selective. In 1989–90 bishops spoke in sixteen out of forty debates on motions for papers (the formula on which general debates are held), but in only two out of thirty-one debates on unstarred questions (which are usually arranged at shorter notice). Most subjects where a moral dimension was self-evident found an episcopal contribution.

Bishops are busy people, and attendance at the House of Lords has to be fitted in around a very full schedule. The occasional high turnout of bishops may arise for quite fortuitous reasons. A meeting of bishops in London took place on the day that eighteen voted on Rhodesian Sanctions in 1968, and when nineteen bishops voted in February 1986 on an amendment to the Shops Bill, none spoke in the preceding debate because they arrived *en bloc* directly from a Synod meeting, just in time to vote (HL Debs, 6 February 1986, col. 1314). A rota ensures that a bishop is present for prayers, which means that at least one bishop is present for the first part of the day's proceedings. Drewry and Brock found a high correlation between bishops' interventions in debate and their reading of prayers (Drewry and Brock, 1971). Given the large cross-bench element and the independent-mindedness of peers generally, individual speeches can sway votes in the Lords, and the contributions made by bishops in general have an impact out of proportion to their numerical strength.

Some bishops give much more attention to the Lords than others, but very few in recent years have attended more than one-third of the sitting days. The Bishop of Norwich, the Rt Revd Maurice Wood, a member from 1975 to 1985, was for several years the most frequent speaker, making up to two dozen speeches annually on a wide range of subjects. When he retired in 1985 several peers hoped he would return as a life peer but this was not to be (Whale, 1985). The Bishop of Rochester, Dr Say, a member from 1969 to 1988, was also a regular attender and quite frequent contributor to debates. Other bishops took very little part, though in recent sessions few have been totally silent.

Should the bishops take their responsibilities in the Lords more seriously? It is certainly reasonable to argue that, given the fact of their membership (in some strength), more effort should be made to ensure that bishops are present and do contribute on a wider range of topics than at present. Even on the Sunday Trading Bill, to which the Church took strong exception, no bishop spoke or voted on several crucial amendments, and not infrequently peers express their regret at the absence of the bishops during debates on social questions. The Bishop of Rochester acknowledged their erratic attendance on Sunday trading, explaining that this had been due to 'our commitments to our parishes and people [which] must always have our first loyalties' (HL Debs, 25 February 1986, col. 949). One view would be that where the Church as a body is openly and publicly critical of the Government, its bishops ought to be prepared to use the forum of the House of Lords to join debate with government ministers – not spasmodically but in a regular, detailed and hence more responsible way.

Law Lords

Legal expertise may be regarded as an essential requirement in any legislature. About one-sixth of the members of the House of Commons are lawyers (far fewer than in many other legislatures, notably the US Congress), but only one-tenth of peers (see Table 2.4). The law officers of the Crown have usually been members of the Commons, though since 1976 one of the Scottish law officers has been a member of the Lords. Legal learning in the Upper House is chiefly represented by the Lord Chancellor, and his predecessors still living, together with the law lords. Serving law lords are not forbidden to take part in any business before the Lords, though there is a predisposition against their participation in matters of political controversy. Their judicial duties also inevitably impose restrictions on the amount of time they can give to the work of the House. Once retired they may have more time to participate, and need no longer feel that the independence of their role as judges is threatened by their entry into matters of political controversy. But advancing years may well limit the activities of some, and others may feel that discretion and a sense of decorum ought still to inhibit participation in political matters.

Some serving law lords hardly ever speak in the House (Blom-Cooper and Drewry, 1972, Ch. 10). Those who are active concentrate their contributions on bills which involve the judicial system, the administration of justice, or law reform. On such matters law lords may play a substantial part, even occasionally dominating the proceedings. Some law reform measures are technical and complex, and political discussion never really emerges, but in other cases matters which do excite party controversy in the Commons may well be debated in the Lords simply from a technical or expert point of view. Law lords are by no means always united, and it is recognised that when they speak, they are simply offering their own views. They may sound out opinion within their profession, or even be subject to a little discreet lobbying from fellow judges, but only in exceptional circumstances do they claim to speak on behalf of their colleagues. An example of the latter occurred in 1976 when Lord Wheatley, a Scottish judge, explained in a debate on the proposed devolution legislation that his speech expressed the unanimous views of all the High Court Judges in Scotland, whom he had specifically consulted and whose views were unlikely to be placed on public record by any other means (HL Debs, 27 January 1976, col. 836). In his speech he expressed serious misgivings about the proposals, but took no part in the subsequent devolution debate. On the question of the death penalty, all law lords who took part in the 1948 debates supported retention; in 1956 seven voted for retention, two for abolition. By 1965 judges were painfully aware of the imperfections of the 1957 Homicide Act (which had categorised murder into capital and non-capital). Lord Chief Justice Parker argued strongly for abolition, undoubtedly exerting an important influence over a number of peers. He was supported by four other law lords, but his predecessor, Lord Goddard, and the Master of the Rolls, Lord Denning, both supported retention.

The most obvious conflict of principle between serving law lords and the Government in the post-war period arose over the War Damage Bill of 1965. It was the retrospective character of this measure – introduced to remove a liability to damages which the courts had found against the Government – which angered the judiciary. The Lord Chief Justice, Lord Parker of Waddington, attacked it at second reading and, along with another law lord and several retired law lords, voted for a wrecking amendment carried by a substantial majority at committee stage. When the Commons returned the bill with the Lords' amendment deleted, Lord Parker again spoke and voted against the Government, but no other law lord supported him in the lobby, and the Government comfortably won. This was a Labour Government bill, but the Conservative Party, which had left office the previous year, had clearly been preparing a similar measure. Two former Conservative Lord Chancellors supported the bill, along with most opposition front-benchers. The law lords were initially united on the War Crimes Bill of 1990, with three serving law lords speaking against the bill and eight voting against it when the House first rejected it in June. However, when the Government brought the bill back to the House in April 1991 under the terms of the Parliament Acts, the law lords were divided; one, Lord Ackner, acted as a teller in the division which resulted in the House again rejecting the bill, while another, Lord Bridge of Harwich, made a speech in which he urged the House to give the bill a second reading, while also making clear that he disliked it and thought it should be amended (see below, p. 252).

Where serving law lords have been asked by the Government to chair commissions or committees of inquiry, their subsequent participation in Lords' debates on these subjects is to be expected. Lord Donovan took an active part at all stages in the passage of the Industrial Relations Bill in 1971 following his chairmanship of the Royal Commission on Trade Unions in the late 1960s. Following inner-city unrest, Lord Scarman was asked to conduct an inquiry in 1981, but several of his recommendations were not accepted by the Government. During the passage of the Police and Criminal Evidence Bill in 1984 he sought a number of changes, one of which was carried on division against the Government; this made racial discriminatory behaviour by the police a specific disciplinary offence, an alteration reluctantly accepted by the Government. In 1987 he gave an ironic welcome to a government statement which, he claimed, marked the acceptance of a recommendation made in his report as 'recently as 1981'. For a serving law lord he was unusually active in the House, prior to his retirement in 1986.

Serving law lords also take some part in the non-legislative work of the House of Lords. Lord Chief Justice Lane made his maiden speech in a debate on crime in 1983, and has contributed to other

debates on this frequently debated subject. When the Lords debated
the report of the committee on Fraud Trials, chaired by Lord
Roskill, a serving law lord, nine of the eighteen speeches were made
by serving or retired law lords (10 February 1986). A serving law
lord always chairs the Law and Institutions Sub-Committee of the
European Communities Committee, and the expertise of law lords is
also made available through their membership of some other select
committees, for example the *ad hoc* Committee on Murder and Life
Imprisonment, which sat during the 1988–9 session and whose
members included Lord Ackner, a serving law lord.

Contrasting approaches to the House of Lords were illustrated by
Lords Devlin and Denning. Lord Devlin retired in 1964 after only
three years as a serving law lord; during that time he rarely attended
the House of Lords and never spoke. He was only 59 at retirement,
and despite his public activities – for example as Chairman of the
Press Council for five years – and his authorship of interesting and
controversial books such as *Trial by Jury* and *The Enforcement of
Morals*, he remained a silent and virtually non-attending member of
the Lords to the time of writing. By contrast, Lord Denning – who
became a Lord of Appeal in Ordinary in 1957 – was a prolific
contributor to debates following his retirement in 1982.

The law lords do play a significant role in the House of Lords. In
part this is a matter of being 'resident technical consultants to the
legislature on legal points arising out of proposed legislation' (Blom-
Cooper and Drewry, 1972, p. 203); in part it is their capacity to
contribute generally to debates on crime and the penal system,
though their contribution here is fairly irregular; in part it is their
readiness to act as guardians over the whole machinery of justice
when they see this being affected by some change they consider
foolish. Among the law lords of each generation there also appear to
be one or two who choose to become House of Lords men, drawing
on their legal expertise but applying it in an unabashed way in
debate on a wide range of topics.

Other Groups of Peers

It is possible to identify many different groups of peers, distinctive
because of their professional background or by reason of such
characteristics as disablement or membership of other bodies such
as the European Parliament. A brief comment about the activities of

some such groups is helpful in developing an understanding of the House of Lords.

Though the few civil servants who received peerages before 1964 had taken little part in the activities of the House of Lords, some of their successors – for example Baroness Sharp, a former Permanent Secretary, and Lord Helsby, formerly Head of the Civil Service – did not regard their examples as precedents to be followed when they entered the Lords in the late 1960s. Both took active parts in proceedings on some bills, including occasions on which the Government was defeated, especially on matters where their specialised knowledge based on their professional experience in the civil service could be deployed. This has also been the pattern for activity within the House of Lords by Lord Allen of Abbeydale, who became a peer in 1976, four years after retiring from his post as Permanent Secretary at the Home Office. Some of the subjects on which he has spoken persistently have been Home Office matters; his courteous yet razor-sharp interventions have occasionally left government spokesmen reeling with discomfiture. Another former civil servant who has taken part in the Lords has been Lord Bancroft, making occasional speeches indicating his disquiet with government attitudes, for example over the summary banning of trade unions at GCHQ (8 February 1984), as did his successor as Head of the Civil Service, Lord Armstrong of Ilminster, who made occasional outspoken speeches in the Lords, for example speaking of the frequent and ill-considered changes which had been made to local government and calling for a royal commission to be set up to report on that subject (27 February 1991). Others have taken no part whatsoever in the proceedings – notably another former Head of the Civil Service, Lord Armstrong of Sanderstead, who never made a speech while he was a member of the House of Lords from 1974 to 1980.

Several peers from the Foreign Service and Diplomatic Corps have been active in the Lords. Lord Strang, former Head of the Foreign Office, entered in 1954 and became the first co-ordinator of the cross-bench peers, a group to which his successors, including Lords Caccia, Garner, Gore-Booth, and Greenhill of Harrow, all belonged. Lord Brimelow, who served for two years as Permanent Secretary at the Foreign Office before his entry to the Lords in 1975, departed from convention by joining the Labour peers instead of remaining on the cross-benches. He has chosen to take little part on the floor of the House, but has actively engaged himself in the work of the European Communities Committee. Lord Gladwyn, whose last diplomatic appointment was as Ambassador to France, entered the Lords in 1960 and has been an active Liberal (and Liberal Democrat) spokesman ever since.

Several former military leaders have taken a regular part in debates on defence and related matters, as well as acting as spokesmen for such interests as the Officers' Pensions Society. The annual debate on the Defence White Paper customarily draws half a dozen or so speeches from such peers. Some ask questions and take a regular part in the business within their particular interests. Such peers invariably sit on the cross-benches, though they may informally link up with peers in whichever party has their sympathy. Many hereditary peers have also had experience as regular officers, and some of these, together with politicians who have had responsibilities for defence, formed the House of Lords all-party defence study group in 1976, an unofficial group which sought to act as a forum within the Lords to develop a better understanding of defence issues.

Several elected members of the European Parliament have been peers (four in 1979, three in 1984, four in 1989); these have naturally used their membership of the Lords to bring European Community concerns to the notice of government and public. Lord Bethell and Baroness Elles, both MEPs, tabled amendments to the 1985 Representation of the People Bill designed to enfranchise all British officials working in EC institutions. Their amendment was carried with the support of Labour peers, but the Labour front bench in the Commons opposed the change, and the Government was unwilling to break a concordat reached across the floor of the Commons, so the changes were eventually reversed.

From the early 1970s onwards a group of disabled peers have taken an active part in the Lords, seeking to improve public awareness of the needs of the disabled and urging Government to take action to alleviate the problems faced by disabled people. Legislation on employment, social security and housing, as well as bills dealing specifically with the sick and disabled, have been amended at the instigation of disabled peers. The presence of several peers in wheelchairs – sometimes four at a time – adds a certain immediacy to debates on the problems faced by the disabled. Individuals who suffer such handicaps are not likely to become sufficiently active as politicians to win election to the Commons, so their presence in the Lords has added significance.

Finally, mention must be made of women peers. Though heavily outnumbered by men, those women who have been peers have tended to be disproportionately active, as was shown by Drewry and Brock (1983). Baroness Young was Leader of the House from 1981 to 1983; Baroness Hylton-Foster has been Convenor of the Cross-bench Peers and Baroness Seear Leader of the Liberal Peers. Baroness Llewelyn-Davies of Hastoe was Labour Chief Whip from 1973 to 1982, and then followed Baroness White as salaried Chairman* of the European Communities Committee before being herself succeeded in the latter role by Baroness Serota in 1986. Proportionately the female element on the front benches in the Lords has been considerably higher than in the Commons. Of the 137 created peers shown in Table 2.7 as speaking more than eleven times in the 1989–90 session, twenty-six were women. Female peers have initiated debates, asked questions and put down amendments to bills on subjects of obvious interest to women, such as Baroness Seear on equal pay, Baroness Ewart-Biggs on female prisoners, Baroness MacLeod of Borve on widows, and so on. When Baroness Lockwood – Chairman of the Equal Opportunities Commission – initiated a debate on the position of women in public life in May 1985, six of the twelve speeches were made by women. But Drewry and Brock's study found that women's contributions in the Lords, taken overall, did not differ substantially from those of their male colleagues in terms of subject matter.

Conclusion

The working House of Lords is hard to describe. A nucleus of peers can be thought of as professional politicians. For some this has been

* These three Baronesses were all referred to as Chairman of this Committee, which follows normal parliamentary terminology under which 'Chairman' has been preferred to 'Chair', 'Chairperson', etc. In this book, as in Parliament itself, female peers who serve as chairmen of committees are referred to as 'Chairman'. In similar fashion the term 'Spokesman' is used rather than 'Spokesperson' or even 'Spoke'! Since all offices are open to both sexes, where the term 'he' is used in referring to the office (rather than to a particular occupant) this should be understood as meaning 'he' or 'she'.

their whole career; for others it is an interlude. Around this nucleus a very large number of peers are part-time members of the Lords – some regular and systematic part-timers, others very infrequent and probably casual attenders. In part, the House has become a meritocratic chamber where leading figures in various walks of life mingle with politicians. In part, it is a representative chamber, not according to any elective principle but simply through the accidental membership, as it were, of doctors, practising dentists, bee-keepers, opticians, accountants, lecturers, social workers, journalists, retailers, and so on. In part, the House remains an aristocratic chamber, some of its most active members being there because of peerages awarded to their forebears, and a high proportion having grown up in families marked by privilege or conspicuous success.

It is a surprising blend. It could be a highly fragmented institution. Certainly, if all peers were like bishops or law lords, eminent and successful but owing their presence in the House of Lords to offices they hold outside it, fragmentation would be likely. Nor do the other groupings we have briefly considered here really bring coherence to the Lords as a working institution. It is the parties which are the great organising force within the chamber, bringing co-ordination to its activities and drawing peers together from all the diverse elements which constitute the House of Lords. It is to the parties, and their role in the Lords, that we turn next.

3

The Role of Political Parties in the House

The party system has been aptly described as the single most dominating feature of the British Constitution. An idealised model of British politics sees one party monopolising government and another party, Her Majesty's loyal Opposition, just as organised and cohesive, taking its place as the alternative government. In practice, third parties may intrude to a greater or lesser degree, but at the parliamentary level it is the two-party model which has predominated.

In modern conditions it is control of the Commons which is crucial in deciding which party becomes the government. The Commons is directly elected and is therefore the centre-piece of the party political struggle. The House of Lords, by contrast, has no role in the making or unmaking of governments, nor do any of its members owe their place to election. Nevertheless, although governments do not depend for their existence on the Lords, they are answerable there and they must get their legislation through both Lords and Commons. All governments must therefore appoint a team of ministers in the House of Lords. For each item of business the government spokesman has his place with his supporters beside and behind him. The opposition spokesman for that business faces him across the table, similarly supported by his colleagues.

Government and opposition parties keep lists of their supporters, to whom a party whip is issued in relation to most of the business which comes before the Lords. This indicates whether votes are expected and, if so, the importance attached to specific items by the party leadership. This is done, as in the Commons, by underlining either one, two or three times, the latter being the strongest summons. The salience of party is heightened in the Lords by the expectations of the many peers who come to the Upper House after a lifetime's experience of the party-dominated Lower House.

Despite these factors, the general environment within which parties operate is very different in the Upper House from the Lower. Fundamental to this is the fact that peers do not owe their position to election, and no election can remove them from the House of Lords. They may be loyal party members, but they were not elected on the basis of any party manifesto, so their obligation to support such is not the same as that of MPs. They have no constituents to bother about, no local parties to humour, no re-selection anxieties to trouble them. Nor do peers receive a parliamentary salary which might generate some obligation to attend regularly. If they disagree with their Party, they need not openly rebel because they can just quietly stay away from the Lords, or at least stay out of the division lobby. The party whips can encourage and try to persuade their colleagues, but they cannot in any sense command, coerce or bully them. A rebellious MP may ultimately face expulsion from his Party and the probable loss of his seat at the next election. If a rebellious peer is expelled from his Party he simply moves to some other quarter of the House, where he may become an even greater nuisance or embarrassment to his former colleagues.

The presence of a large number of non-party or cross-bench peers has also been significant in mitigating the impact of party politics upon the House of Lords. Many cross-bench peers have been active, even in committee on contentious bills, seeking to promote changes which have lain outside the party battle-lines. A description given by a prominent cross-bench peer in 1975 still accurately describes the role of cross-benchers: 'Some are genuinely non-party; some are retired public servants who have served governments of both parties. Some have definite party sympathies, but because they hold some public office prefer for the time being to lay aside their active party allegiance. Some are not in full sympathy with their parties. Some just do not like to be at the receiving end of a whip. In our opinions we range widely from right to left' (Lord Strang, HL Debs, 3 July 1975, col. 382). The presence of a sizeable body of this kind is a highly unusual – if not unique – feature of any legislature. It helps to muffle party politics.

The considerable imbalance between the two major parties has been a final factor restraining the development of competitive party politics in the House of Lords. There is a sense in which the Labour

Party (because it is so markedly smaller than the Conservative) whether in or out of office, is always in Opposition in the Lords, usually losing divisions, just occasionally winning. Competition can never be so keen if teams are so unevenly matched. Yet though the Conservatives retain a marked majority over Labour, the total picture of party strength in the Lords has changed a good deal in recent years; these changes merit closer attention.

The Changing Party Balance in the House

Figures about relative party strength in the Lords need to be interpreted with some caution, since peers who take a party whip may attend the House so seldom (or even never come at all) that their inclusion in party totals is misleading. For many years the parties were reserved about publishing any lists of their supporters, and the information given in reference books was certainly incomplete as well as sometimes unreliable. Not until the 1968 White Paper on reform were authoritative figures about party support published.

Table 3.1 gives the picture for four selected sessions over the last twenty-five years, differentiating between 'regular' attenders, who come on over one-third of sitting days, and mere attenders, but excluding altogether peers who did not attend at all in the sessions indicated. Total Labour strength rose steadily, peaking at 161 in 1979, but then declined to 104 by 1990. There were two reasons for this. The first was the loss of Labour peers to the newly formed Social Democratic Party. By 1985 twenty-three peers had migrated direct from the Labour to the SDP benches. For several years before this, a trickle of Labour peers had made their way to the cross-benches (some of whom moved on to the SDP in 1981). The second was the reduced flow of new Labour peerages following Mrs Thatcher's arrival in Downing Street. As Labour peers became old and frail or died, replacements were slow to follow. Successive Labour leaders urged the Prime Minister to replenish the Labour benches. When she did so, she ensured that the supply of new Conservative peers outnumbered Labour, Liberal and Social Democrats combined (see Table 2.2, p. 36).

The larger number of Conservatives created life peers in the 1980s was one reason for the growth in Conservative strength. Another was Conservative recruitment from new peers by succession (some

Table 3.1 Party Strength in the House of Lords

		Cons	Lab	Lib (and SDP)	Independent incl. cross-benchers, bishops and law lords
1967–8	Attenders	314	113	37	215
	Regulars	125	95	19	52
1975–6	Attenders	292	149	30	281
	Regulars	141	104	24	60
1984–5	Attenders	376	122	76	245
	Regulars	168	91	51	68
1989–90	Attenders	397	104	65	260
	Regulars	186	87	45	68

Sources: 967–8 figures from Cmnd 3799, *House of Lords Reform*. Other sessions: author's calculations based on information supplied by House of Lords Information Office. See also HL 9 (1987–8), Annex B, Tables 1 and 2.

Notes: 'Attenders': Those who attended once or more during the session, excluding any who died during the session (or bishops who resigned before the end of the session).
'Regulars': Those attending who were present on one-third or more of sittings during the session ('regulars' also included in 'attenders'). Figures for total party strength for December 1990 issued by the House of Lords Information Office were: Conservative 449, Labour 112, Liberal Democrat 53, SDP 17, Cross-bench (excluding bishops and Lords of Appeal) 253.

of whom first sat on the cross-benches). From the Conservative point of view, the crucial question was the margin the Party held over the combined opposition parties. Labour's loss to the Social Democrats was no gain to the Conservatives. The increased difficulty faced in the Lords by the Thatcher Government in the mid 1980s no doubt reinforced caution on the Prime Minister's part about her new nominations.

Later in this chapter we examine further the nature of party cohesion in the House of Lords, discussing party organisation and the character of whipping. Before that, however, we examine more closely the front benches in the Lords.

Conservative and Labour Front Benches

There are some striking contrasts between the two major parties'
front benches in the Lords (see Tables 3.2 and 3.3). Labour's has
become dominated by life peers: of the twenty-seven peers who held
office when Labour was in Government from 1974 to 1979, all but
three were life peers, and by late 1990 there were no hereditary peers
in an expanded front-bench team of twenty-seven spokesmen. The
proportion of hereditary peers on the Conservative front bench has
also been declining, but still in 1990 over two-thirds were peers by
succession, though in the early 1970s the proportion had been a
good deal higher.

Because it consists overwhelmingly of life peers, the Labour front
bench tends to have a higher average age and also contains peers
with a shorter experience of the House of Lords than the
Conservative front bench. In 1990 the average age on the latter was
51, while the average age on the Labour front-bench was 64; three
Conservative spokesmen were under 40 but Labour had only nine of
its twenty-seven under 60, and six were over 70 years old. While
Conservative front-benchers were younger than their Labour
opponents, they had on average spent twice as many years in the
Lords as their opposite numbers. However, more of Labour's front
bench also had experience of the Commons, though the proportion
who were former MPs had declined during the late 1980s from about
half to around a quarter.

The Conservative front bench is mainly made up of peers by
succession who have chosen, at least for a time, to follow a political
career. The choice may be made quite suddenly. In 1973 the Earl of
Limerick was appointed parliamentary under-secretary at the
Department of Trade on the day following reports that he had joined
the Conservative Party. He had previously sat on the cross-benches,
and after the Conservatives lost office in 1974 he quickly returned to
his City business interests. For those who happen to inherit peerages
the House of Lords does provide an inside track for rapid
advancement in a political career. In 1986 Lords Beaverbrook and
Hesketh both joined the Government in their thirties without having
had any significant political experience. In 1990 the 33-year-old Earl
of Strathmore and Kinghorne became a government spokesman at a
time when he had yet to make his maiden speech in the House. In
1971, the Earl of Gowrie forsook the teaching of poetry to join the

Table 3.2 (a) Government Ministers, House of Lords, January 1991

Peer	Office (Departments also covered)	Peerage	No. of yrs as member of the House	Age (attained by 1991)
Waddington	Lord Privy Seal / Leader of the House (Civil Service)	LP[a]	0	61
Mackay of Clashfern	Lord Chancellor	LP	12	64
Ferrers	MS, Home Office / Deputy Leader of the House	H 13th E	36	61
Caithness	MP, Foreign & Commonwealth Office	H 20th E	21	42
Belstead	Paymaster General / MS, N. Ireland Office	H 2nd B	32	58
Hesketh	MS, Trade & Industry (Treasury) (Arts & Heritage, Environment)	H 3rd B	19[b]	40
Brabazon of Tara	MS, Transport (Foreign Office)	H 2nd B	16	44
Trumpington	MS, Agriculture, Fisheries & Food (Social Security, Wales)	LP	10	68
Fraser of Carmyllie	Lord Advocate	LP[a]	2	45
Arran	US, Defence (Home Office)	H 9th E	8	53
Ullswater	US, Employment (Energy, Transport)	H 2nd V	27[b]	48
Blatch	US, Environment (Education)	LP	3	54
Hooper	US, Health (Energy, N. Ireland)	LP	5	51
Strathclyde	US, Scottish Office (Employment, Treasury, Trade & Industry)	H 2nd B	5	30
Henley	US, Social Security (Health, Treasury, Trade & Industry)	H 8th B	13	37

Notes: [a] Former Member of the House of Commons. [b] Became eligible to sit at age 21.
Abbreviations: MS: Minister of State; US: Parliamentary Under-Secretary of State; H: Hereditary Peerage; E: Earl; V: Viscount; B: Baron; 2nd: 2nd holder of peerage; LP: Life Peer.

Table 3.2 (b) Government Whips, House of Lords, January 1991

Peer	Office	Peerage	No. of yrs as member of the House	Age (attained by 1991)
Denham	Captain, Gentleman at Arms Chief Whip	H 2nd B	42[b]	63
Davidson	Captain, Yeoman of the Guard (Transport)	H 2nd V	20	62
Long	Lord in Waiting (Defence, N. Ireland, Foreign Affairs)	H 4th B	23	61
Reay	Lord in Waiting (Home Office, Defence, Foreign Affairs, Wales)	H 14th B	27	53
Strathmore and Kinghorne	Lord in Waiting (Employment, Agriculture, Scotland, Treasury)	H 18th E	3	33
Cavendish of Furness	Lord in Waiting (Energy, Transport, Education, Health)	LP	1	49
Astor	Lord in Waiting (Environment, Arts, Trade & Industry, Social Security)	H 4th V	6	44

Notes and Abbreviations: see Table 3.2(a).

Conservative Government. His ability was quickly recognised, but his general political outlook would not have commended him for political advancement under Mrs Thatcher. Nevertheless he received rapid promotion and became a cabinet minister in 1984 – though he resigned the next year because he had come to feel that the pay was inadequate, a point taken up later in this chapter.

The Labour front bench has always contained a substantial number of former MPs who have taken peerages prior to their final retirement from political life, but in the late 1980s the proportion in this category declined as a wider range of party activists were brought into the House. These included several who had stood unsuccessfully as parliamentary candidates, such as Lord Carter, who had spent his life working in agriculture, and Baroness Hollis of Heigham, a lecturer at the University of East Anglia, who had also been leader of Norwich City Council. Academic life, local government and the trade unions were all areas from which Labour recruits were drawn. Unusual on the Labour side was Lord Williams of Elvel, a prominent City figure who continued as a stockbroker after entering the Lords in 1985; he became Deputy Leader of the Opposition in the House in 1989. From 1974 to 1979 Lord Melchett was a Labour minister; he had succeeded to a peerage in 1973 at the age of 25, but soon after Labour lost office in 1979 he left the front bench in order to earn his living elsewhere, though for a time he remained quite active in the House of Lords on behalf of countryside interests. His career pattern was unique on the Labour side, but would have been quite typical on the Conservative side.

Representation of the Government in the House

As Table 3.2 shows, Government is represented in the Lords by some twenty peers who hold salaried offices as ministers or whips. Between them these peers act as spokesmen for all departments. For all items of business peers expect a contribution from the government front bench, even if this is only to declare strict government neutrality in the matter under debate, as is sometimes the case with private members' bills or motions. Generally peers give very close attention to the contribution made by the government spokesmen. The number and relative seniority of ministers in

Table 3.3 (a)   Labour Front Bench (Principal Spokesmen), House of Lords, January 1991

Peer	Principal Spokesman	Peerage	No. of yrs as member of the House	Age (attained by 1991)
Cledwyn of Penrhos	Leader of the Opposition Civil Service, Foreign Affairs, Wales	LP[a]	10	74
Williams of Elvel	Deputy Leader Defence, Trade & Industry	LP	4	57
Graham of Edmonton	Chief Whip (Employment, Tourism)	LP[a]	6	65
Carter	Deputy Chief Whip Social Security (Health)	LP	3	59
Gallacher	Agriculture, Food, Forestry, Fisheries	LP	6	70
Birk	Arts, Libraries, Heritage, Broadcasting & Cable	LP	23	71
Blackstone	Education (Treasury)	LP	3	49
Turner of Campden	Employment (Social Security)	LP	4	63
Peston	Energy (Education & Science)	LP	3	59
McIntosh of Haringey	Environment	LP	6	57
Ennals	Health	LP[a]	6	68
Richard	Home Office (EC Affairs)	LP[a]	1	58
Mishcon	Legal Affairs	LP	11	75
Prys-Davies	N. Ireland (Wales, Legal Affairs)	LP	7	67
Carmichael of Kelvingrove	Scottish Office (Transport)	LP[a]	10	69
Clinton-Davis	Transport (Trade & Industry)	LP[a]	1	62

Notes and Abbreviations: See Table 3.2(a).

Table 3.3 (b) Labour Front Bench (Assistant Spokesmen), House of Lords, January 1991

Peer	Assistant Spokesman	Peerage	No. of yrs as member of the House	Age (attained by 1991)
Dean of Beswick	Whip, Housing Peers' representative on the Parliamentary Committee	LP[a]	6	68
Ewart-Biggs	Whip Home Office, Trade & Industry, Overseas Development	LP	8	61
Hollis of Heigham	Whip Environment, Social Security	LP	1	49
Morris of Castle Morris	Whip Home Office, N. Ireland, Arts, Libraries	LP	1	60
David	Education & Science	LP	11	77
Underhill	Electoral Affairs, Transport	LP	10	76
McCarthy	Employment	LP	13	65
Wedderburn of Charlton	Employment	LP	12	63
Nicol	Environment	LP	6	67
Irvine of Lairg	Legal Affairs	LP	3	50
McCaulay of Bragar	Scottish Legal Affairs	LP	1	57

Notes and Abbreviations: See Table 3.2(a).

Table 3.4 Government Ministers (Including Whips[a]) in the House of Lords

Administration	Total size of Government	Number of peers in Government	Number of peers in the Cabinet
1945–51 (Attlee)	84–95	16–20	2–4
1951–7 (Churchill/Eden)	83–84	18–19	3–7
1957–64 (Macmillan/Home)	82–89	15–21	3–4
1964–70 (Wilson)	100–109	15–19	3–4
1970–4 (Heath)	84–95	16–20	2
1974–9 (Wilson/Callaghan)	98–111	14–17	2
1979–90 (Thatcher)	103–108	19–22	2–4

Source: Derived from Hansard list of ministers; first volume for each
             session.
Note: [a] Includes unsalaried government whips in office 1945.
             Excludes non-political appointments to Royal Household.

the House of Lords are matters of importance to the Lords as a whole.

At the beginning of this century the Prime Minister and up to half the Cabinet were in the House of Lords. Today very few senior ministers sit in the Lords. Furthermore, as the total number of government ministers has increased following the greatly expanded scope of government activity, the number of ministers in the Lords has remained fairly steady. The result is that the proportion of ministers in the Upper House is a good deal lower today than it was generally in the nineteenth century (see Table 3.4).

One obvious reason for this change was the confirmation of the political ascendancy of the Commons provided by the 1911 Parliament Act. Lord Curzon's failure to become Prime Minister in 1923, though not wholly due to his being a peer, was taken as having established a convention requiring the Prime Minister to sit in the Commons. In 1951–2 Churchill had seven peers in his Cabinet, but since then Conservative Cabinets have never had more than four peers, and Labour never more than two. By 1960 it was a matter of some surprise and opposition protest when a peer was appointed Foreign Secretary, and though this post was filled again by a peer in 1979 it had long been obvious that the great bulk of senior ministers must be members of the Commons. That is the elected House, and it is only there that the elected representatives of the people can directly question ministers about the discharge of their responsibilities.

The decline in the proportion of ministers in the Lords also results from a more general change in the nature of political life. At the turn of the century politics was still an activity dominated by the non-professional politician. In that respect Lords and Commons were alike; the members of neither House received salaries, and the great majority followed other occupations. In 1911 pay for MPs was introduced and throughout this century politics has increasingly become a sphere dominated by professional or near-professional politicians. For such people, ministerial office is the natural climax to their career. There is therefore immense demand from MPs for ministerial posts. Furthermore, the workload for all ministers has become extremely onerous. The House of Lords is not generally composed of professional politicians (indeed, if we exclude those who go there towards the end of their political careers, virtually none of its members could be so described). In contrast to the clamour for posts in the Commons, there is some evidence that ministerial posts have been difficult to fill in the Lords. For the non-professional part-time politician, the work involved may be very demanding, the salary offered relatively poor, and – perhaps most seriously – the interruption of another career too serious to contemplate.

Four different categories of government office-holders may be distinguished in the Lords: cabinet ministers, ministers of state, junior ministers and whips. The House of Lords always contains at least two cabinet ministers: the Lord Chancellor and the Leader of the House. The Lord Chancellor acts as front-bench spokesman primarily on legal aspects of government legislation, but he speaks for the government on other matters too. Some holders of this office have been much involved with major policy; others less so. The Leader of the House, who has overall responsibility for the passage of government legislation, always holds a senior non-departmental post. Viscount Whitelaw, who was appointed Leader at the commencement of Mrs Thatcher's second administration, was Lord President of the Council. He was frequently also described as Deputy Prime Minister. (The work within the House of these ministers is described in the next chapter.)

Sometimes Leaders of the Lords have been assigned specific ministerial duties, frequently responsibility for the civil service. Lord Whitelaw had no departmental responsibilities, but as senior Cabinet Minister he chaired a number of important cabinet committees. According to Harold Wilson (1971) Lord Longford felt that leading the House was a part-time job and pressed for a departmental post in 1964–5; he was rewarded by becoming Secretary of State for the Colonies in late 1965. Lord Longford himself argued (1974) that a Labour Leader of the House who lacks a departmental portfolio is at a disadvantage compared with a Conservative Leader, because leading the Lords is regarded as a junior job in a Labour Cabinet.

In addition to the offices of Lord Chancellor and Leader of the House, peers have since 1979 held a variety of departmental cabinet posts including Foreign Secretary, Secretary of State for Trade and Industry and Secretary of State for Employment. Lord Gowrie was Chancellor of the Duchy of Lancaster from 1984 to 1985, and had responsibility for the civil service and the arts. From 1970 to 1974 Lord Carrington was Secretary of State for Defence, then briefly head of the newly created Department of Energy until the fall of the Heath Government. Where departmental cabinet posts have been held by peers, it has been usual to have a second cabinet minister who is an MP attached to the same department and directly answerable to the Commons. Thus, when Lord Carrington was Foreign Secretary, first Sir Ian Gilmour, then Mr Humphrey Atkins were appointed Lord Privy Seal and dealt with Foreign Office matters in the Commons. When Lord Young became Employment Secretary, Mr Kenneth Clarke became Paymaster General and was also described as Minister for Employment. The Labour Opposition were critical of the fact that the senior minister in the department dealing with the politically sensitive and highly important subject of unemployment was in the Lords, but the fact that the department concerned thereby had two cabinet ministers told against their criticism somewhat.

Below cabinet level are ministers of state and parliamentary under-secretaries, all of whom are full ministers, though the former are more senior, with higher salaries and wider responsibilities. In 1990 there were six ministers at each of these two levels in the Lords; when Mrs Thatcher first came to office in 1979 she appointed eight peers at minister-of-state level and three at under-secretary level. The actual balance of numbers between the two ranks depends on a variety of factors, among them the need to recognise seniority and perhaps the need to ensure adequate financial reward to peers who might otherwise decline to serve in the government. A Lords departmental minister will usually answer in the House for all the business of his department (as well as helping as spokesman for at least one other department). He will also be assigned a particular area of responsibility as a minister within the department concerned, and within that area civil servants will seek policy direction from him. For example in 1987 Lord Caithness had particular responsibility for prisons within the Home Office (and was quite frequently referred to as the Minister for Prisons) and Lord Brabazon of Tara had special responsibility for shipping while parliamentary under-secretary at the Department of Transport; in 1990, as minister of state in that department, he carried direct responsibility for aviation and shipping.

The whips' offices are political appointments to the Royal Household. The Chief Whip is styled the Captain of the Gentlemen at Arms (the title was unchanged when a woman, Baroness Llewelyn-Davies of Hastoe, was appointed to this office in 1974); the Deputy Chief Whip is the Captain of the Yeomen of the Guard. Assistant Whips, three or four in number until 1974 but five since, hold offices as Lords in Waiting: they are to be distinguished from the non-political Lords in Waiting, whose functions are in the Royal Household and whose appointments are not affected by changes of government.

Apart from the Chief Whip, all other whips, unlike their Commons counterparts, act as official government spokesmen, supplementing the departmental ministers. Most Chief Whips intervene only in debates on business-of-the-House matters (though exceptionally the Chief Whip and his Labour opposite number made speeches in a debate on 9 April 1987 on the unity of the nation).

Lords in Waiting could usually expect to act as spokesmen for at least three departments – mostly, of course, in a supplementary capacity (see Table 3.2(b)). But this could give them a great deal to do: for example, at committee stage on bills, or generally in answering questions or replying to debates, especially if the departments they spoke for were ones with a lot of parliamentary business. Though not ministers, Lords in Waiting since the mid 1970s have been regularly but not invariably provided with offices in one of the departments for which they spoke. The whole House knew that as Lords in Waiting they were spokesmen and not in any sense originators of policy. When they spoke in the House of Lords it was necessary for them to stick closely to the brief provided by the department concerned, and probably make generous use of the civil servants waiting in the box in the corner of the chamber ready to brief government spokesmen. Being a Lord in Waiting may be viewed as an apprenticeship to ministerial office. It represents an opportunity to get to know the Lords well, and learn how it is best handled; it also gives an insight into the workings of government. Some peers enjoyed the challenge of this office precisely because of the range of topics dealt with and the opportunity for contact with a number of departments. Others found it frustrating and were relieved when a 'proper' ministerial post came their way. But once it did they were likely to find the Lords a little less forbearing. Certainly ministers of state, and even more cabinet ministers, could expect the Lords to press them much harder in debate because of their senior ministerial status.

The Government front bench was organised in such a way that each department had at least two peers who spoke for it. If no minister was in a department, the main spokesman might have been a minister elsewhere, or a Lord in Waiting. Baroness Young dealt with Education while Minister of State at the Foreign Office after 1983; however, she had previously been an education minister, though when at that department she also dealt with health and social security legislation. In December 1990 Energy and Education had no ministerial representation in the House; the business of both these departments was dealt with by ministers in other departments and whips. For major bills the usual spokesmen may need to be supplemented by others drawn in so as to help spread the burden of work. This raises the important question of the adequacy of government representation.

Government Appointments in the House

At no time in recent years have all departments had at least one minister in the Lords. At several points in the 1980s as many as five different departments lacked ministers in the Lords. Sometimes the situation had been even more unsatisfactory. When the Labour Government of March 1974 took office, only fourteen peers (including whips) were appointed, giving direct representation in the Lords to only seven departments. In June 1974 Lord Windlesham, speaking from the Conservative front bench, expressed disquiet at the representation of the Labour Government in the Lords, and argued that the reputation of the House depended to a very considerable degree on the number and seniority of ministers appointed from among peers. In reply the Leader of the House drew attention to the way in which the representation of the Government tended to improve during the lifetime of each administration (HL Debs, 25 June 1974, cols 1322–5).

The implication of these remarks appeared to be that an incoming prime minister first sought to satisfy the aspirations for government office among MPs before looking to the Lords. In time, however, the need for stronger representation in the Lords became obvious, and this resulted in some strengthening of the Government in the Upper House. The Conservative Government started in 1970 with sixteen peers, but this number later rose to twenty. Labour in March 1974 had only fourteen office-holders in the Lords, but by 1975 there were seventeen. When Mrs Thatcher came to office in 1979 the number immediately rose to twenty-one, and though this total was not exceeded during either of her first two administrations, it crept up to twenty-two before she left office. Richard Crossman recorded in his diary the resentment expressed by Labour MPs when Baroness Serota was appointed Minister of State at the Department of Health and Social Security in 1969 because a 'good job has gone to a peeress', though he added that London MPs who knew how good she was from her work as Labour Chief Whip on the Greater London Council 'congratulated me' (Crossman, 1976, p. 380).

The House of Lords, generally, is well pleased when it can deal with senior ministers. If a Secretary-of-State post is conferred on a peer, the expressions of pleasure in the Lords may well be in sharp contrast to the attitudes expressed in the Commons at such appointments. Peers were delighted when Lord Home became

Foreign Secretary back in 1960, but in the Commons Labour MPs secured immediate debate for a hostile motion. Likewise in 1970 the appointment of Lord Carrington as Defence Secretary pleased peers, but in April 1971 a Labour back-bench MP introduced a ten-minute-rule bill seeking to debar the appointment of peers as senior ministers heading departments, on the grounds that they should be 'subject to the scrutiny and if necessary the ribaldry and hostility of the House of Commons' (HC Debs, 7 April 1971, cols 465–70). Lord Carrington's inability personally to speak in the Commons debate following the Falklands invasion in 1982 increased his determination to resign immediately in the face of the strong criticism vented in the Lower House (Carrington, 1988, p. 370). Peers who are senior ministers, if they are prudent, tread cautiously when dealing with MPs. A good junior minister and parliamentary private secretary in the Commons can be helpful. The attitude of the Lords minister himself is important. One ex-minister peer spoke in an interview of his particular care over letters to MPs, which he frequently found he had to modify because they had been drafted by civil servants in a tone suitable for a Commons minister but, in his view, unsuitable for a Lords minister. Others, particularly some who have been recruited direct into senior ministerial posts without having served any political apprenticeship, have not shown such sensitivity.

A prime minister who wants to give ministerial office to a person who has no seat in either House of Parliament may do this by bringing that person straight into the Lords. In 1984 Mrs Thatcher decided to bring a businessman who had been an adviser to the Government and then for two years chairman of the Manpower Services Commission into her Cabinet: he too became a peer, Lord Young of Graffham, and subsequently Secretary of State for Employment and then for Trade and Industry. He left the Government in 1989 and became embroiled in political controversy over the terms on which the Rover group had been privatised, with two Commons select committees criticising his actions. In 1979, Mrs Thatcher decided to include in the Department of Environment ministerial team the Leader of Leeds City Council, who was thereupon created a peer, Lord Bellwin. Sometimes individuals have been brought into the Lords on the nomination of the Leader of the Opposition shortly before an election, with the expectation that if the election brings a change of government, they are likely to be given office. In 1978 Mrs Thatcher, as Leader of the Opposition,

nominated for peerages Sir Christopher Soames, a former Conservative Cabinet Minister turned diplomat, and Sir Arthur Cockfield, a
businessman. Both received office when the Conservatives came to
power a year later. In 1964 and again in 1974 Mr Wilson brought a
small number of non-parliamentarians directly into his Government.

It may be an advantage for the holders of some offices to be peers.
When, in 1964, Mr Wilson wanted to have a government minister
rather than an official as British representative at the UN in New
York, it was understandable that the post should go to a peer – the
more so in view of the Government's very slender Commons
majority. In 1974 Lord Goronwy-Roberts became a junior Foreign
Office minister, the only minister in that department not an MP.
Because of the parlous state of the Government in the Commons, he
was the only one who could go on lengthy overseas trips! Back in
1956 a former Permanent Secretary at the Foreign Office pointed
out how advantageous it would be if the Foreign Secretary sat in the
Lords, though he added that 'in modern conditions this is perhaps
asking the impossible' (Strang, 1956, p. 300). But in this judgement
he was wrong, because in 1960 a peer became Foreign Secretary, as
happened again in 1979.

Work on the Front Bench

While peers who are ministers are relieved of some of the tasks
which fall upon their Commons counterparts – such as constituency
duties and the need to be present in the Commons a great deal, at
least if the Government of the day lacks a secure majority – in other
respects ministers in the Lords may have to work harder. A
Commons minister can expect to speak in his House only on matters
for which he has a very direct departmental responsibility. He will
answer questions only on set days, usually once every three or four
weeks, or less frequently. But as we have noted, Lords ministers may
have to speak on behalf of several departments (they can have a
'long waterfront': Theakston, 1987, p. 137) and may also find
themselves answering oral questions very frequently (see p. 202).
Baroness Young had responsibility for nine bills in less than two
years while she was Minister of State for Education – from 1979 to
1981. Lord Trefgarne was on his feet answering oral questions in the

Lords on 70 of the 147 sitting days in the 1981–2 session while he was a junior minister at the Department of Trade, but also helping with Foreign Office questions.

In 1983 the Top Salaries Review Body commissioned management consultants to investigate and report on relative pay levels for ministers; among those whose jobs were analysed were two peers. The report concluded that because ministers in the House of Lords had to range over a wider area than their Commons counterparts, they needed wider knowledge, and this meant 'perhaps more work (rather than necessarily a more important job)' (Cmnd 881–I–II). The Review Body had recommended in earlier reports that ministerial salaries be the same in both Houses, but because ministers in the Commons were entitled to draw part of their parliamentary salaries too, this in effect meant lower pay for the Lords ministers. In 1981, against the advice of the Review Body, the Cabinet decided to pay a higher ministerial salary to Lords ministers – a decision in effect endorsed by the management consultants' report two years later. The Government had no doubt discovered that low pay was a problem in recruiting Lords ministers. Up until 1980 Lords in Waiting were paid substantially less than back-bench MPs. One former minister told in interview of the amazement of his business associates when in 1979 he felt duty-bound to take ministerial office at a salary so very much lower than he had been receiving for his work outside politics. In 1985, Lord Gowrie – who had been promoted to the Cabinet the previous year at the age of 45, and was widely thought of as a future Leader of the House – resigned altogether from government, publicly stating that his reason for doing so was the low level of pay; he received £33,000 per year, some £8,000 less than cabinet ministers in the Commons.

The resignation of Lord Elton, Minister of State for the Environment, in September 1986 deprived the Lords of another experienced minister, and at the same time Lord Swinton, Deputy Chief Whip, departed. During exchanges on the floor of the House in December 1989 it was suggested that the low level of remuneration for ministers in the Upper House had been the reason for the loss of some experienced members of the government front bench (HL Debs, 14 December 1989, cols 1408–10). In 1991 the Government introduced the Ministerial and Other Pensions and Salaries Bill, which provided for an 'overnight allowance' to be paid to ministers in the House of Lords – a curious way to rectify a situation which really demanded a straightforward increase in salary (see Appendix A). The uncertainty of ministerial life, the absence of anything approaching security of tenure, aggravates the position. One consequence is that some ministers do achieve quite rapid promotion, as the example of Lord Gowrie illustrates. The field from which ministers can be recruited in the Lords is, in practical terms, not extensive. In 1986 Lord Caithness, who had first joined the Government as Lord in Waiting as recently as 1984, was promoted to Minister of State at the Home Office; in October 1987 the difficulties he had in coping with the Criminal Justice Bill caused government embarrassment (and, according to newspaper reports, hastened the departure of the sick Lord Havers from the Woolsack). A good deal of muttering was heard in the Lords in the late 1980s about the overall adequacy of government representation. The business of the House of Lords had become more onerous, and its importance had increased. Was the House being accorded sufficient ministers of the standing and experience it merited?

In a very few cases the general abilities of government spokesmen may be called into question, but most of the time peers have nothing but praise for the individuals involved. But there is a recognition in the Lords that because too few peers hold government office, those who do simply have too many subjects to deal with. Furthermore, if they are spokesmen only, or relatively junior ministers, they do not have the authority to deal with a subject in a way that seems fitting to many members of the Lords. Participants in debates may include peers of considerable expertise and experience in certain areas – for example, former permanent secretaries or cabinet ministers, or those with immense experience of a relevant kind elsewhere. A Lord in Waiting or junior minister answering debate may have received instructions not to give way, and not even to promise another look at a particular clause in a bill. Sometimes the mood of the Lords alters quite quickly in such circumstances; opposition hardens and a division begins to look likely, with possible government defeat and consequent awkwardness. The Chief Whip and Leader of the House may have to be hurriedly summoned, and sometimes a sudden change of tack by the government spokesman at the Dispatch Box may be observed. But equally there can simply be frustration on the part of peers at the difficulties they face in ensuring that their views are being taken seriously enough by Government. Lord Houghton of Sowerby, a senior back-bench Labour peer and vastly experienced parliamentarian, who was formerly Chairman of the PLP as an MP, expressed such frustration during a debate on a government bill in 1985. His remarks are worth quoting:

> I think we are moving into a different regime in this House. We have become more important and more publicised, and there is a desire to become more powerful and to take a more definite place in the combined activities of the two Houses of Parliament . . . the Government Front Bench in this House . . . do not have the authority to do what a Minister in . . . [the Commons] . . . would very frequently feel bound to do, or at least feel that it was desirable to do . . . I think that greater authority, more flexibility and more room for manoeuvre should be in somebody's hands in this House.
>
> (HL Debs, 4 July 1985, col. 1390)

But the generally unsatisfactory nature of government representation in the Lords is a function of the unsatisfactory situation in which the House now finds itself. A full minister in each department would be a minimum desirable improvement. But beyond that, it seems unfortunate that senior ministers are not empowered to speak in either House, while retaining full membership of only one House. In most European countries with bicameral legislatures ministers are entitled to speak in both Houses (though in some cases they are members of neither). It may be objected that this would increase demands upon ministers, but this need not be the case, for example, where answerability in the Commons replaced full membership of that House.

The Opposition Front Bench

Given the legislative role of the House of Lords and the answerability of the Government in the upper chamber, it is incumbent upon the major Opposition Party to make arrangements to ensure that its point of view is officially stated in the debates which take place. When Labour was in Opposition before 1964, the number of active Labour peers was too small to permit anything other than informal, flexible arrangements for the organisation of their front bench. Since 1964, when either Conservative or Labour have been in

Opposition, a front-bench team at least as large as the government team has been maintained. Indeed, in recent years the major parties, when in Opposition, have named more peers to their front bench than when in office. Labour had a list of fifteen principal spokesmen and twelve other spokesmen in 1990 (Table 3.3); the Conservatives in early 1979 had a list of twenty-six front-bench spokesmen. The absence of any pay or extra allowances for opposition front-benchers (other than the Leader and Chief Whip) necessitates using some peers who have careers elsewhere to which they must devote at least some of their time. If this has been one reason for expanding the list of spokesmen when in Opposition, another has been the straightforward desire to make use of whatever expertise is available.

Whenever the Conservative Party has been in Opposition, the Leader and Deputy Leader in the Lords were appointed by the overall party leader. These two peers always served as members of the Leader's Consultative Committee, or 'Shadow Cabinet'. Lord Carrington was Leader of the Opposition from 1964 to 1970 and again from 1974 to 1979. In addition there has always been at least one further peer appointed to the Conservative 'Shadow Cabinet': between 1974 and 1979 Lord Hailsham was a member, described as being 'without specific duties', though not surprisingly he did act as party spokesman in the Lords on legal matters. The chairmanship of the Party has frequently been held by a peer, as it was from 1975 to 1981 by Lord Thorneycroft, and he, too, spoke from time to time from the opposition front bench, though he had no specific sphere of responsibility.

In the Labour Party the offices of Leader of the Labour Peers, Deputy Leader and Chief Whip were all open to election when the Party was in Opposition. The Leader and Chief Whip, together with an elected representative of back-bench peers, were *ex officio* members of the party 'Shadow Cabinet' where, according to Punnett (1973, p. 430), 'their contributions are certainly not restricted to House of Lords matters'. Until 1973 no elections had been necessary because there had never been more than one nomination for each post. But in that year, when Lord Beswick resigned, three nominations were received for his former post of Chief Whip; the victor was Baroness Llewelyn-Davies of Hastoe, who comfortably defeated her two rivals. When she resigned in 1982 Lord Ponsonby of Shulbrede won a contested vote for the post, and following his death in 1990 Lord Graham of Edmonton was elected, again in a contested ballot.

Lord Peart, who had been appointed Leader of the House of Lords in 1976, at the time of his entry to the House, continued as Labour Leader after 1979. But Labour peers became restless with his lack of drive and ineffectiveness. Despite hints and private appeals to step aside, he refused to do so. In 1982 Lord Cledwyn of Penrhos stood against him, and defeated him by 60 votes to 37. A reinvigoration of the Opposition followed, with Lord Cledwyn improving the organisation of the opposition front bench and generally rekindling enthusiasm among Labour peers.

In both the major parties, when in Opposition, it is the party leader in the Lords who selects the team of front-bench spokesmen and allocates duties between them. There does not seem to be much difficulty about this. Once during the 1980s a Labour left-wing peer who thought he had been appointed to the Lords to speak from the front bench on a particular subject found himself quickly shifted to the back benches because of his general rumbustiousness. This was unusual. More often it is a matter of persuading peers to take a role rather than removing them from the front bench. The work involved for an opposition spokesman can be quite onerous, especially when dealing with major and complex legislation. The absence of salaries (except for the Leader and the Chief Whip) is no doubt one reason why some peers, especially younger ones, leave their front bench when their Party is in Opposition.

Back-Bench Party Organisation

The parties and the cross-bench peers each hold weekly meetings every Thursday at 2.15 p.m. The main concern at these gatherings is to outline future business, and to sound opinion about the most desirable way of handling such business. A document is prepared each Thursday while the House is sitting and sent to peers, indicating the timetable for the forthcoming week. For this the party whips are responsible, and the document – or whip – includes mention of expected divisions with appropriate underlining. Cross-bench peers, if they so wish, may receive an 'unlined whip' prepared by the Chief Whip, which indicates the expected timetable and may include other helpful notices (such as when dinner will be available).

On the Conservative side a body known as the Association of Conservative Peers (ACP) is the equivalent of the 1922 Committee in the Commons. All Conservative peers belong, and they elect a chairman and a committee of about ten others, all back-benchers, who retire in rotation. From 1980 to 1990 the Chairman was Lord Boyd-Carpenter, a former MP and sometime Chief Secretary to the Treasury, who left the Commons in 1972. His successor was Lord Colnbrook, formerly Humphrey Atkins, who had been Conservative Chief Whip in the House of Commons in the 1970s, then a cabinet minister until 1982.

The executive committee of the ACP holds a meeting immediately before the general Thursday meeting. At this earlier meeting the members decide what proposals to make to their colleagues – for example, as to the motions to be debated in the time allocated on the floor of the House to the party. Front-benchers do not on the whole attend the 2.15 p.m. meeting (they have their own meeting at 2.00 p.m. instead), but the Chief Whip attends the ACP meeting, and he can relay opinion to ministers as necessary, as no doubt can the Chairman. The Chairman of the 1922 Committee from the Commons is said to attend quite frequently, and the Chairman of the ACP is free to attend the meetings of the 1922 Committee. An average of about forty back-bench peers attend the Thursday meeting, with more coming to the special meetings held up to six times a year, usually with senior ministers giving talks and with the Prime Minister coming once a year. The Chief Whips in both Houses hold a regular weekly meeting. Conservative peers may also attend meetings of Conservative Party back-bench committees in the House of Commons. In 1990 peers constituted up to half the regular attenders for some such groups.

On the Labour side, a Labour peers' co-ordinating committee exists. While the Party was in Opposition in the 1980s this consisted of five elected back-bench peers and the five office-holders within the Party in the Lords; namely the Leader, Deputy Leader, Chief Whip, Deputy Chief Whip and the peers' representative on the 'Shadow Cabinet'. This last post has been held by Lord Dean of Beswick since 1988 (his predecessor had been Lord Oram). The co-ordinating committee of ten peers was chaired by a back-bencher by deliberate choice. It met fortnightly and, among other tasks, considered how to use time allocated to the Party for debate in the House of Lords.

On Thursdays before the 2.15 party meeting, the party whips met at 1.00 p.m., and at 1.30 p.m. all principal opposition spokesmen met. These meetings prepared the ground for the main party meeting at which, in addition to front-bench peers reporting briefly on matters within their area of responsibility, reports were given from the Chairman of the co-ordinating committee and the peers' elected representative on the Shadow Cabinet. Usually about fifty Labour peers attended this meeting. When Labour was in office in the 1970s front-benchers attended the Thursday 2.15 p.m. meeting quite regularly, which contrasts with Conservative peers' practice, but in fact both parties parallel their Commons counterparts in this respect.

Labour peers also hold occasional meetings on an *ad hoc* basis, addressed by leading party members. On most Wednesday mornings the Parliamentary Labour Party (PLP) in the Commons holds meetings to discuss policy issues which are open to interested Labour peers, and quite a few attend. Lord Cledwyn also encouraged suitable Labour peers to participate in PLP subject groups, but it would seem that very few do this; even those who do were excluded from voting in elections for PLP group officers. Before 1983 the PLP in the Commons held a single regular meeting for discussion of policy questions and business matters. Curiously, all Labour peers were entitled to attend these PLP meetings, and indeed to vote on policy matters. Richard Crossman, in his diary, recorded disquiet about this (Crossman, 1976, p. 376). Lord Kennet, in a letter to *The Times* (14 April 1972), claimed that the Labour Government in the 1960s had sometimes put pressure on Labour peers to attend and vote at PLP meetings 'in order to uphold government policy against the objections of Labour back-benchers in the Commons'. By dividing the Commons PLP meeting in the 1980s into a business meeting (at which votes were taken) and a separate meeting for discussion of policy, it became natural to exclude peers from the former.

Liberal Democrats and Other Parties

Relative to their strength in the Commons, Liberals (and from 1981 to 1988 Social Democrats) enjoyed a considerable strength in the Lords. This has from time to time given peers who have been members of these parties a relatively greater prominence within their party counsels. For example, when the Lib–Lab pact was formed in 1977 David Steel announced a 'Shadow Cabinet' which included seven peers along with fourteen MPs. Some Liberal peers remained as leading party spokesmen until 1983, when all such posts were reassumed by MPs. But in January 1987, when a joint Alliance team of parliamentary spokesmen was announced, two peers were included: Baroness Seear on social services and Baroness Stedman on environmental protection.

The Social Democratic Party had over forty peers as members in the mid 1980s. Co-operation with the Liberal peers was always relatively easy in the House of Lords. Though they retained separate party meetings on Thursday afternoons, they also frequently held joint meetings for all party members in the House. Separate whips were issued, but the level of whipping was always the same. When the two parties decided to merge in 1988, a majority of Social Democrat peers became members of the merged Party. But some resisted merger and, like their Commons counterparts, continued as a separate group in the Lords. By the time the Party dissolved itself in 1990, some twenty peers still described themselves as Social Democrats, and continued to do so in 1991.

The old Liberal Party in the Lords always elected their Leader, who then appointed other party office-holders and party spokesmen. Following the death of Lord Byers in 1984, Baroness Seear, who had retired from her post as reader in personnel management at the London School of Economics, was elected Leader. In the same year Lord Tordoff was appointed Chief Whip; he had been Chairman of the Liberal Party before becoming a peer in 1981 (see Table 3.5).

Baroness Seear gave way as Leader to Lord Jenkins of Hillhead following the merger of the two parties in 1988, though she remained as Deputy Leader. Lord Tordoff continued as Chief Whip of the new Party, with the former SDP whip, Lord Kilmarnock, continuing for a time as one of two Deputy Whips, the other being Viscount Falkland. In addition to the Leader, Deputy Leader and two whips, thirteen other peers were named as party spokesmen in 1990. All told, fifty-five peers took the Liberal Democrat whip, so the Party was about half the strength of the Labour opposition in the Lords.

At least two Liberal Democrat peers regularly attended the weekly meeting of the Party's MPs, sometimes more. Attendance by MPs at the meeting of peers was not on any regular basis. Paddy

Table 3.5   Liberal Democrat Party Office-Holders, January 1991

Peer	Office	Peerage	No. of yrs a member of the House	Age (attained by 1991)
Jenkins of Hillhead	Leader	LP[a]	3	70
Seear	Deputy Leader	LP	19	77
Tordoff	Chief Whip	LP	9	62
Falkland	Deputy Whip	H 15th V	6	55

Notes and Abbreviations: See Table 3.3(a).

Ashdown, like David Steel before him, went twice a year or so to talk with party members in the Upper House. Alongside such arrangements, the most important practical liaison between Liberal Democrat peers and MPs probably took place through the policy panels set up within the party organisation.

Cross-Bench Peers

There have always been non-party peers in the Lords. In the post-war period their number grew steadily, and in the mid 1960s some of the more active non-party peers began to meet regularly, with Lord Strang (formerly of the Foreign Office) emerging as their co-ordinator. When he retired in 1974, Baroness Hylton-Foster, widow of a former Speaker of the Commons, was elected in his place. She has been re-elected unopposed every year since. She took the title Convenor of the Cross-Bench Peers.

Every Thursday at 2.15 p.m., when the parties have their meetings, cross-benchers meet as well. Usually some twenty to thirty attend. They decide on the subject matter for debate in time allocated to them, and may discuss any concerns they have about the House. Sometimes they meet earlier in order to hear from a guest speaker they have decided to invite – for example, the chairman of a nationalised industry or a prominent trade unionist. In some respects cross-bench peers may look like another party in the House of Lords, but this is misleading. Their opinions range widely and their organisation is minimal. They have no leader, and could not have one in the usual sense of the term because they do not seek – nor could they – to formulate common views on issues coming before the Lords. But having a regular meeting, a recognised spokesman and an unlined whip are all useful devices for keeping non-party peers in close touch with the work of the Lords. For example, their convenor sits on the various select committees which deal with domestic House of Lords matters, such as procedure, leave of absence and expenses, privileges and the Committee of Selection. She can report back on matters covered by these committees, sound out the opinions of cross-bench peers, and feed these in as necessary.

As Tables 2.4 and 2.5 show, quite a number of cross-bench peers are active on the floor of the House. It is worth particularly noting their role on subject select committees, where a cross-bench figure has frequently been sought for the post of chairman. In recent years most of the chairmen of the six European Communities sub-committees have been cross-benchers. This suggests that non-party status can be seen as a definite advantage for some aspects of the work of the Lords. The voting habits of cross-bench peers are of particular interest.

A few are habitual or at least fairly regular supporters of one or other Party, but most vary their voting pattern. Not having the guidance of a party whip, cross-benchers are slightly more inclined to abstention than are party members. A few, when in doubt, say that they support the Government of the day – whatever Party is in office. More look to other cross-bench peers, taking a lead from those whose opinion on a particular subject they respect. Whips are even known to calculate that an intervention for or against the Government by x on subject y will be worth, say, ten votes. Sometimes gentle overtures are made by party front-benchers to individual cross-benchers whose contributions they have reason to believe may be of particular assistance to them on a certain matter.

Analysis of 222 divisions for which the Government had a whip in the 1983–4 session shows that the balance of cross-bench votes went against the Government 48 times and in support of the Government 174 times. All told, cross-bench peers cast more than twice as many votes with the Government as against it (2,548 to 1,293). However, if the twenty government defeats alone are examined, in fifteen of these the balance of cross-bench votes went against the Government, and in six of these fifteen that balance was crucial to the outcome of the division. A similar result was obtained from an analysis of divisions in the 1988–9 session (see Beamish and Shell, forthcoming 1992).

Such statistical analysis shows that cross-bench votes are of greater assistance to the Conservatives than to the Labour Party in the Lords. Baldwin analysed cross-bench peers in terms of their education, career and peerage, and found that on a comparative statistical basis they were 'overwhelmingly similar' to Conservative peers (Baldwin, 1985, p. 136).

Whipping in the Lords

There may possibly be some validity in talking about the 'black arts of whipping' in the Commons, but such a phrase would be utterly inappropriate in the Lords. Commons whips have a variety of sticks and carrots which they may use to encourage party loyalty. Aspiration to front-bench office, to membership of certain select committees or to positions on delegations to exotic foreign parts, or even hopes of recognition in future honours lists: all these and more may be factors against which a Commons whip can trade. But such inducements are not part of the currency with which a Lords whip deals. For most peers the high-point of their career is over; ambitions have either been fulfilled or subsided. Appeals to party loyalties developed over a lifetime may be an effective approach to whipping, but possibly more effective still are reasoned arguments, carefully framed, possibly put privately by a minister to doubters, rather than publicly on the floor of the House. The whips may be active in identifying waverers, exploring their views, communicating these to party spokesmen and facilitating intra-party discussions.

The arrangements for whipping in the Lords therefore remain low-key. In addition to a Chief Whip, the Conservative and Labour Parties both have Deputy Chief Whips, and several assistant whips. But these all act as party spokesmen on specific subjects. No regional whips exist, as in the Commons, though subjects may at times be allocated as the special responsibility of individual whips. Such arrangements, if made, are flexible, low-profile and short-lived. For a time in the 1970s Labour tried dividing up the entire Party among the various whips on an alphabetical basis, but the arrangement was not sustained.

For many years past Chief Whips have sub-divided their party lists according to the relative availability of different peers and their regularity in attendance. Such categories as 'do not attend', 'age and health make attendance unlikely', 'distance and commitment make attendance unreliable' and 'regular and reliable' have been identified. More recently, during the 1983 Parliament, Labour has made use of a 'telephone whip', with a list of supporters who may be telephoned and urged to attend for particular divisions. Occasionally the Conservative Chief Whip has written a letter to the more likely attenders within his Party's ranks, urging more regular attendance for divisions on particular bills, and possibly including some statistics about attendances and voting figures. In 1983 a *pro forma* was sent to all Conservative peers asking for commitments to attend at particular times, but the response to this was so disappointing that the exercise was not repeated. Later Lord Denham developed different levels of two-line whips, with a carefully chosen form of words indicating whether attendance was urgently requested, most urgently requested, or specially urgently requested. He even differentiated two-line whips according to the thickness of the underlining! Perhaps in some cases such refinements were lost on the recipients of these documents, but his skill as a Chief Whip was widely acknowledged. Appointed when Mrs Thatcher first came to power, he was the only one of her ministers to have remained in exactly the same post throughout her tenure in Downing Street.

Occasionally a party Chief Whip has decided that the voting record or general conduct of a particular peer is such that a talk with that peer is necessary. A Conservative peer who was frequently drunk had the whip withdrawn in the 1960s. The next Conservative to lose the party whip was Lord Alport in December 1984. His offence was to launch what the press described as a stinging attack on Mrs Thatcher during a debate on a Labour motion on unemployment, and to follow this by voting against the Government at the end of the debate. Nor was this an isolated act of rebellion on his part: twice during the 1983–4 session the Government ran a three-line whip, and on both occasions Lord Alport voted in the opposition lobby. According to the *Financial Times* (19 December 1984) the situation was further exacerbated by the fact that 'Lord Alport was unable to make himself available to discuss the position' with his Chief Whip following his rebellion. But the withdrawal of the party whip simply meant that he became an 'independent Conservative', remaining outside the Lords a member of the Party he had earlier served as an MP and Commons minister.

The Labour Party in the Lords frequently uses a three-line whip; it did so for over half of all divisions in the House in the 1988–9 session. Sometimes there has been surprise and disappointment at the relatively modest turnout of Labour peers, though it is important to remember the high average age of these peers. Only twice in the 1983 Parliament did more than a hundred Labour peers vote – both occasions being on the Local Government (Interim Provisions) Bill. In the period 1987 to 1991, only on three occasions did over ninety Labour peers vote. More generally a turnout of over sixty is regarded as quite satisfactory. Sometimes the turnout of Labour peers has been compared unfavourably with that of other opposition parties. On the bill abolishing the GLC, Labour allowed some of the initiative on whipping to be taken by those campaigning outside the House of Lords, notably those assisting the GLC campaign (see Livingstone, 1987, Ch. 8) and peers may have responded less well to this approach. Labour turnout, however, was in general much better than it had been in the 1970s. For the Liberal Democrats a good turnout is something over thirty, though occasionally a much larger number have appeared; when peers voted on whether or not to insist on an amendment to the Health and Medicines Bill on the subject of increased dental charges in November 1988, no fewer than forty-three Liberal democrats and eighteen Social Democrats voted, along with ninety-one Labour peers. But well over 200 Conservatives responded to a three-line whip and turned out to crush the Opposition.

The Conservative Party uses a three-line whip comparatively sparingly. When it does so a turnout of over 200 can certainly be expected; on the second reading of the Local Government (Interim Provisions) Bill, 212 Conservatives voted with the Government, and on the second reading of the Local Government Bill, the next year, 221 voted. To overcome a hostile amendment to the Local Government (Finance) Bill – seeking to relate the community charge to people's ability to pay – a three-line whip brought 274 Conservative peers into the government lobby (with 15 other Conservatives voting with the Opposition). In the 1988–9 session a three-line whip was used on three different days, together covering ten divisions. Lord Denham, Government Chief Whip, was very reluctant to use a three-line whip other than in exceptional circumstances. He argued that heavier regular whipping would in the long term prove counterproductive. In the 1980s, he remembered well the intense pressure put on Conservative peers to prevent any amendments being made to the European Communities Bill in 1972. This, he felt, had a devastating effect on the morale of peers, and he determined to avoid the repetition of such pressure. One cannot put excessive pressure on volunteers, or they may cease to be volunteers.

An analysis of all 222 divisions in the 1983–4 session in which the Government placed a whip shows that some Conservative cross-voting took place in 104 of these, or almost half. In 88 of these 104 divisions the Government won; the number of Conservative rebels averaged between two and three. In fifteen cases the Government was defeated in divisions where the Labour Opposition also had a whip on; the average number of Conservative rebels in these divisions was eight. In one case the Government was defeated outright by its own back-benchers rebelling. This was a division on the Trade Union Bill, which some Conservative peers thought should insist on secret ballots for office-holders (it was even suggested in some quarters that they received a nod and a wink from Downing Street); forty-nine Conservative peers voted against the Government, forty-three in its support. Conservative defeat from the political right had become comparatively infrequent; there was only one other example during the 1983 Parliament – on the 1986 Education Bill (see Chapter 6). In the 1988–9 session Conservative rebellion took place in slightly under half of all divisions for which the Government had placed a whip. Only eleven Conservative peers voted against their Party more than six times in divisions with whips on. Of the Government's twelve defeats during the session, in four of these the result would have been a government victory if Conservatives who rebelled had voted with the Government.

Cross-voting by Labour peers is much less frequent. In the 1983–4 session Labour peers cross-voted in only 22 of the 180 divisions in which both Labour and Government had placed a whip. In only two cases did more than one peer cross-vote, and in thirteen of the remaining twenty, the cross-voting was by the same peer – Lord Plant – who voted against his party whip repeatedly on the Police and Criminal Evidence Bill. Lord Plant, a former trade unionist, had been a member of the Police Pay and Conditions Review Board

before becoming a peer in 1978. He was retained as spokesman by
the Police Federation, and obviously found himself quite out of
sympathy with his Party and its attitude to this major piece of
legislation. One other peer cross-voted four times; this was Lord
Northfield, formerly Donald Chapman, a Labour MP; he voted
against his party twice on the Housing and Building Control Bill,
and on two other different bills. Two other peers cross-voted twice,
and the remainder were isolated instances of disobedience to the
whip. In 1988–9, only in three whipped divisions did any Labour
peers support the Government; in two of these only one peer rebelled
and in the other case rebellion was limited to two peers. Abstention
is a much easier course of action than actually voting against party
colleagues.

Abstention

Unlike the Commons, the House of Lords has no arrangement for
'pairing' absentees, a fact which reflects the more irregular pattern
of attendance and voting in the Upper House. It is difficult to do
other than provide a rough estimate of the extent of calculated
abstention by peers. Sometimes peers indicate in speeches their
opposition to, or misgivings about, their party line on a particular
issue, and then fail to vote in the division immediately following. For
example, four Conservatives criticised the Government in speeches
during the second-reading debate on the Rates Bill in April 1984,
then failed to support it in the division lobby, despite a three-line
whip. The total turnout of peers for particular divisions can also be
considered. Some references have already been made to this – for
instance, to the very low turnout of Labour peers for divisions on
some legislation in the mid 1970s; on the bill nationalising aerospace
and shipbuilding, the average turnout of Labour peers was only
forty. In 1976 the *Sunday Times* published the results of a survey into
the voting records of the ninety-nine Labour peers created between
1964 and 1976, based on the fifty-three most important divisions
over the previous two years. This found that only thirty-five of them
voted in as many as half of the divisions for which they were eligible
as members of the House (*Sunday Times*, 30 May 1976). Baldwin
found that in one month the Labour Government lost forty-six
divisions in the Lords, half of which it would have won if half of its

peers had turned up and supported it in the division lobby (Baldwin, 1985, p. 258).

It is possible for any particular day to consult the *Journals of the House of Lords* to see which peers actually attended, but failed to vote in a particular division. For example, the *Journals* record the names of twenty-eight Conservative peers present on 13 March 1980, none of whom voted in the crucial division on school transport charges held that day. Some were almost certainly deliberate abstentions, but it is impossible to say how many. Peers come and go throughout the day, as a study of successive divisions at the same sitting indicates. Three major divisions took place on the afternoon of 22 July 1980, at report stage of the Housing Bill. The *Journals* list 358 peers as attending that day. The first division took place at 3.44 p.m., and 228 peers voted; the second at 6.55 p.m., with 199 peers voting; and the third at 9.52 p.m., with 136 peers voting. Of the total attending the Lords, 72 voted in none of the three well-spaced divisions, and only 163 or well under half, voted in more than one division. These were keenly contested divisions, the middle one of which the Government lost. On private members' legislation, with the whips not operating, there may be even less regularity about voting. Hindell and Simms (1971) found that in two divisions held at 5.12 and 6.47 p.m. on the same afternoon during the committee stage of the Abortion Bill in 1968, of 140 peers who took part in the two divisions, only 57 voted in both.

Most divisions take place in the earlier part of a day's sitting. In 1988–9 fewer than one in six of all divisions took place after 8.00 p.m. To a considerable extent this is arranged between the whips acting in their role as 'the usual channels'. If the Opposition accepts a timetable ensuring the completion of successive stages on major bills at appointed times, the Government Chief Whip is inclined to acquiesce in arrangements which ensure that divisions take place early in the day's business, or at least before the evening dinner period. In 1984–5 only twenty-nine divisions took place after 8.00 p.m., but eight of these were on items of business for which the Government had no whip (mainly private members' bills). In the remaining twenty-one late divisions, the average turnout of peers, expressed as a percentage of the total recorded as attending the House on the days concerned, was 30 per cent. Only on two occasions did over half the peers who attended vote in divisions held after 8.00 p.m. At the other extreme, only in seven divisions did over

80 per cent of attenders vote, and in all the whipped divisions the average voting turnout was just over half the total of peers attending the House of Lords on the days concerned. The pattern was very similar in the 1988–9 session.

The Opposition does, however, from time to time, arrange an 'ambush'. This involves the deliberate decision to call a late division, while concealing the intention to do this from the Government. For such an occasion opposition peers will be asked to make themselves available in the House at, say, 9.00 p.m., but before that time to keep out of sight, at least from government whips. Sometimes the latter can be seen literally patrolling the corridors of the House and looking in various rooms in an attempt to satisfy themselves that no ambush is being planned. In the late 1980s the Opposition engaged in such tactics perhaps two or three times a session (see below p. 174). Given the overwhelming superiority the Conservatives normally enjoyed, the occasional defeat inflicted in this way was seen as good for the morale of opposition peers. But if employed more frequently, the device would quickly become counterproductive.

Because of the way the House of Lords is composed, the parties cannot organise support in anything like the way they do in the Commons. Most peers subscribe to a party whip, and when they turn out to vote they are almost invariably loyal to their Party. But comparatively few feel an obligation to attend and vote in the Lords in a truly regular manner. It is the relatively casual or spasmodic nature of the participation of peers which limits the hold of the major parties, and the fact that even among active peers only a minority could be described as professional politicians.

4

The Organisation and Procedure
of the House

The previous two chapters have indicated both the similarities and
the contrasts between the House of Lords and the House of
Commons. An examination of the procedure and organisation of
the House of Lords must once again embrace this theme. Many of
the basic rules of debate are very similar in both Houses, as are the
stages of the legislative process. But the style of debate and
the detailed use made of procedures are very different. For example,
the House of Lords, like the House of Commons, has a Speaker, the
Lord Chancellor, but his role contrasts sharply with that of the
Commons' Speaker. In both Houses a prominent part of each day's
proceedings is the asking of oral questions, but the procedures and
practices of the two Houses have developed in quite different ways.

A second general theme to any discussion of procedure and
organisation in the House of Lords must be the increase in the
pressure of business which has taken place over recent decades, yet
alongside this the relative lack of procedural restriction. Despite
higher attendances and increased professionalism among peers, very
few formal restrictions on their freedom have been introduced. Some
consequences of increased activity in terms of changed behaviour
and minor adaptation of procedure have been evident. But broadly
speaking, peers still remain as free as MPs were in the mid
nineteenth century. This matter will also be explored in this chapter.
However, we begin with a brief look at the physical arrangements of
the House of Lords.

The Lords' Chamber: Peers' Facilities and Allowances

Unlike the nearby Commons chamber, that of the Lords was not
destroyed during the Second World War. The present chamber

dates from 1847, and therefore retains the lavish decoration associated with the names of Barry and Pugin. With the Sovereign's Throne as its centre-piece rather than the Speaker's chair, and with the rich deep-red upholstery rather than the mellow green of the Commons, the Lords' chamber is a good deal more spectacular than that of the Commons. In 1980 the ceiling was found to be in need of repair (part of it fell down one day while the House was sitting), and over £2 million was spent in restoration work. Although the chamber is much more ornate than the Commons, it is no less functional. In its centre is the Clerk's Table, furnished with two dispatch boxes, from which Government and main Opposition Party front-bench spokesmen speak.

The seating within the chamber is arranged in three blocks on each side of the Table, unlike the Commons' two blocks (see Figure 4.1). The front benches of Government and main Opposition Party are in the middle block. The side of the House to the right of the Throne is known as the Spiritual side, that on the left, the Temporal side. Nowadays the bishops occupy the front two benches in the first block on the Spiritual side, and the Government of the day and its supporters the remaining benches on that side of the House. Nearest the Throne on the Temporal side are the benches of the Alliance Parties. Facing the Throne and below the Table are the cross-benches, occupied by peers who adhere to no party: in recent years, as their numbers have increased, cross-bench peers have spilled over into some of the benches facing the centre of the House below the Table.

The benches on the floor of the House provide seats for some 250 peers, a number which is small in relation to the total membership of the House of Lords, but until recent years adequate for the active membership. However, with average daily attendance of over 300 by the mid 1980s, for some proceedings there was often the same shortage of seating as for members of the Commons. Peers listening to debates may sit on the steps of the Throne, or stand near by, but these areas are technically outside the House, and may also be occupied by various categories of non-members, such as the eldest sons of peers, privy councillors (senior ministers from the Commons may also sit on the steps of the Throne), peers of Ireland and retired bishops who have had seats in the Lords. On the floor of the House there are no prescribed places for individual peers, though those who attend regularly usually sit in the same spot. In front of the

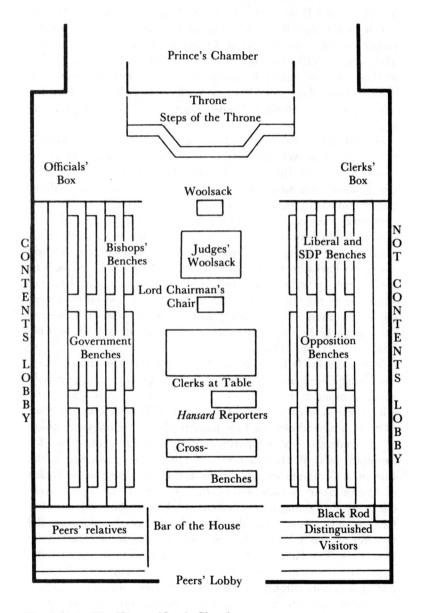

Figure 4.1 The House of Lords Chamber

Throne is the Woolsack upon which the Lord Chancellor sits as Speaker of the House. This is also technically outside the House, which means that the Lord Chancellor steps two paces into the House when he wishes to make a speech himself. To the left of the Throne is an 'Officials' Box' where civil servants sit ready to give briefing to government front-benchers, while opposite this is a 'Clerks' Box' where since 1990 three places have been reserved for advisers to brief opposition front-benchers while debate is proceeding.

Immediately behind the debating chamber is the Prince's Chamber, a relatively small area used by peers as a sort of gossip room. Leading off this is the Royal Gallery, a large and splendid room, sometimes used for a visiting head of state to address parliamentarians, sometimes as the debating chamber when, for emergency reasons, the main chamber has had to be vacated. It is now modestly furnished, so as to enable peers to take guests there for conversation. Through the Royal Gallery the Queen processes when she opens Parliament, on her way from the Royal Robing Room to the Throne. Its walls are covered with 'a vast picture of the battle of Waterloo on the one side and the battle of Trafalgar on the other' (the description is Crossman's, and for his somewhat irreverent description of the State Opening of Parliament in 1968, see his Diary, vol. II, pp. 543–4).

The accommodation available to peers away from the chamber itself is far from generous. There is no equivalent to the Commons' smoking room, and though peers, being without constituents, need offices or rooms in which to hold small *ad hoc* meetings less than MPs, they nevertheless find the paucity of such facilities something of a handicap. The Opposition Party's major spokesmen, for example, must all share a room, as must all six chairmen of the European Communities sub-committees. Certain parts of the Palace of Westminster remain within the control of the Lord Great Chamberlain (acting on the Sovereign's behalf), but responsibility for most of the Palace passed in 1965 to the respective officers of the two Houses, Black Rod in the Lords and the Serjeant-at-Arms in the Commons. The House of Lords Offices Committee looks after the accommodation and services used by the Lords. In 1991 this operated mainly through seven sub-committees, the titles of which adequately indicate their activities: Administration; Computers; Finance; Library; Refreshment Department; Staff of the House; and

Works of Art. Work of considerable practical importance to the running of the House of Lords was carried on through these sub-committees, which tended to be dominated by about a dozen senior peers, mostly office-holders within the party groups in the Lords.

In 1991 peers remained without salaries for their parliamentary work (unless, of course, they were ministers or held one of the very few remunerated offices in the House of Lords). The expense allowance introduced in 1957 had enabled peers to claim out-of-pocket expenses within specified daily maxima ever since, and certainly by the mid 1980s the allowances payable had become relatively generous compared with what they had been in the 1960s and 1970s (see Appendix A for details). But the whole allowance system, while adequate for peers whose work in the Lords is very much a part-time affair, is manifestly inadequate to provide a reasonable recompense for the more or less full-time working peers – on Opposition Party front benches or on the back benches anywhere in the House. (It is, of course, also open to abuse if a peer simply looks in for a short time on most sitting days without actually contributing to the work of the House in any way.)

The Top Salaries Review Board was obviously well aware of the anomalies when it made its 1987 Report (Cd. 131); nevertheless, it felt unable to endorse a recommendation made by its management consultants: namely that parties within the House of Lords should be allowed to nominate a limited number of active back-benchers for a higher level of allowance. The opposition parties in Parliament have since 1975 received a financial grant to defray expenses; this is – perhaps aptly – known as 'short' money (after Mr Edward Short, later Lord Glenamara, who introduced this provision when he was Leader of the Commons). The parliamentary parties are themselves responsible for the distribution of this money, comparatively little of which has been channelled towards peers. Discussions between the Leader of the House and the other parties about the possible introduction of a new allowance or system of support for opposition parties took place in the late 1980s. In advance of a new allowance being introduced, the Labour Party decided in 1990 to direct more of the 'short' money to the needs of the opposition front bench in the Lords. This resulted in Labour employing three research assistants rather than the single research assistant they had had in the mid 1980s.

Arrangements Regarding Peers' Attendance

Certain formalities must be attended to before a new peer becomes a member of the House of Lords. In the case of a peer by succession the claim to a writ must be established, and this can be a lengthy process, especially if the line of succession is complex. For example *The Times* reported on 30 May 1989 that a retired grocer had spent ten years tracing a line of descent through 'fifteen males', and collected some eighty signed documents from around the world, all in order to show that he was entitled to become the tenth Earl of Essex. For straight succession to an elder son, the process is usually speedy. In cases where claims are uncertain for some reason, the Committee for Privileges may investigate; this sometimes involves detailed and complex argument being deployed by petitioners through counsel. In 1989 a barony which had been in abeyance since 1496 was successfully claimed by a former tea-planter in Sri Lanka, who duly became the fifth holder of a peerage – Grey of Codnor – created in 1397. When introducing the report of the Privileges Committee which dealt with this case to the House, Lord Wilberforce remarked that 'even by the standards of your lordships' House 493 years is rather a long time', but that in one case a peerage had been claimed after 547 years in abeyance (see HL 59, 1988–9; HL Debs, 27 July 1989, cols 1569–77). When peerage cases are being heard, at least three Lords of Appeal must be present, and the fact that several days may be taken up delving into arcane matters (such as the precise nature of Scottish peerage law before the Act of Union), inevitably at considerable public expense, has drawn criticism. But hitherto, the House of Lords has not been disposed to recommend any fundamental change: in truth, the amount of time spent on such cases per decade is not large (see HL Debs, 27 June 1977, cols 897–918).

Peers by succession have no ceremony of introduction. When they take their seats for the first time they simply take the oath of allegiance, or they affirm, and are recorded in Hansard, as having 'sat first in Parliament'. Newly created peers must be ceremonially introduced before taking their seats in the House of Lords. The custom is that two peers of the same rank act as sponsors: all appear in their full robes, and the ceremony takes about ten minutes. Usually not more than two introductions take place on any one day, which means that it would take a very long time to introduce the 1,000 peers Mr Benn suggested a Labour Government may create in order to abolish the House (though Mr Benn has argued that mass creations could be effected by an appropriate Commons motion). In 1975 a motion calling for a select committee to examine the ceremony was moved by a peer who argued that it was absurd, time-consuming and open to ridicule, but the Lords decisively rejected his motion by 106 votes to 31.

Peers who have taken their seats may subsequently apply for leave of absence. The reasoning behind the introduction of this facility has been explained in Chapter 1. Under the relevant Standing Order peers may apply for leave for a Parliament, but they are warned not to do so if there is any likelihood that they may wish to attend, however infrequently. In all cases leave may be cancelled at 28 days' notice. Very occasionally a peer on leave has attended, even tried to vote, in which case the party whips will seek to dissuade him, though it is not clear – given the wording of the relevant Standing Order – that they have any power to prevent him.

The leave-of-absence arrangements do allow a peer formally to sign off, as it were, from the House of Lords for a period, and thus 'regularise' his position. The party whips presumably fall silent to a peer on leave. But the arrangements do seem somewhat pointless. They certainly do nothing to discourage infrequent attendances by so-called backwoodsmen. In recent sessions up to 100 peers have not attended at all, but have also failed to take leave of absence. At the same time the numbers taking leave have declined as the House has become a generally more active place. The Procedure Committee acknowledged the relative futility of the arrangements in 1988 when it commented that 'in modern circumstances the scheme is of marginal relevance' and recommended that less effort be made in future to trawl through the list of lords who might take leave (HL 51, 1987–8). It would be sensible – and save both time and money – to scrap the leave-of-absence arrangements altogether.

Peers, like MPs, enjoy certain privileges, notably freedom of speech within the House of Lords and freedom to attend, involving some protection from arrest or detention. This latter point had to be considered by the Committee for Privileges in 1983 when a peer detained under Mental Health legislation asserted parliamentary privilege to secure his release. In a special report the Committee for Privileges recommended that future legislation should make clear that peers could be detained notwithstanding their parliamentary privilege (HL 254, 1983–4; see also Leopold, 1985, 1989).

The Rules and Practice of Debate

Peers do not address the Lord Chancellor or other peers presiding when they speak (as MPs do the Speaker), but make their speech to the rest of the Lords in general. Except in committee, no peer may speak more than once in the same debate, except the mover of a motion, who has the right of reply. Brief interventions to ask questions, or to clarify earlier points, are usually permitted. As in the Commons, peers refer to each other in the third person during debate – for example, the noble viscount, Lord so-and-so. Not all military members are 'gallant', as in the Commons, only Admirals of the Fleet, Field-Marshals or Marshals of the Royal Air Force; similarly, not all barristers are 'learned', but only the holders, or former holders, of high judicial office. Members of the same Party refer to one another as 'my noble friend . . .', relatives as 'my noble kinsman. . .'.

Elaborate courtesy remains the norm in Lords debates. The lack of any disciplinary powers vested in a presiding officer is illustrated by the adoption in 1626 of SO30, 'all personal, sharp or taxing speeches be forborn'; and SO31 of 1641, which enjoins any peer who feels he has been affronted to appeal to his fellow peers generally for reparation. Personal attacks of any kind on fellow peers are rare: a peer who is rude to another peer may find his rudeness simply ignored (as Lord George-Brown did on 10 November 1983 when he attacked Baroness Birk). Lord Hailsham, for many years, displayed a habit of providing his own running commentary on proceedings from the Woolsack, and occasionally his *sotto voce* remarks were not *sotto voce* enough. In particular he directed some disparaging remarks to the bench of bishops. However, when protests about his behaviour were made on the floor of the House, he was quick to apologise (see, e.g., HL Debs, 25 November 1970, cols 129–30; also *The Times*, 26 November 1970).

Peers tend not to interrupt each other and to listen to speeches in near silence. Former MPs may find this a greater ordeal than the noisy hostility they learned to cope with in the Commons, as apparently did the first Earl of Avon (Rhodes-James, 1986, p. 610).

Peers making maiden speeches are expected to avoid controversy. This supposedly allows the next speaker always to congratulate them, and indeed most maiden speeches draw congratulations from almost every following speaker throughout a debate, frequently laced with personal reminiscences about previous dealings with the peer or, in the case of a hereditary peer, his father or even grandfather! The House of Lords is a great place for nostalgia, with peers enjoyably recounting each other's exploits when given the opportunity.

The House of Commons is always called 'another place'. Peers may quote ministers, but may only paraphrase speeches made in the same session by other MPs to which they may wish to refer. Peers are not meant to read their speeches, such a practice being described in the *Companion to the Standing Orders* as 'alien to the custom of the House and an obstacle to good debate'. However, 'extended notes' are allowed, and as any visitor to the public gallery can see such 'extended notes' often amount to a full text, which peers not infrequently then hand in to the editor of *Hansard*, presumably in corroboration of what the shorthand writers recorded. As in the Commons, peers may make minor corrections themselves to the *Hansard* proofs of their speeches, and then to the daily parts before the bound volumes are printed, but not to such an extent as to alter the sense of what they said.

Peers wishing to speak in a debate do not have 'to catch the Speaker's eye', as MPs must in the Commons. Instead they may hand in their names before the debate and, under the general guidance of the Leader of the House, his office prepares a list of peers in the order in which they will speak after consultation with the party whips and the mover of the motion concerned. This list of speakers is then supplied like a programme along with the day's Order Paper to all who attend the debate. This practice has certain advantages: it promotes decorum in debate, and it enables the overall length of a debate to be calculated reasonably accurately. It also ensures that no peer need leave the debate having had no opportunity to deliver his carefully prepared remarks. But it does tend to produce a series of disjointed, if eloquent, speeches, unrelated to each other, even if well-informed. The order is not rigid, and may be varied by mutual agreement; and peers sometimes remove their names, especially if there is a very long list. A peer who has not put his name down can usually speak immediately prior to the closing front-bench speeches, though in some debates this would not be possible.

Peers have no official register of interests as MPs have had since 1975. In 1989 the Leader of the House refused a request from a Labour peer for a register to be set up (HL Debs, 7 June 1989, col. 934). By custom, however, peers begin speeches by declaring any interest they may have in the matter under discussion, though how direct or otherwise such an interest may be has caused some confusion (see HL 50, 1989–90). The declaration of interests is clearly desirable, to safeguard the integrity of peers' debates, but it has an additional purpose in that it enables a peer to explain his credentials for taking part. Where a peer is a member of a public board he is not debarred from speaking in debates which concern that board, but the Addison rules (so called after the Leader of the House in 1951) urge restraint upon him, emphasising that it is ministers and not board members who are responsible to Parliament for the board's activities. The Chairman of the Central Electricity Generating Board, Lord Marshall of Goring, sat through a four-hour debate on the Layfield Report on 2 March 1987 without speaking. This was a particularly sensitive subject at that time, with the Government about to announce its decision on the building of a nuclear power station at Sizewell. Peers who hold offices on public boards do sometimes take part in debates dealing with the work of that body, explaining why they have felt it right to do so (e.g. HL Debs, 26 November 1970, col. 1294). The interpretation of the Addison rules must ultimately be a matter for an individual's judgement.

Servants of the Crown, both civil servants and military officers, who are members of the House of Lords are required to observe restrictions on their participation in the proceedings of the Lords, in the same way as their participation in any political activity is likely to be restricted. The extent of this limitation therefore depends on their seniority and the precise duties they undertake. When a peer who was also a former cabinet minister was appointed a European Community Commissioner, he – Lord Cockfield – was obliged by EC rules to take leave of absence from the Lords, but no other public office requires such detachment from the House.

Peers who speak in debates are expected to attend the greater part of that debate – at least, so the *Companion to the Standing Orders* declares. Frequently this proves difficult: no fewer than four of the first seven peers to speak in a debate on the NHS on 1 April 1987 expressed regret that they had to leave the House during the debate. While general rules relating to the length of speeches have been eschewed, clocks were introduced in 1972 to provide clear indication of the length of each speech as it progresses. In the same year an experiment with limited-time debates was introduced. Subsequently, these have become a permanent feature of Lords procedures, and effectively such debates do involve strict and sometimes very short time limits for speeches (see below, pp. 186–7).

For divisions peers walk through two lobbies, 'content' and 'not content', and are counted by two tellers, whose votes are also included (unlike the tellers' votes in the Commons). If fewer than thirty peers vote during proceedings on legislation, the question is not decided, which in modern conditions very seldom happens except on private members' bills. The peer on the Woolsack or (in Committee) at the Table may vote in a division, which means there is no scope for a casting vote. If there is an equality of votes on legislation, the rule is that the bill proceeds in the form in which it was before the House, while motions are resolved in the negative unless a majority of peers vote in their favour. The quorum for ordinary business is three.

Normal sitting days are traditionally Tuesdays, Wednesdays and Thursdays, though in recent years Monday has become a normal sitting day as well (from approximately one in two Mondays in the late 1950s to almost nine out of ten Mondays in the late 1980s). Friday sittings were once rare, but have become relatively frequent (one in four in the late 1980s). The customary sitting time is 2.30 p.m. (and 3.00 p.m. on Thursdays), but if a Friday sitting takes place it commences at 11.00 a.m., as do the final sittings before a recess. Occasionally these times are varied – for example, when an unusually long debate is anticipated: on two of the three days in July 1971 when the House of Lords held its longest ever debate – 110 peers spoke on entry into the Common Market – the Lords met at 2.00 p.m. The House merely adjourns when everyone who wishes to speak in a debate has finished. There has, however, been a noticeable tendency to sit later in recent years, with the House sitting after 10.00 p.m. on over half the sitting days in 1989–90, an hour regarded as quite exceptional in the 1950s. All-night sittings remain unusual, but over particularly hard-fought bills they do sometimes occur. The longest ever sitting in the Lords was on 3 June 1986, lasting 19 hours and 38 minutes, the main business being the Gas Bill, then in its committee stage.

The Select Committee on Procedure, consisting of about two dozen quite senior peers, keeps under constant review the procedures of the House of Lords. It issues regular reports, usually quite brief, sometimes suggesting slight modifications in procedure, but as often re-emphasising existing rules and conventions of the Lords. Under the authority of this Committee the *Companion to the Standing Orders* is published; this gives peers detailed guidance about the interpretation of Standing Orders, as well as other information concerning the practices of the House.

Broadcasting in the House

It is paradoxical that the unelected House should have become the first part of Parliament to be televised regularly. The concern of peers not to offend the sensitivities of MPs on this matter was eventually overcome by the eagerness of the media and by peers' growing self-confidence. In 1966 the House of Lords debated and approved a motion, moved by Lord Egremont, in which a welcome was extended to television as an additional means of demonstrating the usefulness of the House of Lords. In the various subsequent debates on this subject the confidence of most peers that television would enhance the public reputation of their House has been noticeable.

As a result of Lord Egremont's motion an experiment with closed-circuit television took place over a three-day period in February 1968. Five large cameras, two actually within the chamber itself, were necessary, a degree of intrusiveness which caused some misgivings. None the less, in 1969 the Lords endorsed a report from the select committee it had set up on the subject, which called for a proper public experiment to take place (HL 159, 1967–8). But this did not happen. Broadcasters were clearly not very interested in televising the House of Lords without the House of Commons, and few peers thought this appropriate either.

In 1978 both Houses agreed to the commencement of regular sound broadcasting. This probably enhanced the relative public reputation of the House of Lords compared with the Commons; extracts from Lords debates generally sound better on the radio because the House is quieter and debate more courteous and generally decorous. Sound broadcasting may have contributed a little to the general growth in the self-confidence of the Lords, which certainly had several causes in the early 1980s. After the 1983 election, Lord Soames, formerly Leader of the House, moved a motion calling for a public experiment in televising the House of Lords. The Government made clear that public funds would not be available, but the attitude of the new Leader of the House, Viscount Whitelaw, was definitely favourable, and the Lords voted heavily for an experiment.

In January 1985 regular television broadcasts commenced. The first debate to be carried live was an opposition motion on economic and social policies. A very large number of peers wished to speak, among them the Lords' most distinguished new recruit, the 90-year-old Earl of Stockton, formerly Harold Macmillan. On this and several subsequent occasions over four million people watched at least part of the debate (compared with a daily attendance in the public gallery of between 200 and 900). Varied use was made by BBC and ITV of edited extracts from debates: BBC 2 used material frequently on 'Newsnight'; and Channel 4 produced summaries on the Local Government Bill which were watched on average by almost 300,000 people, despite the fact that they were not broadcast till midnight. A quarter of a million viewers watched a late-night Channel 4 documentary programme on the Lords' Select Committee on Overseas Trade.

In July 1985 the Lords agreed on division to extend the experiment. Expectations were high that the Commons would agree to be televised too, but in November MPs voted narrowly against this, and it was not until November 1989 that the television cameras gained admittance to the Commons. Perhaps the experience of the House of Lords had some part in eventually encouraging MPs to allow television into their chamber. In May 1986, notwithstanding the Commons rejection of television, peers voted to allow the televising of their House to continue on a permanent basis (HL Debs, 12 May 1986, cols 963–1005). Concern about the effect of television on the behaviour of peers had quickly subsided; the television cameras used were relatively unobtrusive and the lighting necessary was not troublesome. Difficulties over achieving party balance in edited summaries were encountered, but the nature of party strength in the Lords, with cross-benchers and bishops to consider as well as the four political parties, meant that no precise balance could ever be defined, let alone achieved. This in a sense obviated the problem: it was more a balance in arguments made on a particular subject for which broadcasters had to strive rather than an exact balance in the political allegiance of individuals televised (see Franklin, 1986).

Officers and Officials of the House

Several peers have roles of particular significance within the House of Lords, as do some non-members who serve the House in various ways. Of first importance is the Lord Chancellor, who is *ex officio* Speaker of the House. But his role is quite different to that of the Commons' Speaker. With regard to the latter, a large body of conventions has grown up designed to ensure that he will be absolutely and irrevocably separated from party politics, but there is no suggestion of the requirement of political impartiality with the Lord Chancellor. As a senior member of the Government he speaks and votes in the House, defending the Government's policies and replying to opposition attacks. When the House goes into Committee, he removes his wig and sits on the government front bench. Indeed, his duties as Speaker are confined to putting the question on motions submitted to the Lords. As far as maintaining order is concerned, the 'Speaker has no controlling powers' (*Erskine May*, 1989, p. 433). In fact it is the Leader of the House who customarily offers guidance when points of order or procedural difficulties arise.

All the most sacrosanct rules regarding the separation of powers are broken by the Lord Chancellor's office. In addition to being an active member of the legislature – and recent Lord Chancellors have been assiduous in attendance at the House of Lords – he is an important member of the Cabinet, with a considerable part in planning legislation. But the most significant anomaly arises from his headship of the third arm of state power, the judiciary. Most recent Lord Chancellors have not sat judicially except on rare occasions, but in 1970 Lord Hailsham determined to depart from this practice, and in order to do so arranged to spend less time than his predecessors on the Woolsack and, with Prime Minister Heath's agreement, largely avoided service on cabinet committees (Hailsham, 1976, Ch. 36). Apart from sitting judicially, the Lord

Chancellor has many important responsibilities in relation to the courts and the administration of the judicial system.

In most legislative assemblies, the presiding officer is chosen by the members themselves, almost invariably from among the more long-serving of their own number. But most recent Lord Chancellors have not had significant experience of the House of Lords prior to their appointment: of the last fourteen, no fewer than nine received their peerages upon taking office. Nor do peers have any say in the appointment. If there is any body of people whom the Prime Minister must consider in making his or her choice, it is the lawyers, because the Lord Chancellor must be a person of the highest eminence in the legal profession. Usually the Lord Chancellor is a barrister who has spent some years in the House of Commons, and been prominent enough in his Party to hold ministerial office, probably as a law officer. Of the last fourteen Lord Chancellors, eight had previously been law officers in the Commons, while three more had, as peers, held other government offices, including Lord Mackay of Clashfern who, as Lord Advocate, had dealt with Scottish law from 1979 until his appointment as Lord Chancellor in October 1987. Two of the remaining three were law lords before their appointment, while the third was Lord Gardiner, who had been a prominent member of the bar before his appointment in 1964. Lord Hailsham, Lord Chancellor from 1970 to 1974 and again from 1979 to 1987, occupied the Woolsack for longer than any other peer this century. Lord Mackay is the first Lord Chancellor not formally qualified in English law.

When disputes or difficulties arise over the interpretation of the rules and procedures of the House of Lords, it is to the Leader of the House that peers look for guidance. For example, during oral question time it is the Leader who tries to move proceedings on if they become protracted, and he will usually do so by suggesting when the Lords should move to the next business. If there is a dispute about the arrangement of business, again the Lords will expect to hear from the Leader. But the advice he offers is not binding. If necessary, disputes can be resolved by votes on the floor of the House, and the Leader, in offering his advice, has to bear in mind that in a formal sense he has no more authority than any other peer.

The Leader is the senior member of the government front bench, and has responsibility for seeing that the Government gets its business through the House of Lords. The Leader has usually been appointed from among peers who know the Lords well from years of personal experience, but three recent leaders were senior Commons politicians created peers simultaneously with their appointment to this office: Lord Peart in 1976, Viscount Whitelaw in 1983, and Lord Waddington in 1990. Another minister in the Lords is usually appointed as Deputy Leader and in the Leader's absence he assumes the role of guiding the Lords on procedural matters.

Opinion among peers has consistently been against appointing a Commons-style Speaker, who would, for example, rule on points of order (HL 227, 1970–1, para. 6; HL 9, 1987–8, paras 12–16). If a peer insists on speaking when it appears that his fellow peers generally think he should give way to another peer, cries of 'order, order' reverberate through the chamber. The Leader or acting Leader may then intervene, and if his advice is still not accepted, it is possible for the motion 'That the noble Lord be no longer heard' to be put. This is a very rare occurrence, having taken place only seven times in the last century (most recently on 29 January 1985, when a prolix Labour peer was silenced at question time).

A third key office held by a member of the House of Lords is that of Lord Chairman of Committees. This is a salaried appointment, made by the House itself, the holder of which withdraws entirely from party politics. The Lord Chairman is *ex officio* Chairman of all committees of the House of Lords, unless the House directs otherwise. When the House of Lords goes into committee on legislation, it is the Lord Chairman (or one of his deputies) who takes the Chair.

In 1974 a new post of Principal Deputy Chairman of Committees was created. This was partly in recognition of the increased workload of the Chairman of Committees, but mainly to enable a salaried Chairman to be available for the European Communities Committee, the Principal Deputy Chairman becoming Chairman of that Committee, the work of which particularly involved the scrutiny of draft legislation from the EC Commission. Counsel are appointed to assist both the Lord Chairman and the Principal Deputy Chairman.

The appointments to the office of Chairman of Committees and Principal Deputy Chairman are always for the current session only, but in practice, like the Speaker of the Commons, the holders remain in office until they choose to resign. The work of the Chairman of

Committees, especially that on private bills, is very complex (see below, Chapter 8). There are obvious advantages in avoiding frequent change in this post; the average tenure of the office of Chairman of Committees since 1800 has been sixteen years.

When the office becomes vacant, informal consultations take place with a view to fixing on a suitable candidate. The peer selected is then appointed by the Lords on a motion moved by the Leader of the House. During debate on this it may be made clear why the peer appointed has been chosen, in preference to another peer who has also been considered. The qualifications most desired appear to be a long experience of the House of Lords combined with comparative youth and the likelihood of occupying the office for a number of years. Not surprisingly, in view of this combination of qualities, appointees have always been peers by succession. Lord Aberdare was appointed Chairman of Committees in 1976, and remained in office in 1991: he had previously been a Deputy Leader of the Conservative peers. Baroness Serota was appointed Principal Deputy Chairman in 1986, after Baroness Llewelyn-Davies of Hastoe had held the post for four years.

There are in addition several Deputy Chairmen of Committees, who really correspond to the members of the Chairman's panel in the House of Commons. They are not expected to renounce partisan activity, and these offices have frequently been held by prominent back-bench peers. As the pressure of business in the House of Lords has increased, so has the number of Deputy Chairmen: in 1966 there were eight; by 1991 there were twenty-three.

The actual arrangement of business is carried out by the party whips who, when this aspect of their work is under consideration, are referred to as 'the usual channels'. The need to take elaborate care in making arrangements for the conduct of business is accentuated by the remarkable degree of freedom individual peers possess both to speak and to initiate debates. What the whips do is simply get together and hammer out an arrangement about the timetabling of the business which is as near as possible to a mutual agreement. The danger is that the whips of the two major parties, in their desire to meet one another's demands, may be neglectful of the wishes of others. Occasionally there are protests on the floor of the House about the arrangements made, and in such cases hasty rearrangements may sometimes take place. For example, in early July 1986 the Alliance Parties were angered by the fact that business was altered at less than a week's notice without their spokesman for the item concerned being consulted. In exchanges on the floor of the House the SDP whip asked for an assurance that he would be consulted when business was altered in this way in the future, but the Leader of the House in reply could only promise consultation 'when possible' (HL Debs, 8 July 1986, col. 179). In 1989 the Liberal Democrat Chief Whip described himself in interview as 'a tributary to the usual channels'.

Some peers have expressed unhappiness with the degree of control exercised by the 'usual channels'. Lord Alport suggested that a committee with back-bench representation as well as party whips, perhaps under the chairmanship of the Chairman of Committees, should be set up for this task. But no widespread support for such a change has been evident. In fact the party whips appear to constitute a body well suited to the difficult and delicate task of arranging business. They certainly cannot afford to ignore the wishes of back-benchers. They want to keep party morale high and to secure good turnouts in divisions, so they are predisposed to meet the wishes of back-benchers whenever they can.

Certain officials have an important role as the professional servants of the House. The permanent staff is under the Clerk of the Parliaments, who is the Lords' equivalent to the Clerk of the Commons. All told, the number of clerks working in the Lords is approximately one-third of the number who work in the Commons. Like their Commons counterparts they service select committees, take responsibility for the formal records of parliamentary proceedings published in the *Journals of the House*, prepare the Order Papers for each day's business and generally advise peers on matters of procedure.

Of particular importance to the smooth running of the House of Lords is the clerk seconded to be private secretary to the Leader of the House and to the Chief Whip. He is the official who services the 'usual channels'. Party whips are constantly in touch with him about the timing of business, and individual peers anxious for advice about when or how to raise a matter in the Lords may go to him. In his office details about the organisation of business, both large and small, are settled. Here in the mid 1980s a good-sized board was kept with the future timetable of business throughout a session provisionally marked out (together with information about hazards which might reduce attendance, such as Ascot Gold Cup Day!).

There is constant liaison between this official and civil servants in departments with legislation before the House of Lords. This is chiefly a question of pinpointing matters likely to cause delay to bills, and seeking to make arrangements which balance the needs of the Lords with those of departments. This is a job which demands a thorough knowledge of the procedures of the Upper House, together with real sensitivity to changes in the political mood of the Lords, as well as copious discretion and a capacity to command and retain the confidence of various groups of peers.

The Organisation of Business

Despite the increased activity of the House of Lords, compared with the Commons (and most other legislative assemblies) it remains relatively free of procedural rules. There is provision for a closure, but the *Companion to the Standing Orders* emphasises that this is a most exceptional procedure; it was in fact last used in 1927! There is no provision for allocation of time orders, nor is there any formal restriction on the right of any peer to initiate a debate on any subject on any sitting day. Yet it must be emphasised that alongside this formal freedom, powerful constraints can be applied within the House of Lords, through the demands made by governments (which need to get their business passed), buttressed by the strong tradition of collective self-discipline which still pervades. *Erskine May* takes 21 pages to deal with the order of business and the conduct of debate in the Lords and 144 pages to do the same task for the Commons, a difference indicative of the contrast between the two Houses. In this section we first consider the daily order of business and then discuss some of the procedures a little more fully, before returning to the question of the pressures imposed on the House of Lords by increased business.

Usually oral questions immediately follow prayers, though certain items of business may intervene, such as messages from the Crown, personal statements by peers (for example, correcting erroneous remarks or making apologies) or obituary tributes (confined in practice to the exceptionally distinguished, the exceptionally old, or those who have died suddenly while office-holders). There is no fixed length for question time, as in the Commons; instead, the number of oral questions is limited. Since 1959 the limit has been four per day, and while SO32 provides that 'no debate may take place on such questions and supplementary questions must be confined to the subject of the original question', exchanges on questions are frequently quite lengthy – at least compared with the Commons – and it usually takes at least twenty-five minutes to get through four questions. Periodically the Select Committee on Procedure has expressed concern at 'the growing disorderliness of question time' (to quote a 1971 report: HL 37, 1971–2), but no new or more rigid rules had been introduced to limit the practices the Committee deprecated, which included the reading of supplementary questions and the giving of lengthy replies by ministers (which provoke lengthy rejoinders and hence precipitate a kind of mini-debate). Oral questions are starred, as in the Commons, and in theory are asked for information only. Oral questions may be set down up to one month in advance for any sitting day. On most days in recent sessions the maximum of four per day have been asked, and not infrequently the Order Paper shows all available spaces for such questions already taken. Suggestions for a further increase in the number, or the introduction of a regular slot for short-notice 'topical' questions, have not been taken up. As in the Commons, attendance is usually high for questions, and the proceedings relatively more lively than those which follow.

At a typical sitting the Lords will move rapidly from oral questions to the main business of the day, but it is possible for several types of business to intervene. Immediately after starred questions, private-notice questions are taken. These deal with matters of urgency, and must be submitted in writing to the Leader of the House by twelve noon of the day concerned. The Leader decides whether the matter is one of genuine urgency, but his judgement may be challenged on the floor of the House. A similar procedure is available to MPs, and the practice in the mid 1980s was to repeat answers given to such questions in the Commons as ministerial statements in the Lords (rather than create artificial private-notice questions in the Lords whenever such a question was accepted in the Commons, as had been the practice before 1983). As a result, only one or two such questions have been asked in the Lords in each recent session.

Ministerial statements are made immediately after questions in the Commons, and repeated in the Lords, but because it is considered important to synchronise the time at which statements are made in the two Houses, in the Lords they usually interrupt the main business of the day, maybe coming after the first or second speeches in a debate – or, as it is euphemistically described by the Government Whip, 'at a convenient moment after 3.30 p.m.'. Statements are frequent, with two sometimes being made on the same day. Front-bench responses follow a statement, and back-bench questions may be asked for information, but SO33 stipulates that statements 'should not be made the occasion for immediate debate, unless the House so order'. None the less, exchanges can be quite lengthy, as indeed can statements themselves, and the interruption they cause can be disruptive to the flow of debate. In the early 1970s the practice developed of not repeating all statements; instead, if agreement was reached through the 'usual channels' a statement was simply printed in *Hansard*. For a while about one-third of statements were dealt with in this way, but in recent sessions the number has declined to half a dozen or fewer out of up to one hundred per session. Opposition spokesmen generally wish to have statements repeated in the Lords. If the senior minister concerned is a member of the Lords, the statement is made by him immediately after questions, and repeated later in the Commons. If one House is not sitting, statements may be made in the other alone, and sometimes this means that important statements are made only in the Lords because the Commons is in recess.

Messages from the Commons may then be read out by the Clerk of the Parliaments from his position at the Table in the Centre of the House, and business of the House motions may be taken – for example, altering business already set down on the Order Paper, or suspending SO44, which disallows more than one stage of a bill to be taken on any one day. The Chairman of Committees may also bring forward business, for example, concerning private bills; this is usually dealt with quickly, sometimes not so – as when, for example, a private bill receives a full debate at second reading. Motions to appoint select committees or to approve the report of a select committee may be taken. Again these are usually quite brief, occasionally not so.

Essentially there are two types of business which follow: proceedings on bills and general debates. On Wednesdays proceedings on motions have precedence, but on all other days Standing Orders give precedence to legislation. This does not mean that days other than Wednesdays are 'government days'; private members' bills as well as government bills may be taken, and the precedence given to legislation does not inevitably squeeze out all other debate. Wednesdays are, however, generally reserved for debates on motions.

Finally on the Order Paper are unstarred questions. These are questions on which speeches may be made; they may be put down on any sitting day, and they always come last in the day's business. Unlike Commons adjournment debates, no time limit exists for debate on unstarred questions, which may range from half an hour or less to three hours or even more. Questions for written answers receive replies printed in *Hansard* at the end of the record of each day's proceedings.

How the House Spends its Time

Table 4.1 indicates, for the 1989–90 session, how the total time of the House of Lords was allocated as between various categories of business. Though it is not possible from these figures to state precisely what proportion of time was spent on business initiated by the Government, or by front-benchers generally as opposed to back-benchers, the table does show that well over half the time was spent on government bills. However, most motions are moved by back-bench peers, and almost all questions come from back-benchers. Thus around a quarter of the time of the House was spent on motions, questions or bills initiated by back-bench or cross-bench peers. The proportion of the total time of the House spent on government bills has increased in recent years: from an average of 47 per cent of the time of the House in the period 1979–82 to an average of 58 per cent in the period 1987–90. But because this increase has been accommodated through adding to the total number of hours which the House sits – up from an average of 1,040 hours per session to 1,170 during the 1980s – it has not resulted in a significant decline in the number of hours spent on non-legislative debate and on questions. The House sits longer than it did a decade ago in order to spend more time dealing with government legislation.

Public bills may be introduced into either House, by government ministers or by private members. Private members' bills which are successful in the Commons are brought to the Lords, but peers may also introduce their own private members' bills. On the more important public bills about half the time is spent in committee, the remainder on the other stages (see Chapter 5).

Table 4.1 Allocation of Time to Various Categories of Business (1989–90)

Category of business	Percentage of total time
Prayers and introduction	1.5
Legislation	
Public bills	61.2
Government bills	58.0
Private members' bills	3.2
Lords' bills	21.3
Commons' bills	39.9
Private bills	1.1
Statutory Instruments and measures	3.2
Motions and questions	
Starred questions	5.9
Motions for general debates	15.2
Debates on Select Committee reports	3.1
Unstarred questions	3.7
Statements	2.0
Other (including formal business and adjournments during pleasure)	3.1

Source: Adapted from figures provided by House of Lords Information Office.

Private bills (not to be confused with private members' bills) are largely dealt with off the floor of the House in select committees, though all must be accorded a second and third reading by the Lords; and sometimes extended debate takes place. Most debates on Statutory Instruments are brief, occasionally not so. Instruments must be approved by the Lords. Sometimes the House debates a motion of regret at the content of an Instrument, while at the same time formally approving it (see Chapter 8). 'Measures' are the form in which Church of England business comes before the House of Lords: this relates to those few areas where Church matters are still subject to parliamentary control. They are introduced by bishops, but in recent sessions the time taken by such business has been negligible.

Motions in the Lords may be of four kinds. First is a motion for address, the form used for debate on the Queen's Speech and for certain items of formal business. The Queen's Speech debate typically extends over three days, usually with a concentration on foreign affairs and defence one day, home affairs and social policy another, and the economy and industry on the third. Second are motions to 'take note', the formula usually used by Government when it wishes the Lords to debate a situation or a document without coming to a positive decision. Select Committee reports, almost invariably, are debated on 'take-note' motions. Third are motions calling for a definite decision of the Lords, which, if not withdrawn or agreed without a division, result in a vote taking place. Fourth, and most frequent, are motions for papers. These call attention to a particular subject, but are not usually worded in a contentious manner. The motion ends with the somewhat cryptic formula 'and to move for papers', the addition of this phrase ensuring that the mover of the motion has the right to reply to the debate, at which point the motion is withdrawn. Thus a motion for papers enables a debate to be held without the Lords formally expressing any opinion or, as the *Companion to the Standing Orders* states, 'The opinion of the House is expressed in the speeches made by its members rather than on division' (p. 84).

On most Wednesdays only one motion is debated as the day's main business. But in 1972 a procedure was introduced whereby one Wednesday a month, up until the Whitsun recess, was set aside for two limited-time (two-and-a-half hours maximum) debates on motions chosen by ballot. Back-bench and cross-bench peers only are entitled to enter the ballot, which they do simply by placing their motion on the Order Paper. The ballot is conducted by the Clerk of the Parliaments, but not at the Table; instead it takes place in the office of the Chief Whip, in the presence of the 'usual channels', a minor example of the relatively relaxed procedures in the Lords. For limited-time debates peers indicate their wish to speak as they do for other business, and at the commencement of the debate the Chief Whip announces how much time is available for each speaker. In 1984 the Lords agreed to extend the principle of limited-time debates to allow for some five-hour debates. An increasing proportion of debates on motions have been subject to the two-and-a-half or the five-hour time limit in recent years (see below, p. 182). It is argued that the advantages of time limits are as follows: they encourage short, and hence perhaps more pithy, speeches; they make it more reasonable for peers to attend throughout a debate; and in the case of motions for resolution they ensure a definite time at which any division can be anticipated. However, time limits tend to make peers very unwilling to give way to allow other peers to put questions or interject, and this, in turn, can inhibit peers from expressing controversial views. Those who value the cut and thrust of debate more highly than the eloquence and charm of set-piece speeches have been lukewarm about time limits.

Those Wednesdays not set aside for balloted debates are allocated to various party groups in the House of Lords. A formula has been established which gives eight days to Labour, five to government back-benchers, three to the Liberal Democrats and three to cross-benchers. In the 1970s, when Labour was in office, the formula used gave half the time to the Conservative Opposition, a quarter to government back-benchers and a quarter to cross-benchers and Liberals together. The changes since then reflect changes in the political complexion of the Lords, although the Liberal Democrats press for a still larger share. A Party may decide to use one of its Wednesdays for two 'short' debates rather than one longer debate.

Increased demands on the time of the Lords – both from the Government, with more legislation to consider, and from a more active body of peers – have made it less easy for individual members to obtain opportunities to initiate debate and to secure the discussion of private members' bills. Whilst any peer can put down a motion or introduce a bill, it is only with the co-operation of the 'usual channels' (or possibly by the luck of the ballot for a motion) that this will be taken as early business on a particular day. If this is not forthcoming the peer concerned will find that his only opportunity to raise the subject will occur very late in the evening.

Motions and unstarred questions usually make their first appearance on the Order Paper under the heading 'No day named'. A peer may approach the secretary to the Leader of the House and Chief Whip directly to explore possible times for an unstarred question, and may seek the support of his own party whip. But there can be no guarantee that time at a reasonable hour will be made available. SO41 lays down that no motion or question may be put on the Order Paper for a date more than one month of sitting time ahead. Informally, however, debates on motions are frequently arranged at longer notice, especially when it is considered desirable to secure the participation of peers with very heavy commitments away from the House of Lords.

There is no weekly announcement of forthcoming business as in the Commons, but a provisional future business paper is prepared by noon on Thursday each week in the Chief Whip's office. This contains a detailed statement of business for the forthcoming week, as well as provisional information for later weeks. It has been drawn up by the 'usual channels' and is the basis both for discussion at the parties' Thursday afternoon meetings, and for the party whips issued by the parties to their members at the end of each week.

The House of Lords is often said to have more time than the House of Commons, and therefore to be well placed to revise legislation hurriedly considered – maybe under a 'guillotine' – by the Lower House, as well as to debate issues which MPs overlook or ignore. But these are only partial truths. Commons financial privilege is one clear factor which limits the time spent in the Lords on some bills compared with the Commons. But almost all legislation is debated a great deal more expeditiously in the Upper House than in the Lower (see Tables 5.2 and 5.3). This is because peers conceive of their work as being the revision of bills, and therefore give most bills much less scrutiny than does the Commons. Furthermore, the House of Lords is not engaged in contesting the will of the Government as the Opposition in the Commons seeks to do. Much less time is spent in the Upper House on the repartee of party politics. The whole style of speaking in the Lords tends to be much more concise. In moving amendments to bills, peers more usually go straight to the point of the amendment without accompanying political banter. They are less inclined to repeat points made by earlier speakers.

On second-reading debates and debates on motions the same sort of points apply. In the Commons party whips know a debate must be kept going until 10.00 p.m., and not infrequently in the 1980s opposition whips had to cajole back-benchers into speaking, so as to fill up the time available. But this kind of thing simply is not necessary in the Lords (even if occasionally party leaders are embarrassed at the small number of speeches from their members in a particular debate).

Of course all this is generalisation, the description of a tendency. Sometimes debate in the Lords is protracted, repetitive and generously laced with party rhetoric. On other occasions it is brief,

Table 4.2 Increased Activity of the House of Lords, 1959–90

Session (at approximately 4-yearly intervals)	Total number of peers on roll	Total number who attended	Total number who spoke	Average daily attendance	Number of days House sat	Total number of hours House sat	Average length of sittings in House (hrs)	Number of sittings after 10 p.m.
1959–60	907	542	283	136	113	450	4	1
1963–4	1,012	525	289	151	110	534	4¾	3
1967–8	1,061	679	424	225	139	803	5¾	31
1971–2	1,073	698	419	250	141	813	5¾	28
1975–6	1,139	752	486	275	155	969	6¼	39
1981–2	1,174	790	503	284	147	930	6⅓	41
1985–6	1,171	798	529	317	165	1,213	7⅓	93
1989–90	1,186	826	521	318	147	1,072	7⅓	74

Sources: Calculated from information supplied by House of Lords Information Office and from the sessional index to *Hansard.*

not because peers are well informed but because on some subjects the spokesmen concerned appear so very ill informed that they have little or nothing to say.

A Busier House

Indisputably, though, the Lords' timetable has become much fuller in recent years. Sessions vary a good deal according to a government's legislation programme, but an unmistakable trend towards a busier House is clear both throughout this century, and in particular over the last thirty years. A more active membership is one cause for this increased activity. Another is the heavier legislative programme imposed on Parliament by Conservative as well as Labour governments. Table 4.2 summarises some of the changes of the last thirty years consequent upon both the altered membership of the House of Lords and the increased burden of government legislation.

In this table figures have been given for sessions of normal length at roughly four-yearly intervals. Of course no session is absolutely typical: certainly both 1975–6 and 1985–6 were unusually heavily congested. But a clear overall long-term trend is evident. More peers attend the House of Lords; more speak; the House sits on more days and until later in the evening than used to be the case. It is true that the House of Lords sits fewer hours than the Commons: in 1989–90 the Commons sat 1,468 hours (excluding time spent in standing committees, which in that session held 454 sittings). But the Lords still sits for longer than any other European legislative assembly. It is not the relatively short hours of the Lords but the immensely long hours of the Commons which are unusual in an international perspective.

The most serious timetable problems faced by the House of Lords result from the uneven flow of legislative business, a matter discussed further in the next chapter. Here we may simply take note of the fact that even when the House of Lords has been manifestly, if not hopelessly, overburdened with work, the 'usual channels' have never broken down, nor indeed has there been any serious threat of this happening. The House of Lords has retained its flexible procedures and in a formal sense individual peers have retained their unusual freedoms. This has been possible because, collectively, there has been the acceptance of a remarkable degree of self-discipline. A group of peers, appointed in December 1986 to examine the working of the Lords and suggest alterations, conducted a survey of opinion among all members of the House of Lords. Its report, published in summer 1987, strongly endorsed the existing system of self-regulation and made only minor recommendations for changes in procedure. The case for a Speaker with controlling powers received virtually no support whatsoever (HL 9, 1987–8). When this report was debated in the House, the pride peers take in their lack of procedural restriction was very evident, and peers who were former MPs seemed especially inclined to contrast favourably the procedures of the Upper House with those of the Commons (HL Debs, 4 November 1987, cols 988–1053).

5

The Legislative Work of the House

The legislative work of the House of Lords is generally regarded as its most important task. Bryce emphasised this in 1918, as did the White Paper on Lords Reform in 1968. Surveys of peers' opinions suggest this is the view of active members of the Lords (Baldwin, 1985; Bromhead and Shell, 1967). Since almost all major legislation is introduced first into the Commons, it is the revision of bills brought from the Lower House which must be regarded as having first importance. But some bills are introduced into the Lords, and the work of the House on these is by no means insignificant. Private members' bills can, of course, be introduced in either House.

The Upper House is often spoken of as a revising chamber. But in an important sense both Houses are revising chambers because, in the modern legislative process, bills are shaped and drafted in government departments and the work of both Commons and Lords is chiefly one of revision. Nevertheless the Lords is clearly the junior chamber, and its role in relation to legislation is formally circumscribed, a point which is best discussed before the legislative procedures and the use made of them are examined.

Limitations on Power

The formal powers of the House of Lords are limited, first by the financial privilege of the House of Commons, and second by the Parliament Acts. These two limitations need to be considered separately, though the terms of the Parliament Acts differentiate, for special treatment, a category of bill known as 'Money Bills'.

Financial privilege arises from 'the ancient rights and privileges' of the Commons: these require that all proposals dealing with 'aids and supplies' must originate from the Commons, and that once approved by the Commons they cannot be altered by the Lords. These principles were embodied in the seventeenth century resolutions passed by the Commons (see Chapter 1, p. 8) and have never been disputed. In modern times 'aids and supplies' are brought together in Finance Bills which deal with taxation and Consolidated Fund Bills which authorise expenditure. Together these are known as Supply Bills.

Though the power of the House of Lords in relation to such bills is strictly limited, they must nevertheless be passed by the House. The current House of Lords never even debates Consolidated Fund Bills (though a peer attempted to speak on such a bill in 1981 – see HL Debs, 22 December 1981, cols 395–400; HL 86 [1981–2]).

As regards the annual Finance Bill, embodying budget proposals and authorising taxation, debate at second reading is usual, generally, on the overall economic situation, though sometimes particular aspects of the Finance Bill may be attacked – as for example in 1978, when Conservative peers were critical of the allegedly retrospective character of clauses on tax avoidance. After second reading, remaining stages are taken formally.

The seventeenth-century resolutions, however, were incomplete in two respects. First, though the Lords could neither initiate nor amend any bill of aid or supply, the House could still reject such a bill in its entirety. This is what happened to the 1909 Finance Bill, and that episode resulted in the Parliament Act which introduced a quite distinct limitation on the power of the Lords, considered below.

Second, the resolutions left room for debate over definition. Complaints were soon heard that some bills of aids and supplies included clauses dealing with extraneous matters, which the Lords was prevented from amending because they were 'tacked' on to bills protected by Commons' privileges. So in 1702 the Lords adopted a Standing Order which condemned 'tacking', defined as 'the annexing of any clause . . . to a bill of aid or supply the matter of which is foreign to and different from the said bill'. In modern times the question of 'tacking' has rarely been raised, though it was in 1976 when a peer argued that the power conferred in that year's Finance Bill (to allow Inland Revenue staff to seek a court order empowering them to break into private premises to take away papers) altered the law on trespass, and *prima facie* appeared to breach the House of Lords SO No. 50 (quoted above). His view was not accepted by the Lords as a whole, though his assiduity in raising the matter was widely welcomed (see HL Debs, 7 July 1976, cols. 1225–9; 15 May 1978, cols. 6–44). In effect the House of Lords Standing Order on 'tacking' is the Upper House's way of safeguarding *its* privilege, which could otherwise be eroded by a creeping extension of the Commons' financial privilege.

Other bills, besides Supply Bills, frequently contain some provisions which deal with taxation or public expenditure (technically, 'charges', imposed either on the people or on public funds), and where this is so the Commons' financial privilege is involved. However, it may often be difficult to disentangle in such bills provisions dealing with 'charges' from other provisions concerned with policy and administration. Some relaxation of the Commons' financial privilege is therefore desirable, otherwise the legislative role of the Lords could be unduly inhibited. In practice, the Commons is less emphatic in asserting its privilege in relation to such bills. If, for example, the House of Lords introduces amendments which infringe the Commons' financial privilege, the Commons may accept such changes, and even if it disagrees with them, the Lower House does not necessarily assert privilege in order to get its way. However, if the Commons does reject a Lords' amendment on grounds of financial privilege, the Upper House will not press the matter, though peers may sometimes try to find another form of amendment which circumvents financial privilege. For example, in 1985 the House of Lords carried on division (by 77 votes to 62) an amendment (opposed by the Government) to the Films Bill. This would have enabled financial assistance to be given to film production from funds derived by levies on films shown on TV, levies on video cassettes of films, and blank videotape. The Commons rejected this amendment, advancing financial privilege as its reason for doing so. Back in the Lords a further amendment was proposed to remove the suggested levy on blank videotape (a form of tax), but retain the other two levies; this alteration, it was argued, would mean that the amendment no longer infringed the Commons' privilege. The Government, however, secured a better turnout in the division lobby, and the compromise amendment was rejected by 100 votes to 83.

If the Lords amend a bill in such a way as to impose a charge which goes beyond the authorisation embodied in the accompanying financial resolution, then the Lords' amendment can be rejected by the Commons without debate. This happened on the Education (Student Loans) Bill of 1990, when peers voted to allow continued eligibility for housing benefit, payment of which, however, was authorised by the Social Security Act 1986, not the bill under consideration. Such an amendment would have been ruled out of order without debate in the House of Commons (see HC Debs, 4 April 1990, col. 1259).

Bills which deal with 'charges' are quite often introduced into the Lords before being dealt with by the Commons. When the House deals with a bill which involves any kind of financial provision, a 'privilege amendment' is moved at third reading specifically disclaiming that the bill affects 'charges'. When the bill arrives in the Commons, this amendment is removed. Such procedural nicety illustrates further the care taken to avoid even a technical infringement of financial privilege.

The second major limitation on the power of the House of Lords arises from the Parliament Act of 1911 (amended in 1949). This introduced a wholly new category of legislation, Money Bills, over which the power of the Lords was limited to a single month's delay. Somewhat simplified, a Money Bill is one which deals exclusively with 'charges'. This means that Finance Bills embodying budget changes have frequently not been certified as Money Bills, because they deal with other matters besides 'charges'. At the same time, other bills, which are not supply bills, may be certified as Money Bills; such are generally brief bills, the specific purpose of which concerns public expenditure. It is the Speaker of the Commons who alone decides what qualifies as a Money Bill (see Table 5.2 for examples from the 1981–2 session).

It is sometimes erroneously stated that the House of Lords refrains from debating Money Bills, but in fact such bills usually are debated at second reading and very occasionally at later stages as well. In 1985 the Lords debated – and only narrowly rejected (by 110 votes to 91) – a reasoned amendment to the second reading of a Money Bill, the London Regional Passenger (Transport) Bill, with some peers expressing concern at the allegedly retrospective character of this bill, and other peers arguing that it was inappropriate on constitutional grounds to debate such a motion at all. This was unusual. In fact the House is extremely cautious about its handling of Money Bills.

Moving away from Money Bills, the Parliament Acts also provide for a Commons bill brought forward in one session to go for Royal Assent in the following session, notwithstanding disagreement by the Lords, providing twelve months have elapsed since the bill had its second reading in the Commons. The bill must be reintroduced in the second session substantially in the same form as it was when first brought from the Commons. In the 1975–6 session the two Houses failed to agree on the Trade Union and Labour Relations (Amendment) Bill, which accordingly fell at the end of the session. It was reintroduced in the following session and, after second reading in the Commons, proceeded straight to the House of Lords with an accompanying certificate from the Speaker in accordance with Parliament Act procedures. The same thing happened in the 1976–7 session to the Aircraft and Shipbuilding Industries Bill, which was reintroduced in the 1977–8 session (see Chapter 9, p. 249). On both these bills the Parliament Act procedures were activated, but in neither case did these procedures run their full course because compromise between the House of Lords and the Labour Government was eventually attained, though only after the bills concerned had been delayed by the Lords.

In 1990, however, the House of Lords did reject outright the War Crimes Bill. Before this measure had been brought forward, both Houses had debated the recommendation of a Committee of Inquiry that such legislation should be introduced so that Nazi war criminals, who had found their way into Britain at the close of the Second World War, might be prosecuted. Though no vote was taken in the Lords, speeches made in the debate (held on 12 December 1989) indicated clear and overwhelming hostility to legislation being introduced. However, MPs voted in favour, and the Government duly came forward with a bill. This passed through all its Commons stages, but was then rejected by the House of Lords at second reading on 4 June 1990 by 207 votes to 74. Despite this huge adverse majority the Government quickly indicated its intention of reintroducing the bill in the following session, and if necessary securing its enactment by using Parliament Act procedures. In March 1991, a year after the bill had first been given a second reading in the Commons, MPs again voted for it (by 254 to 88). The bill then went directly to the House of Lords, where peers debated it on 30 April;

some who opposed the bill felt that it would be better for the House now to accept it at second reading, and then try to improve it in committee, rather than reject it outright and so lose any chance of securing amendments. However, the House still rejected the bill, though by the much smaller majority of 131 votes to 109. The Parliament Acts provide that a bill approved by the Commons in two successive sessions, but rejected by the Lords, shall go forward for Royal Assent unless the Commons direct otherwise; accordingly, since the Government decided to provide no time for a further debate in the Commons, a few days later the bill was taken forward for Royal Assent. The procedure of the Parliament Acts was thus used for the first time since 1949. The significance of this episode is considered in the concluding chapter.

The language of the Parliament Acts is entirely in terms of Commons bills, so it would be impossible to use these procedures to ensure the passage of bills introduced into the Lords. The 1911 Act specifically exempts any bill to extend the life of a Parliament beyond five years (upon which the Lords' veto remains absolute). Nor do the Parliament Acts apply to private legislation or to Statutory Instruments, upon which the Lords' power of veto remains.

Legislative Stages in the House of Lords

Although bills can be introduced in either House, most major and controversial bills must, in practice, be introduced in the Commons. This is because opposition leaders in the Commons, as well as other MPs, feel that it is their right as the people's elected representatives to be the first parliamentary discussants of major bills. Senior ministers usually want to introduce their prize departmental offspring personally, and since almost all senior ministers are in the Commons, this necessitates the introduction there of bills about which ministers have strong feelings of paternal jealousy.

The stages a bill goes through in the Lords are, in outline, the same as in the Commons, though there are differences in the detailed procedures and in the use made of these. As in the Commons, the first reading of a bill is almost always a formality. Sometimes a Lords private members' bill has been debated and even rejected on first reading, but this occurs only if the peer concerned exasperates the House by persistently introducing bills which have no hope of success. After first reading a bill is printed, and an explanatory memorandum is usually made available.

The second-reading debate is generally taken as an opportunity to consider the principle of a bill. The government spokesman frequently makes a speech very similar to that made by his Commons colleagues on a bill which has already passed that House, though he may, in particular, indicate alterations made to the bill by the Commons, and perhaps areas where the Government itself intends to amend the bill during its passage through the Lords. Again the main opposition spokesman is likely to make a speech reiterating many of the points already made by his colleague in the Commons. But while the Commons debate has almost certainly been dominated by Government and main Opposition party spokesmen, in the Lords contributions from peers less closely involved with the party political struggle can be anticipated. In some cases these will be reflective speeches from retired ministers; others will be speeches from experts of various kinds – for example, trade-union leaders or industrialists – who may take a party whip but who nevertheless speak very much as individuals knowledgeable about the subject concerned. Speeches from members of minor parties, as well as from cross-benchers and, in some cases, from law lords and bishops, will be made, and some of these may contain powerful attacks on the legislation concerned. Peers also make frequent second-reading speeches, which act as trailers for amendments they would like to see made to a bill at later stages. For a bill first introduced in the Lords, the second-reading debate affords the government spokesman the first opportunity to explain the purpose of the bill and to expound its contents.

Whereas in the Commons a vote against a government bill at second reading is taken as a normal part of the Opposition's attack, such a vote in the Lords would inevitably constitute a direct challenge to the Government, and indeed to the Lower House in the case of a bill which has already been passed by MPs. This creates difficulties for the Opposition in the Upper House. For a bill introduced by a Conservative Government, opposed at every stage in the Commons by the Labour Opposition, it can be difficult for Labour leaders in the Lords to explain to the party faithful outside the House why they have not even bothered to force a division at second reading. On the other hand, while a Labour Opposition might do this, secure in the knowledge that any such division would be lost and the will of the Government not thereby frustrated by the unelected House, the danger remains that such an action could be held to set a precedent which, if followed by a Conservative Opposition, would almost certainly have a very different outcome.

There are two procedures by which peers hostile to a government bill have forced divisions at second-reading stage without risking loss of the bill itself. One is to move a reasoned amendment which can specify which aspects of the bill are deprecated by the Lords. For example, when the Local Government Bill (abolishing the GLC and Metropolitan counties) was debated at second reading on 15 April 1985, the Labour front-bench spokesman moved an amendment which stated: 'this House regrets the failure to provide a local and democratic framework for the strategic services essential to the capital city and the metropolitan area.' This challenged the basic principles of the bill. The amendment was voted on (and lost) prior to the second reading of the bill being approved.

The other procedure is to move a resolution at the same time as the second-reading debate takes place, which is then voted on after the bill has been formally given its second reading. This procedure was pioneered by Lord O'Hagan (at the time a cross-bench peer) on the 1971 Immigration Bill. His motion, spelling out reasons for regret at the bill, was debated simultaneously with the second reading, but then voted on after the second reading had been approved (24 June 1971).

While both these procedures have been used with some frequency by Labour Oppositions, never have such motions yet been carried because the Conservative Government has taken enough trouble to ensure their defeat. That being so, whether there is any tactical advantage to be gained by moving such a motion is a moot point. In 1990 the Liberal Democrats proposed a motion adjourning the second reading of the Education (Student Loans) Bill on the grounds that the Government had provided insufficient detail in the bill to show how it would operate. After Labour made clear that it would not support this amendment (which would have amounted to rejection of the bill), a motion simply regretting the lack of information available in the bill was moved, upon which the opposition parties were united. However, the Government secured a comfortable victory, which some peers believed made opposition to the bill during its later stages more difficult. Never (yet) has the

Conservative Party in Opposition adopted such a procedure. If it did so, it could expect to win such a division, and though formally a bill might still be accorded a second reading, it would be inconsistent thereafter not to amend it in a sufficiently drastic way to ensure that the features deprecated in the resolution carried at second reading were removed. In practice a Conservative Opposition can content itself with passing whatever 'wrecking' amendments it considers appropriate at committee or report stage.

After second reading the presumption is that bills will have a committee stage for detailed debate and amendment. But the House does not go into committee on Supply Bills, and almost never does so on Money Bills. For such bills the committee stage is negatived immediately after second reading, and remaining stages may be taken formally forthwith. For other bills the committee stage can be cancelled (the order of commitment discharged) if no amendments are put down, and no peer indicates a wish to speak at that stage on any motion concerned with a particular clause remaining in the bill.

The committee and report stages for the detailed amendment of a bill vary very much according to the character of the bill. Controversial bills can attract large numbers of hostile amendments, with many divisions taking place. Complex bills may require much detailed amendment – not least by the Government adjusting earlier proposals, and the draftsmen improving their handiwork. Other bills may have brief, straightforward treatment. For bills brought from the Commons, these stages in the Lords present opportunities for further consideration of proposals for change already made in the Commons, and vice versa on Lords' bills.

There are several important differences between committee stage in the Lords and in the Commons. First, while most bills in the Commons go to an *ad hoc* Standing Committee consisting of between sixteen and fifty members, almost all bills in the Lords are dealt with on the floor of the House. While in the Commons party whips can take steps to exclude back-benchers whose contributions might be unwelcome, in the Lords no such opportunity is afforded. Lords whips never know who may turn up at committee stage, and even if the proceedings tend to be dominated by a few peers, divisions are much less predictable than in Commons Standing Committees.

Further contrasts between the two Houses in relation to the stages for detailed discussion of a bill derive from the absence of a Speaker in the Lords capable of exercising power to select amendments, or to rule on the admissibility of amendments. This is a matter left to the Lords as a whole. Amendments which would not be allowed in the Commons because they would be considered irrelevant to the purpose of a bill can be debated in the Lords. As on other procedural questions, the Leader of the House may ask for an amendment to be withdrawn on the grounds that it is irrelevant to a bill (see, for example, HL Debs, 29 October 1979, cols 484–93). Behind the scenes considerable efforts are made by clerks, and then – if these are unavailing – by party whips, to dissuade peers from tabling irrelevant amendments, though if this does happen the Lords may still take a fairly relaxed and flexible attitude. Thus, on a bill dealing with agriculture, amendments about fish farming may be debatable in the Lords but not in the Commons; and on a bill dealing with the protection of aircraft, amendments to include airports may be out of order in the Commons but not in the Lords.

At committee stage a bill is considered clause by clause, with amendments being dealt with according to groupings (proposed by the government department concerned with the bill). The names of up to four peers may be put down as sponsors to an amendment (or five if the peer in charge of a bill chose to add his name). Close observers of the House of Lords suggest that in recent years much more careful consideration has been given to the question of amendment sponsorship, with important amendments being drafted in such a way as to secure cross-party support, reflected in the names of sponsoring peers (see Miers and Brock, forthcoming, 1992).

Following committee stage, a bill is reported to the House. Given that almost all bills are dealt with on the floor of the House at committee stage, the report stage affords an opportunity for exactly the same people to go through the bill again. Procedure is slightly different (no 'clause stand part' debate, for example), but the main value of this stage is to debate amendments drawn up in the light of committee stage discussions. The third reading follows, but this, unlike the Commons third reading, provides a further opportunity for substantive amendments. Though the *Companion to the Standing Orders* states that repetition should be avoided, in practice very similar amendments may be debated at committee, report, and third-reading stages (see Miers and Brock, forthcoming, 1992). In the Commons the Speaker can rule out of order amendments at one stage which repeat the substance of earlier amendments. Some ex-MP peers complain of the laxity of Lords procedures in this regard (see Bruce-Gardyne, 1980).

When amendments are moved at third reading, the House of Lords has a final consideration of the bill on the motion 'that the bill do now pass'. This is usually brief, the opportunity for a quick summary of the changes made to a bill, often linked with collective self-congratulation, and the exchange of compliments among peers active on the bill. Occasionally, at the final stage of a bill, a hostile or critical motion is moved. If the Government has resisted all amendments at every stage, the Opposition may register its disapproval in a motion deploring this fact, as happened at third reading of the European Communities Bill in 1972 and at the final stage of the Transport Bill in 1983. Where amendments have been made, a motion spelling out reasons for regret at the passage of a bill may still be moved; Labour did this at the end of proceedings on the British Nationality Act in 1981.

When a bill has completed its passage in both Houses, it is returned for the first House to consider amendments made by the second House. In the case of a Commons bill, if MPs reject any amendments made by peers, then the bill is returned again to the Lords with the Commons' reasons for disagreeing to the amendments in question attached. Such reasons are usually expressed very briefly in a single sentence. A full explanation for the disagreement can be found in the record of speeches printed in Commons *Hansard*. The Lords usually acquiesce at this stage, though peers may make speeches – some in sorrow, some in anger – deprecating the Government's foolishness in rejecting Lords' amendments. Sometimes one or other House will propose amendments in lieu of amendments already made, or amendments to amendments, and in this way some to-ing and fro-ing may take place before an agreed version of a bill can go forward for Royal Assent. If at the end of the session no agreed version has been attained, the bill concerned falls.

It is clearly conducive to careful consideration of a bill that sufficient time should be available between successive stages to allow for consultations and preparation of amendments. SO44 stipulates that no two stages of a bill should be taken on a single day. This Standing Order is sometimes suspended in order to deal rapidly with a particularly urgent bill, but on other occasions to allow government business managers freedom to arrange business as they please at times of congestion. In 1977 the Lords agreed to a procedure committee report recommending minimum intervals between successive stages for lengthy and complex bills; these were two weekends between first and second reading, fourteen days between second reading and committee, fourteen days between committee and report, and three sitting days between report and third reading. Though not incorporated in Standing Orders, these intervals are stipulated in the *Companion*, which also states that notice should be given on the Order Paper if they are departed from in relation to any bill. This has been by no means infrequent, especially when the business of the House becomes heavily congested late in a session.

The Problem of Legislative Congestion

Given the fact that all legislation must complete all its parliamentary stages in both Houses within a single session, the introduction of most major bills in the Commons first can lead to a legislative bottleneck in the Lords towards the end of the session, and this can so seriously impair the thoroughness of the work of the House in scrutiny and revision of bills that the problem deserves separate discussion. The very fact that such problems have occurred regularly under governments of both major parties indicates their intractable nature.

In the 1971–2 session, under the Conservative Government of Mr Heath, difficulties were acute. Peers returned after the summer recess four weeks before MPs. One task before them was to debate over 1,000 amendments to the Local Government Bill, of which over 600 were passed and sent back to the Commons. A motion calling for more legislation to be introduced in the Lords was passed without a division (25 October 1972) and in the following session the major bill reforming the National Health Service was introduced into the House of Lords, an arrangement which pleased peers and seemed satisfactory to MPs also.

In 1975 and 1976 difficulties were again considerable, especially in the latter year, aggravated by the Government's loss of its Commons majority during that session. When the Lords rose for the summer recess in 1976, the committee stage of ten bills, including six major ones (five of which had been guillotined in the Commons), had not begun. As well as bringing peers back early, the

Government extended the parliamentary session, which meant that for eight weeks in the autumn peers sat five days a week, usually till after 10.00 p.m. Again, it was not simply the long hours but the deleterious effect on the quality of the legislative work of the Lords which angered peers. In some cases time schedules were so tight that it was impossible to get amendments made to a bill at one stage printed before the next stage commenced. The opposition front bench moved a motion formally expressing the regret of the House at the inadequate time to deal with legislation, which was carried by a large majority.

In the first session of the following Parliament, with the Conservatives back in office, the legislative timetable again became seriously congested. One bill which caused particular difficulty, the Companies Bill, had actually been introduced in the Lords, but after it went to the Commons the Government had introduced forty-three new clauses, some at a very late stage in that House. The Upper House was then asked to deal with 246 amendments on a Tuesday which had been published only the previous Friday, 48 pages of complex proposals with much cross-referencing to other legislation. Opposition leaders protested and moved a motion deploring the way the Government had handled the House which, though lost by 119 votes to 80, did give rise to critical speeches from all quarters. Lord Boyd-Carpenter, the senior Conservative back-bencher, referred to the timetable as 'making a mockery of the revising function of this House' (HL Debs, 27 October 1980, col. 922). During this debate Lord Denham, Government Chief Whip, argued that more notice had been given of amendments on this occasion than had been given in 1977 when the Lords had hurriedly to consider 252 amendments to the Patents Bill, or in 1975 when 300 amendments to the Children's Bill had to be dealt with. (Whereas, in the Commons, front-bench spokesmen cite precedents exemplifying previous governments' mismanagement of business when debating guillotine motions, in the Lords such exchanges take place when the House is asked quickly to dispose of large numbers of recently tabled government amendments!)

The most satisfactory solution to the problem would be to introduce more of the major bills in the Lords. All governments have attempted this, but the obstacles to so doing have already been described. However, in the 1985–6 session, the end of which was again heavily congested, a major bill was introduced in the Lords, but ironically this was the Shops Bill (on Sunday Trading), which the Upper House spent seven days dealing with, but only as a prelude to its outright rejection at second reading by the Commons. When the House of Lords returned after the summer recess it faced repeated late sittings throughout a five-week 'overspill' period during which the detailed stages of five major bills had to be undertaken. A question in the House elicited the information that over 700 government amendments had been put down to these bills, one of which in particular, the Financial Services Bill, was a very complex measure largely rewritten at the tail end of the session. Again opposition peers protested, especially when they felt that the Government had broken a private undertaking not to table amendments incorporating quite new material to this bill. In his response the Leader of the House, Viscount Whitelaw, argued that the House 'had a much greater role as a revising chamber' than it had known in the past. This was both an explanation for the extra work involved and also an assurance to the Lords that it had become quite simply a more important place and was doing more work (HL Debs, 14 October 1986, col. 687). The 1987–8 post-election session was not only unusually long but also heavily congested. Several major bills reached the Lords late in the summer, and as a result the 'overspill' period was extended by two weeks. The question arises as to whether the House of Lords could more adequately cope with its larger workload by adapting its procedures in some way.

Reform of Legislative Procedure

Proposals for reform in the way Parliament deals with legislation have frequently been made. Generally attention is focused on the Commons, though some proposals – for example, a sessional carry-over of legislation – would involve both Houses. The Lords has considered some reforms involving the Upper House alone.

From time to time the idea of taking the committee stage of bills off the floor of the House has been considered. In 1968 this was done on an experimental basis with one bill, the Gaming Bill, and over the next eight years the experiment was repeated five times. The committees were composed in such a way as to favour the Party in office, but without giving it an overall majority. Peers not appointed to public bill committees were allowed to attend their proceedings, to speak and to move amendments – which several did – but not to vote. Bills chosen for this treatment were ones upon which party political controversy was not anticipated.

How much time did such committees save? Borthwick (1973) estimated that the Gaming Bill committee saved two to three days, but that subsequent committees saved less time. After an interval of ten years, this procedure was used again following the difficulties over congestion in the 1985–6 session. The Pilotage Bill in the 1986–7 session was sent to a public bill committee, which spent eleven hours spread over five days dealing with it, but subsequently the same bill took ten more hours on the floor of the House. The use of such a committee was not judged a success (HL Debs, 5 March 1987, cols 807, 812; see also HL 9, 1987–8, para. 26). It seems doubtful that a reform of this kind can on its own make any significant difference.

More fundamental reform of the legislative procedure was advocated by the 1976 Select Committee on Practice and Procedure. This recommended that the Lords establish committees to commence work while bills were still before the Commons, reviewing the proceedings there and noting commitments given by the Government. Such committees would be given evidence-taking powers, like select committees. These proposals were not designed simply to save the time of the Lords, but to improve the quality of consideration given to bills. A sessional carry-over for bills was also recommended. However, when this report was debated in the House on 5 July 1977 its proposals did not receive any clear endorsement, and some peers, notably Lord Carrington (Conservative Leader), were highly critical of its suggestions. These were not taken up.

A Labour peer, Lord Northfield, himself a member of the select committee, described its recommendations as 'modest proposals', and in an interesting article he argued that experience gained in the work of the European Communities Committee should be applied in the area of public bill procedure (Northfield, 1978). This would entail the widespread use of pre-legislative select committees. It is not a reform which Government or Parliament generally shows much inclination to accept. He raised similar points in the House when peers agreed to set up an inquiry into the use made by the House of select committees in 1991 (see HL Debs, 18 April 1991, cols 1561–3).

In 1983 Lord Diamond initiated a debate on public bill procedure, but his proposals, which involved standing committees composed with regard both to expertise and 'to the proportion of the votes cast for the main political parties at the last general election', implied the recognition of wholly new principles for the composition of parliamentary committees – and seemed more like an argument for electoral reform. They were given short shrift by peers (HL Debs, 3 November 1983, cols 642–60).

Amendments to Government Bills

Table 5.1 gives statistics for the number of amendments made by the House of Lords to government bills during the first three sessions of each Parliament since 1970. The inclusion of sessions terminated early by the calling of an election can produce a distorted picture because in such circumstances arrangements are made for the rapid enactment of some legislation and the abandonment of other items.

These figures need elucidation and qualification. The number of amendments made is a very crude index of the legislative impact of the House of Lords. (On this, see especially Griffith, 1974, Ch. 7.) Yet the figures do provide a starting point for an assessment. Many bills are not amended at all in the Upper House. Money and Supply bills have already been excluded from this analysis, but of the eighty other bills indicated in this table as having been introduced between 1979 and 1982, the House of Lords amended only thirty-nine. The figures for the 1981–2 session may be used to illustrate this point in more detail (Table 5.2). In that year, of twenty-two bills brought from the Commons (excluding Money and Supply Bills) only eight were amended, leaving fourteen to which the Lords made no alteration. Of these fourteen, five were bills the main object of which 'was to create a charge on the public purse' (introduced under a Standing Order specifying this in the House of Commons), and on only one of these did the House of Lords go into committee, and that for a mere half-hour. The Upper House can amend such bills (which may even be introduced into the Lords); but, equally, it is not surprising to find it refraining from doing so because such bills are mainly concerned with 'charges'. Of the remaining nine bills not amended in the Lords, five were not amended in the Commons either, and three of the remaining four received very brief Commons

Table 5.1 (a) Government Bills Brought from the House of Commons
(Excluding Money and Supply Bills)

Sessions	Total number of bills	Number of bills amended by House of Lords	Number of amendments made by House of Lords
1970–3	79	31	2,366
1974–7	68	49	1,859
1979–82	82	39	2,231
1983–6	69	43	4,137
1987–90	61	38	5,181

Table 5.1 (b) Government Bills Introduced into the House of Lords
(Excluding Consolidation Bills)

Sessions	Total number of bills	Number of bills amended by House of Lords	Number of amendments made by House of Lords
1970–3	39	29	488
1974–7	58	38	1,594
1979–82	33	20	1,604
1983–6	42	28	1,373
1987–90	29	18	2,687

Source: Calculated from figures supplied by the Public Bill Office, House
of Lords.
(See also HL 9, 1987–8, Tables VI and VII.)

discussion and only slight amendment. The exception was the
Northern Ireland Bill, debated for some ninety hours in the
Commons (including a committee stage on the floor of the House
with hours spent 'filibustering') but for only nine hours in the Lords.
If we look at bills introduced in the Lords in the same session, we
find that five of ten such bills were unamended by peers, but four of
these five were also unamended in the Commons.

Thus most bills which did not receive amendment in the Lords
were either not amended in the Commons or received very slight
amendment there. This illustrates the point that public bills vary
enormously in importance and complexity. Table 5.2 shows that in
the 1981–2 session the Currency Bill took 48 minutes for all its stages
in the Commons and 19 minutes in the Lords. This simple bill,

Table 5.2 Government Bills Introduced into the House of Commons, 1981–2*

Title of bill	Total time in Commons (hours)	Total time in Lords (hours)	Number of Lords' amendments	Time in Commons considering Lords' amendments (hours)
Canada Bill	21.45	7.14	0	–
Civil Aviation	12.06	1.33	0	–
Coal Industry	11.30	1.49	0	–
Criminal Justice	88.30	52.06	300	0.14
Currency	0.48	0.19	0	–
Derelict Land	5.30	0.46	0	–
Duchy of Cornwall	6.48	0.19	0	–
Employment	91.00	62.00	41	6.48
Finance[a]	127.00	–	–	–
Housing Amendment (Scotland)[b]	2.12	0.23	–	–
Industry[b]	4.40	0.10	–	–
Local Government Planning (Scotland)	101.15	0.52	16	0.26
Local Government Finance (No. 2)	77.45	26.36	32	5.38
Local Government (Miscellaneous Provisions)	23.15	31.31	225	2.48
Merchant Shipping (Liner Conferences)	14.00	1.51	0	–
New Towns	7.30	0.30	0	–
Northern Ireland	90.00	9.00	0	–
Nuclear Industry (Finance)[b]	4.00	0.26	0	–
Oil and Gas Enterprise	87.00	36.00	67	3.27
Shipbuilding	6.30	0.26	0	–
Social Security and Housing Benefits	68.30	12.40	27	0.11
Social Security (Contributions)	7.30	7.18	0	–
Stocks Transfer	2.06	1.07	0	–
Transport	83.00	31.45	134	4.26
Transport (Finance)	14.45	0.41	0	–
Travel Concessions	8.45	1.55	0	–

Notes: [a] Supply Bill; [b] Money Bill; * Excludes Consolidated Fund Bills.

passed without amendment, redefined 'new penny' as 'penny', so that the shortly-to-arrive twenty-penny piece could be described officially as the twenty-penny piece rather than as the twenty-new-penny piece, though of course it became known colloquially as the twenty-pence piece. In the same session the bill taking the longest parliamentary time was the Employment Bill, debated for almost a hundred hours all told in the Commons and over sixty hours in the Lords; this was both a complex and politically controversial bill, introducing restrictions on picketing and strike action.

The fact that public bills vary so greatly and yet all go through the same basic parliamentary processes can be expressed as a criticism of these processes, but it can also be taken as an indication of their flexibility. The stages a bill must go through are the same, but the use made of these stages varies greatly (Drewry and Burton, 1980, discuss this point).

While in both Houses time is heavily concentrated on major and controversial bills, Tables 5.2 and 5.3 show that in the 1981–2 session the House of Commons spent more time than the House of Lords on almost all bills, including those first introduced in the Upper House; the only Commons bill on which peers spent longer than MPs was the Local Government (Miscellaneous Provisions) Bill. A similar analysis of time spent on all government bills in the 1988–9 session likewise showed the Commons spending more time on almost all bills, though analysis of this latter year also reflected the increased time spent by the Lords on legislation. The time spent by peers expressed as a percentage of the time spent by MPs had risen from 30 per cent to 36 per cent for Commons bills, and from around 50 per cent to near parity for Lords bills (see Beamish and Shell, forthcoming 1992).

Table 5.1 gives figures for the total of Lords' amendments made to government bills. Some of these were subsequently rejected by the Commons, and in other cases amendments were proposed in the Commons in lieu of particular Lords' amendments. The proportion of Lords' amendments accepted or rejected by the Commons has varied greatly according to whether the Conservative or Labour Party has been in office. When Labour was in office the Lords made many more amendments against the Government's wishes, but these were mostly reversed by the Commons. Thus in the period 1974–7, of the 1,859 amendments made by the Lords, over 400 were rejected by the Commons, and in almost every case the House of

Table 5.3 Government Bills Introduced into the House of Lords, 1981–2

Title of bill	Total time in House of Lords (hours)	Total time in House of Commons (hours)	Number of Lords' amendments	Number of Commons' amendments
Administration of Justice	15.30	12.15	93	58
Civic Government (Scotland)	33.00	66.00	188	367
Civil Jurisdiction and Judgments	4.45	4.52	47	62
Fire Service College Board (Abolition)	0.15	0.04	0	0
Harbours (Scotland)	0.30	1.24	0	0
Hops Marketing	1.30	0.42	0	0
Legal Bill	4.45	14.00	20	18
Mental Health (Amendment)	32.15	75.00	119	123
Reserve Forces	0.02	0.19	0	0
Taking of Hostages	0.45	2.30	0	2

Lords agreed not to insist on its amendment. Between 1979 and 1983 only 6 of the 2,283 amendments made by the Lords were rejected by the Commons.

One may generalise by saying that when Labour has been in office it has experienced frequent defeat in the Lords and therefore, as a matter of routine, seeks the cancellation of large numbers of Lords' amendments in the Commons – which, providing its majority there is secure, does not normally present any difficulty. When the Conservatives are in office comparatively few amendments are carried in the House against the Government's wishes, though when this does happen, a Conservative Government is much more hesitant about simply asking the Commons to reverse such amendments. This is because their acceptance by the Lords has frequently depended on support by some Conservative peers, if not on substantial cross-bench support, and may well have been foreshadowed by rebellion in the Commons as well. There may well be political embarrassment for the Government in the Commons if it simply insists on trying to reverse the defeat already suffered in the Lords. Therefore, the pressure to compromise can be considerable.

If one looks at the number of legislative defeats suffered by governments in the Lords, it may appear as if the House had greatest impact on Labour legislation. But if one looks at the extent to which bills are actually amended in ways contrary to the wishes of the Government by the House of Lords, the impact is probably just as great on Conservative legislation. When Nicholas Baldwin asked active peers whether the Lords carried on to the Statute Book many more amendments against the wishes of a Labour Government than against the wishes of a Conservative Government, fewer than 7 per cent said 'yes', the great majority reckoning that the end result was very similar (Baldwin, 1985, App. 10).

The statistic showing the total number of amendments made fails to distinguish amendments of greatly differing importance. Some can be described as 'purely drafting' amendments, which means they involve no intention to alter, in any way, the substance or impact of the bill, but simply seek to clarify its wording. Some are 'technical' amendments which are intended to improve the bill by making its impact more precise; others are 'substantive' amendments which may concede important points without altering the basic purpose of the bill; while still others can be described as 'wrecking' amendments because they do change the basic nature of the bill, and may indeed result in the whole bill having to be abandoned.

Nor does the statistic of total amendments made reveal anything about their source. It is possible to identify the immediate source by consulting *Hansard* and seeing who moved the amendment concerned, but even the names of peers sponsoring an amendment do not, by any means, necessarily reveal its origin. This is most clearly seen in the case of government amendments, which constitute the bulk of all successful amendments. Not infrequently these are put down by the Government as concessions in direct response to criticisms made at earlier stages of a bill's passage, sometimes even as a result of a defeat the Government has suffered, after which it brings forward amendments to clarify the change it has been forced to accept. A good many government amendments to bills in the Lords are the result of undertakings given during the bill's passage through the Commons. Often these result from pressure brought to bear on the Government by groups outside Parliament altogether, though in such cases spokesmen within both Houses will generally move amendments on behalf of outside groups as part of the whole process of exerting pressure on the Government.

It is therefore impossible to be precise about the origin of all amendments. Nicholas Baldwin found that almost half of all amendments moved in the Lords to government legislation between 1970 and 1983 were moved by government spokesmen, but he then sought to identify from within this group the proportion which were actually initiated by the Government and found this to be something under three-quarters, the remainder being government responses to undertakings given at earlier parliamentary stages or as the direct result of an identifiable undertaking given to an interest group.

When a bill is going through Parliament, groups with interests in its subject matter are likely to be continuously active. Depending on the kind of bill and the nature of the group concerned, part of this activity will be continuing discussions with ministers and civil servants. But even when these are taking place, contact with MPs and peers is also likely to be sustained to ensure that the group's point of view is put forward in Parliament during detailed discussion of the bill. Lobbying of this kind has always taken place, but there is good reason to believe that it has increased in recent years. Furthermore, the House of Lords has undoubtedly become a more frequent object of attention by group leaders than it was in the past.

Some peers in interview expressed the view that it was the 1980 Wildlife and Countryside Bill which first alerted professional lobbyists to the potential usefulness of Lords proceedings for securing alterations to legislation. This was a major conservation measure introduced into the House of Lords, where countryside interests have traditionally been strongly represented. The 'usual channels' found debate on this bill almost impossible to control, and eventually the Lords spent eight days in committee dealing with it, making, in all, 520 amendments.

Whatever the importance of this particular bill, it also became evident in the early 1980s that as far as actually getting detailed changes made to bills was concerned, the House of Lords could be at least as useful as the Commons. Interest groups responded accordingly, and peers on all sides reported increases in their postbags. A survey of organised groups in 1986 found that of 211 which said they had been concerned about legislation before Parliament, no fewer than 163, or 77 per cent, said they had responded by contacting one or more members of the House of Lords. The same survey found that 177 groups had 'used the House of Lords to make representations or to influence policy', and that of these 144, or 82 per cent, had found the House either useful or very useful. Indeed, almost as many groups had found the House of Lords more useful than the Commons as vice versa (forty-two as opposed to forty-six), while about half the groups concerned had found the two Houses about equal in value (see Norton, 1985, p. 183; Baldwin, pp. 160–64 in Rush, 1990).

When an important bill is before the Lords, groups will usually arrange meetings to which interested peers are invited. Here draft amendments may be distributed and detailed explanations on particular points given. Thereafter group spokesmen will make themselves available throughout the passage of a bill, perhaps holding regular meetings at successive stages to provide ready-drafted amendments to interested peers. A well-resourced group such as a trade union may provide a near-full-time researcher to assist opposition spokesmen to a bill. In other cases the assistance may be much more spasmodic, and opposition spokesmen may bemoan the unwillingness of groups to offer greater assistance.

One way in which some groups seek to advance their cause is through private members' legislation. This chapter concludes with a brief discussion of such bills, after which we return in Chapter 6 to

examining the role of the House of Lords in relation to government
bills since 1979.

Private Members' Bills

While Government may be dominant within Parliament, it does not
monopolise Parliament's law-making role. Back-benchers in both
Houses have opportunities to bring forward bills on their own
initiative, and every session sees quite a number of such bills –
private members' bills – enacted. Mostly these are minor measures
enjoying the benevolent neutrality (if not open support) of
Government. Some are significant changes in areas of law where
parties traditionally fear to tread, issues left to the consciences of
individual members. Such bills must – like other public legislation –
go through all stages in both Houses before reaching Royal Assent.
It is therefore necessary to consider the treatment of both private
members' bills introduced into the Lords and those brought to the
Upper House following their passage through the Commons.

As regards the latter, the difficulties that face MPs who wish to
introduce private members' bills are well known. The time available
for debating such bills is strictly limited, which means that for all
but the most innocuous a precondition of success is that the MP
introducing the bill draws a high place in the ballot of private
members' time.

Almost all private members' bills which complete their Commons
stages are passed by the House of Lords (between 1978 and 1990, of
131 bills brought from the Commons, only 10 failed to reach Royal
Assent). The greater procedural flexibility in the Upper House
ensures that all private members' bills receive some debating time,
so that those bills passed entirely without debate in the Commons
are always accorded at least a brief explanation in the House of
Lords. Since few private members' bills arrive from the Commons
before Easter, their consideration does add to the pressures the
Upper House usually faces late in the session, though most take
relatively little time. Of seventeen private members' bills brought
from the Commons in 1985–6, only one took more than two hours
for all its Lords stages. This was the Disabled Persons (Services,
Consultation and Representation) Bill, which peers debated for five

hours and to which the Lords made 102 amendments, a quite exceptional number for a private member's bill. Only because this measure enjoyed wide support was it safe for peers to give it such close, time-consuming attention.

Any amendments made to Commons bills by peers must, of course, be approved by the Lower House. Usually the last private members' Friday of each session is devoted to taking Lords' amendments, but some may be dealt with earlier. Governments in the 1950s and 1960s were, in general, much readier to provide time for the later stages of private members' bills than more recent governments. (According to a Commons written answer published on 26 January 1987 (cols 106–23), virtually no government time had been provided for any private member's bill at any stage since 1979; whereas between 1954 and 1970 government time was provided for consideration of Lords' amendments to forty-nine bills.) This has had the effect of severely inhibiting the House of Lords from exercising its revising role in relation to private members' bills brought from the Commons. To insert any changes may be tantamount to killing a bill, and peers have complained several times about this.

On the other hand, when peers have amended bills their subsequent demise in the Commons may reflect quite extraneous factors associated with the lower House or the attitude of the Government. In the 1988–9 session the Licensing (Scotland) Bill was introduced into the Commons late in the session, not in balloted time. The only debate on the bill in the Lower House had been in a Scottish Standing Committee. It had government support, though as various outside groups became more aware of its implications, concern either to amend the bill or to stop it appeared to grow. The government attitude became very lukewarm in the Upper House. When peers decided to amend the bill (on 21 July) those present were well aware that their action would also kill the measure, because the Commons would have no opportunity to consider any amendments before the end of the session. In the 1989–90 session of the twelve private members' bills brought from the Commons, four were amended by the Lords, two of which failed to attain Royal Assent. In one case, that of the Consumers' Guarantee Bill, even before the bill reached the Lords it had been emasculated, so much so that it had 'a title which bore no relation to its contents' (HL Debs, 16 May 1990, col. 364). The other, the Road Traffic

Table 5.4 Private Members' Bills Introduced into the House of Lords

Parliament	Total number introduced	Number of bills completing HL stages	Number of bills gaining Royal Assent
1966–70	49	15	12
1970–4	48	16	10
1974–9	77	28	9
1979–83	91	27	11
1983–7	59	31	14
1987–90	25	16	4

(Temporary Restrictions) Bill, fell at the final stage in the Commons when two MPs forced a division which was inquorate, a tactic to which they resorted in protest at the way in which proceedings on the bill were being elongated in order to prevent a subsequent bill being reached.

Such examples illustrate the difficulties faced in the Commons in regard to private members' bills, and these also explain the low success rate for private members' bills first introduced in the Lords. Table 5.4 shows that since 1979 only 40 per cent of bills which completed their Lords stages also got through the Commons. This was a higher proportion than in the 1974–9 Parliament, but a good deal lower than earlier Parliaments, notably 1966–70. A Lords private member's bill taken to the Commons can be taken up by any MP, but only if the bill is given an unopposed second reading on a Friday afternoon is it likely to be successful. However, mere statistics are slightly misleading in this case because some private members' bills passed by the House of Lords in one session were taken up in the Commons in a later session, and their passage as Commons private members' bills may well have been facilitated by their prior debate in the House of Lords.

This was undoubtedly the case with some very significant private members' bills in the 1966–70 Parliament, especially the so-called permissive society legislation. Twice the House of Lords passed bills legalising homosexuality (previously always a criminal offence) before such legislation was successful in the Commons. The legalising of abortion was likewise heralded in the Lords, again with the House both pushing public opinion along on the subject and showing how some of the difficulties inherent in legislating in such an area could be overcome. For a time it seemed that the Upper House was the 'place for all social reform to be first discussed' as Lord Gardiner – Labour Lord Chancellor at the time – claimed (HL Debs, 23 November 1966, col. 251). The presence of bishops, law lords, eminent doctors and other experts, as well as the freedom from constituency pressures, were all factors which made the Lords well suited to the difficult task of producing viable legislation on complex issues (see Richards, 1970).

The impetus for reform of this kind appeared to decline in the 1970s, though frequent attempts at relaxing restrictions on Sunday observance were made and abortion continued to be a highly controversial subject, with more emphasis in the 1980s on the need to restrict availability and introduce legislation on the 'beginnings of life' issues reported on by the Warnock Committee in 1985. After several private members' initiatives in this area had failed, the Government introduced the Human Fertilisation and Embryology Bill in the 1989–90 session. A recent example of a matter upon which legislation was eventually passed, but which proved extraordinarily difficult to get right, was female circumcision, a subject on which the House of Lords worked hard before a Commons private member's bill – the 1985 Prohibition of Female Circumcision Bill – was enacted (see Sochart, 1988).

A number of private members' bills introduced in the Lords in recent years have been referred to select committees. These are discussed in Chapter 8, but we may note here that no similar recent practice giving opportunities to both the advocates and opponents of a proposed bill to assemble evidence in support of their views has developed in the Commons.

Most successful private members' bills introduce minor changes, possibly removing anomalies in earlier legislation – or introducing small alterations recommended by committees of inquiry – but ignored by governments. Even if a bill is unsuccessful, it may stimulate a response from Government. Several all-party campaigning groups within Parliament have used private members' bills to try to achieve their ends. In the 1970s an all-party group was formed to help the racing industry. Several peers have been prominent in this group and several Lords private members' bills have been directed to this end. Lord Newall, Chairman of the British Greyhound Racing Board, introduced a bill in 1980 to allow an increase in the number of races at meetings, and another in 1985 to relax, in a minor way, restrictions on betting at dog races. Both these attained Royal Assent.

Animal welfare and conservation is another area where private members' bills have proliferated – again, success is much more likely for bills with specific and limited aims. Eight successive private members' bills introduced in one or other House on scientific experiments on animals failed, until eventually in 1985 the Government sponsored legislation on this subject. Three bills introduced by Lord Janner in the early 1970s sought to regulate zoos. This culminated in the Zoo Licensing Act of 1981 which, though a Commons bill, entered into an inheritance prepared by the Upper House.

Sometimes all-party groups are rather more partisan, an example being the so-called 'All-Party' Repeal Group which, in the early 1980s, set about introducing bills to repeal statutes which imposed restrictions of various kinds. A Rent (Abolition of Control) Bill was introduced by Lord Vaizey in 1982 which sought to abolish all controls on rents; needless to say, this did not succeed, though much of what the bill sought was eventually enacted in the 1988 Housing Act. The late Lord Spens, who was Chairman of the Group, introduced a Wages Council (Abolition) Bill in 1984, a subject taken up in modified form by the Government's 1986 Wages Act. In 1982 Lord Rugby introduced a bill to remove the monopoly enjoyed by opticians, which he withdrew after a three-and-a-half-hour second-reading debate (described by the government spokesman as 'extraordinarily interesting' (HL Debs, 18 February 1982, col. 727)), and again this subject was later taken up by the Government. So was Baroness Trumpington's bill on Sunday trading of the same session. The 'Repeal Group' was a kind of ginger group of cross-benchers and Tory back-benchers, eager to encourage the Thatcher Government along the path of liberalisation.

Constitutional reform is another subject frequently ventilated by private members' bills. As well as a bill of rights, the House of Lords has debated electoral reform, with a bill allowing district councils to opt for a single transferable vote system for elections being introduced first in 1983 (when it was defeated) and again in 1985, when Lord Blake, a Conservative peer and formerly Chairman of the Hansard Society Commission on Electoral Reform successfully took a bill through the Lords, with the only opposition coming from the two front benches. Such sources of hostility were of course sufficient to ensure the bill a rapid burial in the Commons. In 1990 the Lords passed a bill introduced by Lord Bonham-Carter which would have reformed the electoral system used for the European Parliament, but this again made no headway in the Commons.

Private members' bill procedure is used in both Houses to give prominence to debate on certain subjects, without any very serious legislative purpose being evident. In the Commons many so-called ten-minute-rule bills fall into this category. In the Lords, peers whose concern is simply to initiate a debate generally use other procedures. But sometimes private members' bills are introduced which do not appear to be serious attempts at legislation. If the House feels this to be the case, such bills may be refused a second reading. Two bills on Namibia introduced by Lord Hatch of Lusby in 1985 and 1986 were obvious examples. In 1984, Lord Sudeley introduced a Prayer Book Protection Bill, but after a four-hour debate he withdrew it (rather than risk its rejection on a division); his main aim appeared to be the establishment of a select committee of the House of Lords, but opinion was against this. In 1983 Lord Jenkins of Putney introduced a bill to allow trustees of the British Museum to return objects to countries of origin (such as the Elgin Marbles), but the Chairman of the Trustees, followed by the ex-Chairman, followed by two more trustees and the Minister for the Arts, all roundly condemned the bill which, not surprisingly, expired there and then – a fate Lord Jenkins must have anticipated.

Private members' bills are introduced in the Lords by peers from all parts of the House, including occasionally the opposition front bench. In 1974 Lord Hailsham of Saint Marylebone introduced a bill to remove any doubt about the possibility of a Roman Catholic becoming Lord Chancellor. Serving law lords, including the Lord Chief Justice, have introduced bills, as have bishops and the Archbishop of Canterbury (the latter a bill to facilitate the sharing of Church buildings, enacted in 1969).

Given the unwillingness of governments to legislate in some areas, and the apparent reluctance of ministers to introduce minor bills, usually – so it is said – because they are untimely in advance of more general legislation (which, however, can seem interminably delayed), private members' legislation is an important safeguard. The role of the House of Lords is circumscribed by the procedural rigidity of the Commons, but this is also a factor which contributes to the usefulness of Lords proceedings.

6

The Treatment of Government
Legislation, 1979–90

The purpose of this chapter is to examine the impact the House of Lords had on government legislation in the period 1979–90. This is potentially a vast subject, and selectivity is inevitable. The approach adopted here is to begin by giving particular consideration to occasions on which the Government suffered defeat in the division lobbies; next to consider the effect of the Lords on legislation in a number of specific areas, notably the 'right to buy' council housing legislation, and measures relating to local government. The chapter will conclude with a brief discussion of the changing attitude of the Government to the legislative role of the House during the 1987 Parliament.

Government Defeats

Of the total of 155 defeats suffered by the Government in the Lords' division lobbies between 1979 and 1990, 148 involved legislation (the remainder involved defeats on non-legislative motions or procedural matters). Defeat can result in the Government accepting the decision of the House, or rejecting that decision, or reaching some definite compromise. However, deciding into which of these categories the outcome of every defeat is to be placed is not easy. For example, the Government may offer what it describes as a compromise, but one which appears to go so little of the way to meet the amendment carried by the House that those responsible for that amendment see the government response as one of rejection. Accepting, then, that no categorisation can be wholly precise, analysis of the 148 defeats shows that in 63 cases the change thereby made to a bill was accepted in principle by the Government (though further amendments to tidy up the details were often necessary); in 55 cases amendments were rejected (though in a few cases, after a second defeat in the Lords, the Government accepted the will of the House); while in the remaining 30 cases a definite compromise was reached.

These amendments varied greatly in importance. Some were minor to the point of triviality, while a few were very significant indeed. In between were many which made changes to bills which could be described as minor from the perspective of the Government's overall legislative programme but which, nevertheless, were important to particular groups.

It so happens that the first three defeats suffered by the Thatcher Government in the 1979–80 session illustrate rather well the varied circumstances and importance of government defeat in the Upper House. In chronological order these were: a defeat of a very minor kind on the Bees Bill in February; a defeat on the Criminal Justice (Scotland) Bill, also in February; and third, a major defeat on the Education Bill over school transport charges in March 1980.

The Bees Bill had been introduced by the Government in response to pressure from bee-keepers. It concerned the threat posed by a lethal bee disease – varroasis. Under the bill, hives found to be infected would be compulsorily destroyed. In the Commons the question of compensation for commercial bee-keepers who lost hives in this way was raised, but the Government resisted amendments on this point, and did so again when the same change was advocated in the Lords, arguing that it had agreed to bring the bill forward only because no public expenditure was involved. Eventually peers voted by 33 votes to 25 to amend the bill to make possible the payment of compensation without obliging such payments (18 February). Back in the Commons the Government Minister indicated willingness to accept this amendment, but at the same time he emphasised that the Government had no intention of using the permissive power it had thus been given. The amendment therefore made no practical difference to the implementation of this bill. Had peers altered the bill more drastically – for example, to require the payment of compensation – their amendment would have been rejected. This was a hollow victory, but perhaps one considered at the time to have some symbolic value, the putting down of a marker of opinion to which a subsequent government might choose to respond more sympathetically.

A further example of a minor defeat with cosmetic rather than substantive implications occurred when peers amended the 1980 Health Services Bill. The bone of contention here concerned the salaries reimbursement scheme operated for GPs' employees, which disallowed reimbursement to GPs who employed their relatives, because, according to the Government, it would be impossible to prevent abuse in such cases. Peers protested that a system which compelled two doctors married to two nurses to employ each other's wives (rather than their own) or forgo salary reimbursement was ludicrous. Again the amendment did not require the Government to act on this matter, but established that a change could be made at some point in the future by Statutory Instrument. The Lords carried the amendment against the Government's wishes by 71 votes to 41 (10 July). The Government made no effort to reverse the change, but made clear that it had no intention of bringing forward the necessary order. Nevertheless, the fact that the Lords voted by so large a margin for this change ensured continuing pressure on the Government in coming years, and further questions on the subject were regularly asked in the House (for example 20 February 1985, cols 567–9).

The second government defeat, chronologically speaking, occurred in 1980 on the Criminal Justice (Scotland) Bill. Again this was a minor affair, but it was different from those just discussed in that it illustrated the role of the House in an area where it feels a high degree of self-confidence. The bill followed recommendations of the Emslie Committee in stipulating that when sentencing a convicted murderer a trial judge should, in open court, give reasons for the sentence imposed, together with his recommendation concerning the minimum term to be served. Lord Keith of Kinkel, a law lord with Scottish judicial experience, opposed this, arguing that the purpose behind the proposal was simply to ensure that the views of the trial judge would be available subsequently to the Parole Board, an objective by then routinely secured by other means. The Minister made an unconvincing reply and the Lords supported the amendment by 47 votes to 39 (26 February). When the bill went to the Commons, the Government allowed a free vote, in which the Lords' view was upheld.

On matters to do with the courts and the administration of justice, the presence of senior judges as well as the Lord Chancellor, and former occupants of the Woolsack, enhances the authority which the

House of Lords feels entitled to exercise. On the 1982 Criminal Justice Bill, peers passed minor amendments against the Government's wishes, dealing with bail conditions and the sentencing of young offenders, neither of which the Government overturned (22 June). More significant examples occurred when the Lords inflicted three defeats on the Government during the passage of the Police and Criminal Evidence Bill in 1984. One of these restricted police powers to stop and search to constables in uniform, and this was rejected by the Commons (31 July). Another, moved by Lord Scarman and carried against the Government by 71 votes to 65 on 19 October, required that racially discriminatory behaviour by the police would be a disciplinary offence, and this the Government eventually accepted, while the third – also moved by Lord Scarman – concerned the rules of evidence, and resulted in a government compromise.

A further example of government defeat on matters judicial occurred when the Lords voted by 140 votes to 98 to delete a clause from the 1985 Prosecution of Offences Bill, which would have enabled the Attorney-General to refer to the Court of Appeal any sentence, imposed by a Crown Court for an indictable offence, which appeared to him to be too lenient. Such a reference would have been for an opinion, which would have constituted authoritative guidance for the courts in subsequent cases, but without altering the particular sentence in question. On this occasion the Lord Chancellor found his views rejected in debate by at least eleven peers who had substantial judicial experience, and supported only by Baroness Phillips 'speaking on behalf of various women's organisations' (26 January 1985). The Government accepted the defeat, though after further public outcry about apparent leniency in sentences for some rapists, it brought the matter back in the 1988 Criminal Justice Bill. By this time some peers (including Lord Denning) had changed their minds, and after a lengthy committee-stage debate a government amendment allowing such appeals was agreed by 151 votes to 108 (26 October 1987). In April 1991 peers voted heavily (by 177 votes to 79) in favour of an amendment to abolish the statutory life sentence for murder – against government advice, but in line with the recommendations of one of their own select committees (see below, p. 240).

The third defeat inflicted in 1979–80 was entirely different again. This was the much-publicised rejection by peers of the clause in the

1980 Education Bill which would have allowed local education authorities to impose school transport charges for children in rural areas. The Government was eager to facilitate expenditure savings of some £20–30 million by this means, but the proposal offended both rural and religious interests (because children travelling to denominational schools would be particularly affected). Some local authorities announced the kind of charge they proposed to make while the bill was still before Parliament, and in so doing catalysed opposition to this proposal. In the Commons thirteen Conservative MPs voted against the Government on this issue, and a further sixteen abstained. To try to head off defeat in the Lords the Government offered a compromise package (limiting charges to two children per family, and so on), but to no avail. The Duke of Norfolk, a Conservative back-bench peer and well-known as a leader among Roman Catholics, led the assault (13 March 1980). He was supported by strong speeches from two former Conservative Secretaries of State for Education, Lord Butler of Saffron Walden and Lord Boyle of Handsworth. Public interest had been aroused, and many peers spoke of their heavy postbags on this subject. The Government went down to a convincing defeat: by 216 votes to 112 (with 40 Conservatives rebelling). An attempt to reverse such a defeat in the Commons would probably have led to further humiliations for the Government, so instead ministers gave way.

This was a crucial episode in revealing the importance the House of Lords could have under the new Conservative Government. The greater readiness of back-bench MPs to rebel – a noticeable change in the Commons during the 1970s – meant that the reversal of Lords' defeats could certainly not be taken for granted by the Government. Furthermore, the mail received by both peers and MPs indicated widespread resistance to the proposed change, not least among grass-roots Conservative Party supporters. In most subsequent cases where the Lords inflicted significant defeats on the Government it is plausible to argue that the Conservative Party in the country was at least as sympathetic to the Lords' view as it was to the Government's.

Such an example occurred on the British Nationality Bill in 1981 over proposed treatment of Gibraltarians. By 150 votes to 112 the Lords accepted an amendment moved by Lord Bethell, a Conservative back-bench peer and a member of the European Parliament, to alter the status of Gibraltarians (22 July 1981). During the final stages of debate on this bill in the Lords, reference was made to the possibility of the Government rejecting this amendment and a constitutional crisis ensuing, but Lord Boyd-Carpenter argued that if the Government did reject the change no such crisis would occur, because all the Government had to do was to wait a year and invoke the Parliament Act in order to secure the passage of the bill (HL Debs, 20 October 1981, cols 731–2). But the Government had already been under pressure in the Commons on this issue and decided that its better course was to give way to peers, which it did. By contrast, on another matter upon which the Government suffered a defeat on this bill, an amendment to make discretionary decisions taken by the Home Secretary subject to appeal to the courts if an applicant alleged discrimination, the Government sought and obtained approval in the Commons to reverse the Lords' amendment. When the bill returned to the Lords, Lord Elwyn-Jones from the Labour front bench urged peers to insist on their amendment despite its rejection by the Commons, but the Government successfully resisted this by 116 votes to 96. It is worth noting that thirteen of twenty-two Conservative peers who voted against the Government on this matter of appeals in July 1981 voted with the Government (thus reversing their former position) in October; the remaining nine stayed away. But this was an issue upon which the Government had much more solid support from its Commons backbenchers.

Towards the end of the decade the Government appeared readier to overturn Lords' amendments despite the risk of defeat in the Commons. This is a point we return to below. Meanwhile, having illustrated the varied character of defeats suffered by the Government in the Lords, we look more closely at the impact the House has had on legislation in two particular areas.

'Right to Buy' Legislation

A jewel in the crown of the Thatcher Government was its 'right to buy' legislation, enacted for the benefit of tenants of public-sector housing. To begin with, the basic principle of this policy was strongly contested, but as far as the House of Lords was concerned debate focused on where the precise boundaries of the policy should be drawn. How far should central government go in enforcing such a policy, especially in areas where the only housing within the financial means of many was local-authority-owned? What discount should be allowed to tenants who purchased their homes? Should all accommodation, including that purpose-built or specially adapted for the elderly or disabled, be included? If local-authority tenants enjoyed the right to buy, should this be extended generally to all tenants of those housing associations which had received public funds?

During the first two Thatcher Parliaments three major bills were enacted: the 1980 Housing Bill, the 1984 Housing and Building Control Bill, and the 1986 Housing and Planning Bill. On each of these measures the Government suffered important defeats in the Lords which it was unable to reverse. Peers generally were inclined to impose limits on the individual's right to buy. Pressure groups such as Shelter and Help the Aged were behind some of the more important amendments made by the Lords.

Take first the question of accommodation suited to the needs of the elderly. The 1980 Bill originally excluded from the right to buy only the tenants of 'sheltered' accommodation – that is, houses or flats with warden services or the like provided. By 109 votes to 74 the House of Lords extended this exclusion to all dwellings designed or specifically adapted for the elderly and habitually let to them, an estimated additional 220,000 homes (21 July 1980). The argument for such extension lay in the need to preserve such housing for occupation by the elderly; the argument against centred on the desirability of making as uniform as possible the individual's right to buy, without discrimination on the grounds of age.

Even before the 1980 Bill had completed its Lords stage, a government minister announced in the Commons (30 July) that this amendment would not be accepted. Peers took umbrage at this tactless treatment of their House, and marked their displeasure by initiating a further defeat on the Government in voting to adjourn their House in protest. A week later, however, the Government changed its mind and accepted the Lords' amendment, motivated to do so by a desire to see the legislation on the Statute Book before the summer recess.

The alteration, thus forced by the Lords, involved difficult decisions about what precise accommodation qualified as being adapted for elderly tenants. The Department of the Environment was clearly unhappy about administering the resulting rules, and the suspicion quickly arose that some unsympathetic local authorities simply advised elderly tenants that they had no right to buy their houses or flats. Should the Government seek to define the criteria used in assessing accommodation adapted for the elderly more precisely, and chase up recalcitrant local authorities? Or should it go for a radical solution, namely to extend the right to buy to all elderly persons (save those in sheltered accommodation)? After the 1983 election a new bill was introduced which initially contained no proposals on the subject. However, late in its Commons passage – at report stage – the Government introduced amendments going for the radical solution – extending the right to buy to all elderly tenants. Commons scrutiny of these changes was inevitably perfunctory, but in the brief debate which took place several Conservative MPs expressed disquiet. *The Times* (23 December 1983) criticised the Government, saying: 'It has slipped in important changes at an obscure stage', and urged the House of Lords to examine the bill very carefully. On 28 February 1984, an all-party initiative in the Lords led to the rejection of the Government's proposal by 113 votes to 90. Ministers then put forward a compromise – involving enhanced local-authority rights of repurchase – but this was again rejected by peers, who voted 101 to 100 (10 May) to insist on their version of the bill, thereby continuing the exclusion from the right to buy of accommodation purpose-built or adapted for the elderly. A four-week hiatus followed before the Government announced its acquiescence.

Under the 1984 Act local authorities had to seek approval from the Secretary of State if they wished to retain accommodation which an elderly tenant wanted to purchase. Only in a small minority of cases did the Secretary of State withhold approval for a sale. When the 1986 Housing and Planning Bill came forward proposing further extension of the right to buy, peers sought to amend this to maintain the principle established – albeit against the Government's wishes – in the earlier legislation. Once again the Commons reversed a Lords' amendment (5 November 1986), but peers voted the following day (by 148 to 124) to insist on their amendments, and a day later, up against the sessional deadline, the Government asked the Commons to acquiesce to the Lords' views. On this occasion several back-bench Conservative MPs expressed their anger at the Upper House's intransigence: one even suggested that this was 'a very black day for the constitution' (HC Debs, 5 November 1986, col. 974).

On three different occasions the House of Lords had thus prevented the Government carrying through its avowed aim of obliging local authorities to sell properties to pensionable-age tenants, and twice this had involved peers voting a second time to insist on their amendments in the face of clearly expressed opposition from the Commons. It would have been possible for the Government to have used the Parliament Act to secure the passage of this legislation in the form ministers wished. But to do so would have involved delay, and in 1986, in particular, the Government was very eager to see its legislation placed quickly on the Statute Book because another part of the same bill involved further incentives (in the form of higher discounts) to the tenants of flats, the sale of which the Government was anxious to encourage further.

The Lords' amendments to the 1986 Act gave to local authorities rather than the Secretary of State the duty to decide whether accommodation fell within the definition of being suitable for occupation by the elderly. The effect of this change was to bring about a rapid growth in the frequency with which the elderly were denied the right to buy. The Local Government and Housing Bill of 1989 afforded an opportunity for the Government to adjust matters again to its own preference. At Lords committee stage ministers decided simply to remove the exception from the right to buy accorded to the occupants of accommodation suitable for the elderly. Despite the sustained interest shown by the House in this subject over many years (or perhaps because of that interest!) the amendment concerned was moved very late in the evening – at 11.15 p.m. (11 October 1989). The Government won the division by 29 votes to 17, but the Opposition were angry at the tactics used, and a fortnight later the Government went down to heavy defeat (94 votes to 36) on the same issue. Ministers decided to accept the continued exclusion of elderly persons' accommodation, but further amended the bill to return to the earlier position whereby the responsibility for defining qualifying accommodation was once again exercised by the Secretary of State rather than the local authorities. Later, ministers added another amendment stipulating that the exception would not apply to any new lettings made from 1990 onwards. The House of Lords had thus for a decade limited the right to buy in respect of elderly persons' accommodation, but eventually the Government had secured its wishes.

A similar conflict took place over accommodation for disabled people. While the 1980 Act had excluded dwellings purpose-built or adapted for the disabled, the 1983 Bill sought to extend the 'right to buy' principle in this area. However, an amendment moved in the Lords by a disabled peer, Lord Ingleby, to exclude most such accommodation was carried against the Government (by 136 votes to 104 on 28 February 1984), and this the Government decided not to try to overturn, while making clear in the Commons, on 12 April 1984, its disagreement with the Lords' decision. On this matter the Government's decision was perhaps surprising because the disabled lobby was far from united on the question, with two disabled peers speaking against the change made in the Lords. When the House debated the 1988 Housing Bill peers returned to this subject and reversed their former position. Some peers who had earlier argued for the exclusion of accommodation for the disabled now admitted that they had changed their minds. The effect of their earlier decision had been to discriminate against disabled people by denying them the right accorded to other members of the community. In fact the House seemed almost to have a sense of guilt about its earlier mistake, and peers voted to extend the right to buy to all disabled people, including those living in purpose-built accommodation, without the further consultation that the Minister argued was desirable (HL Debs, 27 October 1988, cols 1743–59).

Other aspects of the 'right to buy' legislation were impeded by the House of Lords. In 1982 the Government decided to extend the right to buy to two groups of tenants not covered by its earlier legislation: those whose landlords were charitable housing associations and those whose landlords owned the leasehold, but not the freehold, of their properties. Its bill to this effect, the Housing and Building Control Bill, received an almost unprecedented verbal mauling at second reading in the House of Lords, on 11 April 1983, when only one of the twenty-six non-ministerial speeches made offered any support at all to the Government. In particular it was the implied threat to charitable bodies which worried peers. The Government argued that under the 1974 Housing Association Act much public money had been put into charitable housing associations, and tenants of such bodies should be able to purchase their dwellings in the same way as local-authority tenants. But to the Government's opponents its proposal involved the compulsory expropriation of assets held by charitable bodies, since any such accommodation would be sold at a heavy discount. At committee stage the Lords voted overwhelmingly (182 votes to 96 on 26 April 1983) to remove from the bill the right to buy for tenants of charitable housing associations, and shortly afterwards the Government announced that it would not attempt to restore this proposal. The early dissolution of Parliament then led to the bill's demise.

A successor bill introduced in the new Parliament did not refer to charitable housing association tenants, but the Government made clear its intention to find a means to give such tenants a right to buy. Not until the day the bill – again the Housing and Building Control Bill – got its third reading in the Commons did an announcement appear, as a written parliamentary answer (21 December 1983). This outlined a scheme whereby the Government would provide to tenants of such associations funds equivalent to the discount they would have obtained if they had possessed the right to buy, which the tenants concerned could then use towards the purchase of a property on the open market. Thus the housing associations would not be compelled unwillingly to sell, but their tenants would not be disqualified from receiving a financial discount equivalent to that available to local-authority tenants, though in this case to spend on a property of their choice on the open market.

This wholly novel scheme received its first parliamentary examination when the Lords debated government amendments at the bill's committee stage. On division at report stage the Lords narrowly approved the scheme (by 99 votes to 94), which then duly received Commons endorsement when the bill returned to the Lower House for consideration of Lords' amendments. The House of Lords had thus obliged the Government to adopt a wholly different method from that which had originally been envisaged to extend the right to buy to some 80,000 or so housing association tenants. In so doing it had arguably safeguarded an important principle of charity organisation.

The House of Lords defeated the Government in fourteen other divisions on its 'right to buy' housing legislation between 1979 and 1990. In some cases the Government simply reversed amendments thus made: for example an amendment in 1980, to reduce the discount payable to tenants. In other cases a compromise was reached: for example, on an amendment facilitating the possibility of elderly tenants taking option mortgages, also in 1980. Finally, some were accepted, notably amendments made in October 1986 to both the Housing and Planning Bill and the Housing (Scotland) Bill regarding the responsibilities of local authorities towards the homeless.

Notable in the treatment of legislation on housing was the determination – indeed, intransigence – of peers, including Conservative back-benchers. The general principle of selling public-sector housing was not in question, but what the House of Lords did was to insist on definite limits and exceptions to that principle. Lord Simon of Glaisdale, a former Lord of Appeal and a cross-bencher (also a former Conservative MP and minister) expressed well the tensions felt between the House of Lords and the Government on this matter, supporting the principle of the 'right to buy' policy but disagreeing with the 'passionate logic' which sought to carry that 'good principle into every corner of our social and legal life in the face of commonsense, humanity and all experience' (HL Debs, 10 May 1984, col. 1040).

Local Government Legislation

During the 1983–7 Parliament the House of Lords came into greater public prominence through its hostility to certain aspects of the Government's legislation affecting local authorities. Given the unitary character of the British Constitution, local authorities derive their powers ultimately from Parliament, and legally these may be altered at any time by Parliament. But unwritten conventions of the Constitution have customarily spoken in terms of partnership between local and central government, a mutual recognition of states and spheres of competence. Mrs Thatcher's Government took the view that some local authorities had themselves broken the terms of this partnership by, for example, failing to co-operate with government expenditure plans: her Government's response was to tighten central control over all local authorities. This process provoked strong objections from many involved in local government, Conservatives included, who felt that their problems were needlessly multiplied through continuous and thoughtless Whitehall interference. Local authorities generally found some able spokesmen for their interests in the Upper House, as well as a large number of peers with some experience of local council activity, who were sympathetic to their viewpoint.

The Greater London Council and the metropolitan county authorities were particular targets of government displeasure. The Conservative manifesto of 1983 promised their abolition, but the legislation necessary for this complex process could not be brought forward until 1984. In the preceding session the Government introduced a Local Government (Interim Provisions) Bill, a 'paving' bill concerned with transitional arrangements. As part of these, the legislation included provision to cancel elections due in 1985 and to set up, in their place, bodies nominated by the relevant lower-tier authorities to run the affairs of these doomed authorities during their final year of existence. This proposal was open to criticism, not only because it involved the cancellation of elections but also because in London at least it would have entailed the replacement of a Labour-controlled GLC by a Conservative body nominated by London boroughs. The proposal was heavily criticised in the Commons (nineteen Conservatives voted against the Government at second reading on 11 April 1984). In the Lords the Government narrowly avoided defeat – by 237 votes to 217 – on a critical amendment at second reading (11 June), but was then decisively defeated (by 191 votes to 143) on a 'wrecking amendment' at committee stage (28 June), the effect of which was to prevent the cancellation of elections until the main abolition legislation had completed its parliamentary passage. This would have imposed too tight a timetable for the Government, which therefore decided to offer a compromise by allowing existing councils to run on for an extra year (rather than seek their replacement) while still cancelling elections due in 1985. Peers accepted this compromise by 248 votes to 155 on 16 July.

For the Government the ironic consequence of this was to allow the GLC leader, Ken Livingstone, a further year in office without the need for him to submit to re-election. It involved the Government seeking a whole new strategy for actually carrying through the abolition of these authorities, and one that involved much greater complexity. But the House of Lords had safeguarded what was widely perceived to be a constitutional principle, even if in so doing it had proved itself highly inconvenient to the Government. The House found itself the bemused recipient of plaudits from the Labour left (a banner on the GLC headquarters over the Thames proclaimed 'Thank you peers for saving London') and from such an organ of the establishment as *The Times*, which declared the episode 'a triumph for the principles of constitutionalism, and specifically for the principle of a bicameral parliament' (30 June 1984).

In the following session the substantive abolition legislation appeared. On this the Government suffered four defeats in the

Lords, but none of these was a matter of major importance. In general, peers sought to strengthen the role of London boroughs and metropolitan districts and to limit the power of central government to regulate the subsequent activities of authorities established under the bill.

One aspect of the GLC campaign against abolition was a lavish advertising campaign. Government annoyance at the use of public funds by local authorities for 'political advertising' led to the introduction of a further Local Government Bill in 1985, the main purpose of which was to ban such material. The House of Lords made two important changes to this bill, both as a result of Government defeats. The first narrowed the scope of the prohibition proposed in the bill by removing the ban on material which 'can reasonably be regarded as likely to affect' political support, leaving a ban on material which 'appears to be designed to affect such support', a change which the Government Minister argued 'would seriously undermine the effectiveness of the prohibition on party political material as a whole' (HL Debs, 18 February 1985, col. 537). The second altered the status of the code of practice to be issued by the Department of the Environment, making clear that this would be for guidance only and not obligatory for local authorities.

Because this bill also contained provisions requiring local authorities to fix their rates by 1 April each year, the Government was very anxious to see it on the Statute Book before the Easter recess. In the Commons there had been difficulties over the bill which had already resulted in Government concessions in order to get it out of Standing Committee early enough in the session to meet this deadline. When the bill returned again to the Commons with the Lords' changes the Government accepted them, but at the same time made clear its reluctance and its determination to return to the point again in the future (HC Debs, 25 March 1986, col. 881).

By 1987, the readiness of the House of Lords to be awkward and even intransigent over such legislation appeared to be a factor in slowing down the introduction of further legislation. For example, a major bill obliging local authorities to put their services out to competitive tender and imposing limitations on their freedom to publish political material was foreshadowed in the 1986 Queen's Speech but later postponed. Commenting on this, *The Economist* (21 February 1987) said that the prospect of the bill being 'ignominiously savaged in the Lords' was good reason for its delay.

The Government's considerably more circumspect handling of the House of Lords (compared with its handling of the Commons) on the Teachers' Pay and Conditions Bill of 1986–7 was also noticeable. This 'emergency' measure was rushed through all its Commons stages in three days in December 1986. The House of Lords debated it over a four-week period in early 1987. After the bill's second reading in the Lords, the Government announced a number of concessions which (as a *Times* headline stated) appeared designed 'to head off Lords' revolt'. Amendments made in the Lords ensured that teachers would be represented on the Advisory Committee established under the bill, and that the Committee's reports would be published. These changes were made without government defeat in the lobbies, though several other more significant amendments were resisted only through a large turnout of Conservative loyalists. When these were debated back in the Commons, the opposition spokesman described them as 'relatively trivial', although he also paid tribute to the high quality of debate in the Upper House (HC Debs, 26 February 1987, col. 438). Nevertheless, in terms of alterations to the bill, the impact of the Lords was definitely greater than that of the Commons.

The torrent of legislation impinging on local government was by no means abated after the 1987 election. The contracting out of local authority services was taken up in the Local Government Bill of 1987–8, as was the imposition of curbs on local authorities in respect of their publications so as to eliminate so-called party propaganda. Lords' amendments to this Bill were very minor. One would have allowed local authorities to take account of the number of disabled people employed by private firms when awarding contracts, but this was overturned by the Government in the Commons. In the following session, 1988–9, the House of Lords had more success in securing a relaxation in the constraints imposed under the Local Government and Housing Bill on the political activities of higher-paid local council employees; originally the bill proposed that a ban on such activities should operate for all employees earning over £13,500 per year, but following a defeat in the Lords the Government accepted that restrictions should affect only those earning over £19,500.

Such measures were, however, all eclipsed by the Local Government (Finance) Bill of 1987–8, which replaced the rates system with the community charge or so-called poll tax, a change opposed not only by the Opposition Parties but also by the local-authority associations and by significant sections of the Conservative Party itself. While the bill was going through the Commons the Government's majority sank to twenty-five when thirty-eight Conservatives voted with the Opposition in favour of banding the tax according to ability to pay. In the Lords a former chairman of the Conservative MPs' back-bench 1922 Committee, Lord Chelwood (formerly Sir Tufton Beamish MP), moved an amendment seeking to establish the same point. Anxious to avoid a defeat – which would have necessitated further difficult votes in the Commons – the Government imposed a heavy three-line whip which brought a massive turnout of 550 peers. Only 15 Conservative peers cross-voted, giving the Government a comfortable victory by 317 votes to 184. The whole episode, however, discredited the House, with newspaper reports showing how many very rare attenders came to the House to vote for a measure which would save them a great deal of money (the *Observer*, 29 May 1988). Thereafter the Lords did pass two amendments against the wishes of the Government, concerned with student nurses and the disabled, but both of these were rejected back in the Commons despite further rebellion by Conservative MPs.

The same session also saw the passage of the Education Reform Bill, in relation to which Lord Whitelaw predicted that the Government might suffer serious defeats early in the session (see above, p. 27). In the event, however, although the Government was defeated six times on this bill, the resulting changes were relatively minor. One highly contentious issue of great concern to local authorities was the provision under the bill for schools to opt out of LEA control if, in a ballot of parents, a majority voted for such a course. The House approved an amendment moved by the Bishop of London which stipulated that in order for a school to opt out, a majority of all parents (not simply a majority of those voting) would have to vote for such a step. The Government offered what ministers described as a compromise: namely, that if less than 50 per cent of eligible parents voted in a ballot which approved opting out, a second ballot would be required, though in this second ballot no specific turnout was necessary. The Bishop found this compromise acceptable, and peers accepted it, though not without a further division. This was a crucial issue in a bill which fundamentally altered the education service. Its general effect was to devolve power away from local authorities, either to school governing bodies or to central government departments. When it went back to the Commons it contained 569 Lords' amendments, but MPs disposed of these in eleven hours under a 'guillotine'.

During the 1980s local authorities came to look to the House of Lords for support in moderating the impact of government legislation, the general effect of which appeared to local councils to be the removal of their powers and the erosion of their functions. In the middle years of the decade the House did have some success in obliging the Government to adjust its policies, or slow down their implementation, but by the end of the decade its capacity to do this seemed to have largely disappeared. At the time of writing the whole poll tax saga is unfinished, but whatever the outcome might be, it is apparent that the relationship between central and local government has been radically altered. Conventions which spoke in terms of partnership and of the need to generate consensus before introducing fundamental change vanished, and the House of Lords showed itself unable to arrest this development. This is a point taken up again in the Conclusion.

The 1987 Parliament

As already indicated, both in this chapter and in Chapter 1, the Government appeared to take a less conciliatory attitude to the House of Lords after the 1987 election. As far as legislation was concerned, a greater willingness to overturn Lords' amendments made against government advice was matched by a greater determination to resist such amendments in the first place. The frequency of government defeat in the Upper House was just as great as it had been earlier, but instead of the majority of resulting changes being accepted (as had happened from 1979 to 1987), rejection was three times as frequent as acceptance in the period 1987–90. The turning point seemed to occur in the 1987–8 session. Reference has already been made to two major post-1987 bills, introducing the poll tax and reforming education, which illustrate this point.

In the same session the Government met sustained opposition to its plans, contained in the Health and Medicines Bill, to introduce charges for eye tests and to increase dental charges. At report stage in the Commons in April some twenty Conservative back-benchers cross-voted on these proposals. On 19 July the Government went down to defeat on both these matters in the Lords. Two days later it was reported that sixty-one Conservative MPs had signed an Early Day Motion in the Commons calling on the Government not to reverse the Lords' amendments. However, when MPs did debate the changes made by the Lords on 2 November they were reversed, but the Government's majority sank to sixteen on dental charges and only eight on fees for eye tests. The announcement of an extra £2 billion for the National Health Service the previous day probably assisted the Conservative whips in their task of persuading MPs to support the government line. A week later peers again voted on the matter, but a three-line Conservative whip ensured a massive turnout and the Government got its way by 257 votes to 207.

In the following session, when Lords' amendments to the Social Security Bill concerning child benefit and the extension of mobility allowances were rejected outright by the Commons, opposition peers gave vent to their anger at what they considered the contemptuous attitude displayed by the Government towards the Upper House. Lord Russell, who had taken an active part in the House as a Liberal since his arrival there in 1987, protested that he could not 'recall any amendment passed on a division in the Lords which had been fully accepted in the Commons'. A leading Labour peer, Lord Stoddart of Swindon, said that the Government's attitude made the House of Lords nothing more than a curiosity and that if the electorate realised how useless the House was in the face of Government 'diktats', they would demand its closure. Conservative back-bench peers spoke more in sorrow than in anger, both about the way ministers were treating the House and about the deeply mistaken policies some felt the Government was following (HL Debs, 20 July 1989, cols 918–27).

In the 1989–90 session the House defeated the Government twenty times, but on only three occasions were the amendments so carried accepted. The legislation on student loans was subject to sustained attack in both Houses. While it was going through the Lords a stream of small concessions was announced, and these probably helped the Government to escape with only three defeats. One of these was plainly the result of an Opposition 'ambush' on 26 March 1990, but the resulting amendment – restoring student rights to housing benefits – was deleted in the Commons. Amendments to the National Health Service and Community Care Bill – to 'ring-fence' funding for community care – commanded widespread support and were carried against the Government in the Lords on 8 May 1990, but rejected in the Commons. Amendments to introduce the so-called 'Valdez' principles on environmental audit to the Environment Protection Bill were likewise passed by peers but rejected by MPs.

Most surprising, and perhaps most starkly indicative of its attitude, was the Government's insistence on deleting Lords' amendments to the same bill which sought to introduce a compulsory scheme for dog registration. Again this had been the subject of earlier rebellion in the Commons by forty-nine Conservative MPs. Peers voted heavily for registration (by 155 votes to 83 on 5 July). But rather than give way the Government decided to fight the issue again in the Commons. In a vote on 29 October MPs rejected the Lords' amendments by 274 to 271. So narrow a majority encouraged some peers to force another vote in their House, but this the Government won on 31 October. The possibility that this vote might have resulted in a further defeat, and therefore in the need for the Commons to vote again on the matter, caused the whips in the Commons to summon at least four ministers back from overseas visits (from America, Brazil, Barbados and Japan) to maximise the Government's chance of victory. It could hardly be argued that any great issue of political principle was at stake. One would have thought that on an issue of this kind, where the Government could sustain its position only by resorting to such heavy whipping, and then by so narrow a majority, giving way to a second chamber was a thoroughly reasonable course of action. At least if the Conservatives had been in Opposition, and such high-handed treatment of the second chamber had emanated from a Labour Government, such a point of view would undoubtedly have been been vigorously expressed from Conservative quarters.

The same session also saw the Government introduce its War Crimes Bill. Ministers chose to go ahead with this bill despite the very clear hostility to it from the House of Lords (see p. 132). For the first time ever a Conservative government resorted to the Parliament Act in order to overcome opposition from the House of Lords. Why the Government chose to act like this is a point taken up in the concluding chapter.

Conclusion

What can be concluded from this somewhat cursory examination of the treatment of government legislation? First, we do well to remind ourselves of the sheer complexity of the legislative process. Almost any proposal made by Government has repercussions for numerous groups and identifiable interests within society. Many of these become involved in the legislative process, not infrequently dealing directly with government departments. Some also alert MPs and peers to their concerns, who in turn may press these upon Government. Part of this activity takes place within Parliament, during the formal legislative stages of a bill. But the parliamentary stages may be likened to the visible tip of the iceberg, nine-tenths of which lies beyond public view. Nevertheless, a study of what is public and visible can help to develop our appreciation of what goes on elsewhere.

The fact that the initiative for most successful amendments to bills lies outside Parliament does not diminish the importance of parliamentary proceedings. Where these are accepted by Government (and frequently then introduced as government amendments) a public explanation of the change made has to be given in Parliament, and this is subject to debate and criticism. Where Government resists amendments, and these are pressed upon it during parliamentary proceedings, the arguments both for and against proposed changes are ventilated. The fact that most of such debate is of no interest to the public (and often beyond the comprehension of all but a few experts in that field) does not invalidate its importance. Interest group leaders interpret what goes on to their members, just as Government seeks to develop a favourable view of the position it takes among the interested and informed (the 'specific publics' involved). But this must not be taken as implying too ordered and rational a view of the whole legislative process. Interest groups sometimes completely fail to notice the possible effect of a bill within their area of concern, and much of what goes on in Parliament – especially in the part-time House of Lords – is a matter of accident or luck rather than deliberate plan or foresight.

Paradoxically, the value of the House of Lords in the legislative process appears to lie precisely in its complementarity to the Commons, based as this is on the former's non-elected (and

undemocratic) character. It is the less party political character of
the House which is the single most important fact differentiating its
legislative role. Some peers at least approach any item of legislation
devoid of a party stance, while many who basically subscribe to
government or main opposition party views do so with considerably
greater flexibility than their Commons counterparts. The expert, the
political and the truly lay contributors all mingle in the House of
Lords, and in so doing almost invariably seek to exert influence over
legislation rather than contest power.

The House of Lords has a value to the Government first, because
it enables parliamentary debate on some bills to start elsewhere than
in the Commons, and this offers a helpful flexibility, especially in
relation to bills the party political significance of which is slight or
non-existent. Second, the House is useful to the Government as a
kind of legislative long-stop, enabling ministers to introduce
amendments fulfilling undertakings given in the Commons, or at
least brooding on arguments and counter-arguments put forward at
earlier stages, and having the time for further opportunities for
discussion and consideration of the interests involved. In 1969,
Richard Crossman suggested that if no second chamber existed the
Commons would need at least two further stages for dealing with
legislation. There seems little reason to dissent from that judgement
today.

But the House of Lords is also useful to the Opposition, and
indeed to many outside groups of all kinds. It is true that debate in
the Lords can be repetitive of what has already been fully discussed
in the Commons. But frequently debate in one House does, so to
speak, clear the ground in relation to a particular bill, and enable
debate in the second House to focus more sharply on particular
provisions and possible changes. Exploring possible options for
change, and their various consequences, is arguably an activity best
carried out by two separate bodies over an extended period of time,
with several opportunities being given for possible amendments to
be made. It is often parliamentary debate which first alerts outside
groups to a bill's potential effect on their interests, and the
opportunity to raise issues through the second House is important to
them. Most changes made to bills appear very minor, but their
importance to particular groups can easily be underestimated. At
the same time some significant changes are made, and appear to be
made as a result of pressure focused on and through the House of

Lords. This was clearly the case with the 'right to buy' housing legislation in the early 1980s.

The whole legislative process is far too subtle to permit any simple quantifiable index of the comparative influence of the two chambers (or of outside bodies) to be constructed. But detailed examination of the role of the Lords in getting particular changes made to bills shows that this grew significantly in the 1980s.

7

The Deliberative Work
of the House

One of the main functions which the Bryce Commission, in 1918, considered to be appropriate to the House of Lords was the discussion of general subjects connected with the Government's stewardship. Repeatedly since then this aspect of the work of the Lords has been emphasised. The White Paper on Lords Reform in 1968 identified six main functions, the first of which was 'the provision of a forum for full and free debate on matters of public interest'. As a check upon the executive, a body which discusses what the Government is doing, or is failing to do; has done or has not done; ought to do or ought not to do, the House of Lords has functions which closely parallel those of the House of Commons. The House of Lords spends about one-third of its time debating motions and dealing with questions. What kinds of subject are dealt with? How important is this activity, and who is influenced by it? Does the House of Lords deserve the high reputation it is often accorded for the quality of its debates? These matters are dealt with in this chapter.

Parliamentary Debate

In some fundamental respects the activity of debate is similar in both Houses of Parliament. Crucial is the fact that the Government is obliged to define its attitude to the subjects raised in motions or in questions. It is this obligation on Government to state its view, to argue its case, to defend its policy, which is the distinctive feature of *parliamentary* debate. Outside Parliament, Government has no such

direct obligation, and while within Parliament government spokesmen may evade or vacillate or even contradict each other, none the
less the fact remains that their responses are taken as authoritative
indications of the Government's attitude to an issue. To an
important extent, speeches made during a debate serve to provide
the context within which the adequacy, or otherwise, of the
Government's position can be assessed. That is a major purpose of
debate. In preparing to reply to a debate a minister – and, perhaps
even more important, his advisers – are required to consider
arguments brought to bear against the Government's position. The
realisation that there are relevant facts unthought of by Government, implications of policies unanticipated by Government,
perhaps policy ideas which deserve more serious attention by
Government – any of these can result from debate.

Beyond Parliament and Government, the influence of debate is
exceedingly hard to determine. Only a tiny fraction of the public pay
any continuing attention to what goes on in either House of
Parliament, but this fact must not be taken as proof that
parliamentary debate has no influence on the electorate. Particular
interest groups and specialised media do give attention to what is
said in Parliament on specific subjects, and these in turn influence a
wider public. Furthermore, the mass media's coverage of political
news is to some extent shaped by parliamentary activity. It is not
simply a matter of how much news about Parliament is reported,
but also a question of the extent to which journalists, feature writers,
producers of documentary programmes, and so on make use of
parliamentary proceedings in researching topics. While the whole
process of influence is difficult to analyse, just as the nature of public
opinion is hard to define, it is reasonable to argue that parliamentary debate is not without some influence on the electorate.

If the House of Lords, in principle, shares with the Commons the
fact that through debate the Government must publicly define its
view of subjects discussed, and that in doing so both Government
and public may be influenced by the activity of debate, there are also
important differences between the two Houses. Crucial is the fact
that the Commons may still aspire to the exercise of political power,
while the Lords can only hope to exert influence. The Government is
responsible to the Commons in the sense that it must retain its
majority in the Commons in order to survive. A motion of no
confidence in the Government has a place in the Commons, but such

a motion would be meaningless (and offensive) in the Lords. While in a formal sense the Government may not be obliged to comply with a motion specifying some action by the executive passed in the Commons, it nevertheless finds a motion of this sort passed by the Lords much easier to ignore than one passed by the Commons. While the Government is responsible to the Commons because it is ultimately removable by the Commons, it is in effect only answerable to the Lords.

The junior status of the House of Lords in political terms inevitably results in its debates being accorded very much less public attention than those of the Commons. But so long as it exists it cannot be ignored, and in recent years it has almost certainly been gaining rather than losing importance. Among the distinctive characteristics of the House which, it can be argued, enhance its role as a debating chamber are the presence of a wide range of expertise and a degree of procedural flexibility unparalleled in the Commons.

The procedures available for debate and for the asking of questions have already been outlined in Chapter 4. Table 7.1, on p. 182, categorises all non-legislative debate and questions in the 1989–90 session. Debate can take place on motions, and also on unstarred questions at the end of the day's business. Though debate as such does not take place on ministerial statements, comment and questions are allowed, and in practice a kind of 'mini-debate' takes place. Both ministerial statements and private notice questions have been discussed in Chapter 4. Peers sometimes wish to debate a Statutory Instrument without in any way threatening the use of the formal power the House of Lords possesses to kill such Instruments; in such cases motions may be put down and votes can take place which register the opinion of the House on an Instrument. In a formal sense this is non-legislative debate, so it is included here, though it is discussed in Chapter 8.

Debate on Motions

Tables 7.2 to 7.5 give information about all debates on motions in the 1989–90 session. Taking first motions debated in time allocated to the parties, these are almost always held on Wednesdays and formulated as motions for papers. Until the mid 1980s such motions

Table 7.1 Non-Legislative Debate and Questions, 1989–90

		Total number	Total time (hours and minutes)	Time as a percentage of total time in session
Motion for address (Queen's Speech debate)		1	25h 18m	2.4
Motions to 'take note'				
Government (see Table 7.5)		3	17h 50m	1.6
EC Committee Reports ⎱	see Table 7.4	9	25h 27m	2.4
Science & Technology Committee Reports ⎰		2	7h 08m	0.7
Motions for papers				
In time allocated to Parties (see Table 7.2)		26	83h 16m	7.8
Balloted 'short' debates (see Table 7.3)		12	23h 56m	2.2
Other (see Table 7.5)		2	7h 42m	0.7
Unstarred questions (see Table 7.6)		31	39h 49m	3.7
Motions on subordinate legislation (Excl. Motions for Approval of Affirmative orders)		4	4h 07m	0.4
Ministerial statements		36	21h 40m	2.0
Starred (oral) questions		551	63h 15m	5.9
	Total		319h 28m	29.8

were usually the subject of a full day's debate, with no time limit. In the late 1980s, however, parties with increasing frequency chose two motions, each debated for up to two-and-a-half hours (rather than a single motion), and where a single motion was favoured these had become much more frequently the subject of a five-hour time limit. Table 7.2 shows that in the 1989–90 session, seven of the nineteen days given over to motions chosen by the parties were used for two-

and-a-half hour debates, while a five-hour time limit was applied to debates on ten of the remaining twelve days (see above, p. 122).

How the 'Wednesdays' are used and the choice of subjects debated are matters decided by the parties. When the Conservative Party was in Opposition prior to 1979 the front bench decided; since 1979 the Association of Conservative Peers (see pp. 86–7) have decided on a draft motion, which is then always shown to the Chief Whip, who may then consult the government department concerned and subsequently lean a little on the ACP Committee to try and ensure a form of wording congenial to the Government. On the Labour side the front bench decide after discussion at the weekly party meeting, but when the Party was in office, the Labour Peers' Co-ordinating Committee was responsible for the choice.

A Party may decide not to use the supposedly neutral 'motion for papers' form, but instead to put down a motion for resolution, in which case the debate will terminate with a vote (unless the Lords accepts the motion without a division). No Party did this in the 1989–90 session, but as an example of such a motion that of 12 December 1984 may be cited; this was put down by Labour for its second Wednesday of that session, and read: 'This House recognises the human misery and waste caused by current unemployment of labour and resources; deplores the lack of urgency shown by HMG in tackling this problem, and calls for a statement of the positive steps to be taken to enable available labour to be used to meet undoubted national needs'; it was lost by 105 votes to 134. In this case the Government clearly felt it necessary to resist the motion, but when a Liberal peer's motion calling for the repeal of Section 2 of the Official Secrets Act was debated later in the session (20 March 1985) ministers did not resist and the motion was accepted without a division.

Some motions are worded in such a way as to express a definite point of view, though typically this will be done in a mild manner. For example Labour, on 28 March 1990, initiated debate on a motion calling attention to 'the problems currently accompanying the imposition of the community charge . . .'. But motions are usually cast in a neutral form, for example 'to call attention to the situation in Hong Kong' (Lord Bonham-Carter, 24 January 1990).

Clearly many subjects are chosen with an eye to the anticipated political mileage the debate may offer to one or other Party. Sometimes this is a matter of timing – for example, motions for

Table 7.2   Motions Debated in Time Allocated to Parties, 1989–90

Date	Party	Peer	Subject of motion	Length of debate	No. of speakers
29 Nov.	Lab	Ewart-Biggs	Family	4h 49m	22
6 Dec.	Cross-B	Hunter of Newington	Future of National Health Service	4h 52m	26
20 Dec.	Cons	Campbell of Croy	Environmental Protection	2h 56m	14
24 Jan.	Lib D	Tordoff	Traffic in London	2h 29m	22
31 Jan.	Lib D	Bonham-Carter	Hong Kong	2h 25m	16
7 Feb.	Lab	Peston	Education and training	5h 0m	28
21 Feb.	Cons	Boardman	Free-market economy	4h 45m	23
28 Feb.	Cons	Williams of Elvel	Manufacturing industry and the economy	4h 45m	20
	Cross-B	Annan	Higher education	2h 22m	11
14 Mar.	Cross-B	Birkett	Proposal for National Lottery	1h 53m	8
	Lab	Carter	Rich & poor in society	2h 26m	15
	Lab	Mishcon	Legal Aid	2h 23m	10
21 Mar.	Cons	Home of the Hirsel	Eastern Europe and the Soviet Union	4h 46m	22
28 Mar.	SDP	Stedman	The community charge	2h 31m	19
4 Apl	Lib D	Jenkins of Hillhead	House of Fraser Holdings Report	2h 14m	12
	Lab	McIntosh of Haringey	City dwellers: social problems	4h 23m	18
18 Apl	Cons	Stanley of Alderley	The tenant-farmer	2h 09m	15
	Cons	Radnor	The forestry industry	2h 31m	15
2 May	Lab	Underhill	Channel Tunnel: road and rail links	4h 35m	24
9 May	Cross-B	Shannon	Waste: environmental policy	1h 54m	7
	Cross-B	Baldwin of Bewdley	Medicine: complementary and conventional	2h 29m	15
23 May	Lab	Irvine of Lairg	Civil liberties	2h 18m	9
	Lab	Rea	Population growth	3h 36m	16
6 June	Lib D	Jenkins of Hillhead	European political and monetary union	4h 55m	19
13 June	Lab	Williams of Elvel	Industrial and economic recovery	4h 43m	19
20 June	Cons	Caldecote	Industrial relations	3h 19m	11

debate in the pre-budget season are often chosen as convenient pegs on which peers can hang speeches adding to the advice being given to the Chancellor. Labour's motion on 21 February 1990 drew attention to the 'role of manufacturing industry in creating a sustainable balance in the economy, and to the case for policies to achieve that end'. In June 1989 Conservative peers chose to debate the Monopolies and Mergers Commission Report on the brewing industry. This followed a statement made by the Minister then responsible, Lord Young of Graffham, that he was 'minded' to accept the report; the debate provided an array of speeches opposed to its implementation, with even a bishop talking of the great damage this would do to English life by destroying country pubs. Much other pressure was brought to bear on Lord Young, who substantially modified his earlier acceptance of the report.

Sometimes a motion is debated before the introduction of a bill, in an effort to develop opinion about a subject with a view to amendments being made to the expected legislation. Baroness Cox introduced a debate on politicisation in education shortly before the arrival of the 1986 Education Bill, which was subsequently amended heavily by the House (see Chapter 6).

It is noticeable that on a Labour motion there are usually fewer Conservative than Labour speakers, and vice versa. Sometimes the imbalance is very marked, as for example when only one Conservative (other than the Minister replying to the debate) spoke compared with twelve Labour speakers on Lord McIntosh of Haringey's motion on 'the social, financial and environmental problems facing the inhabitants of our cities', debated on 4 April 1990. On this occasion Lord McIntosh, in opening the debate, referred to the dearth of speakers from the government side. In his reply to the debate the Minister, Lord Caithness, said by way of explanation that he had discouraged Conservatives from putting their names down to speak the previous week, because only three peers had then indicated their intention to take part in the debate! The following week was a 'Conservative Wednesday', and in the two limited-time debates which took place, out of fifteen speakers in each, only one was Labour; the motions on this latter occasion were, however, good traditional Conservative Party fare: one dealt with farming and the other with forestry.

Table 7.3 lists all balloted motions debated in the 1989–90 session. The ballot is one for motions already placed on the Order

Table 7.3 Balloted (Two-and-a-Half-Hour) Debates, 1989–90

Date	Peer	Party	Subject of motion	Length of debate	No. of speakers
13 Dec.	Parry	Lab	Rural and suburban communities	1h 33m	7
	Perth	Cross-B	Museums & galleries: current problems	2h 23m	14
17 Jan.	Callaghan	Lab	German unification	2h 25m	22
	Bruce-Gardyne	Cons	Health care: elderly	1h 41m	7
14 Feb.	Campbell of Croy	Cons	North Sea pollution	1h 30m	5
	Rippon of Hexham	Cons	Legislation: scrutiny proposals	2h 12m	10
7 Mar.	Ewart-Biggs	Lab	Citizens' Advice Bureaux	2h 21m	10
	Molloy	Lab	NHS: pressures on staff	1h 37m	6
25 Apl	David	Lab	Educational governing bodies	1h 29m	7
	Simon of Glaisdale	Cross-B	Constitutional powers of second chamber	2h 22m	11
16 May	Bp Worcester	Cross-B	European co-operation	2h 08m	10
	Monkswell	Lab	Nuclear disarmament	2h 12m	10

Paper, so peers enter it simply by putting down a motion. As can be seen, a very wide range of subjects were thus debated. The two shortest 'short' debates of the session were on Baroness David's motion calling attention to the 'place for balance on the governing bodies of places of education' and Lord Campbell of Croy's motion calling attention to 'the state of the North Sea and the need to continue to prevent further pollution', with only six and five peers respectively taking part. No time limits for speeches were necessary for these debates. By contrast, twenty-two peers spoke in the balloted debate initiated by Lord Callaghan of Cardiff 'calling attention to German unification' on 17 January 1990, which meant that the time limit for speeches was only five minutes.

Motions for short debate are usually – but by no means always – worded in such a way as to indicate the particular concern of the peer who has put down the motion, and are therefore frequently more specific than motions for unlimited-time debates. In this respect they are more like unstarred questions. The procedure of the balloted debate does give back-bench peers the chance to raise subjects which their party leaders or more senior colleagues would not choose.

The debate initiated by Lord Bruce-Gardyne on 17 January was on a motion calling attention 'to the case for extending the entitlement of those of 65 years and above to offset the costs of their prescriptions to private health-care insurance schemes, created by the Finance Act 1989, to include payments direct to medical practitioners and hospitals for private health care at the customer's choice . . .'. In his opening speech Lord Bruce-Gardyne explained that he had put this motion down after writing a newspaper article on BUPA (a leading private health-care insurance company) which provoked more letters from readers than any other article he had written. His speech, like the letters he had received, criticised BUPA, but he also argued his case on the grounds of freedom of choice and the Government's stated preference for tax neutrality. The chairman of BUPA was Lord Wigoder, who – in typical House of Lords style – responded to Lord Bruce-Gardyne's outspoken criticisms by saying: 'We have other subscribers who occasionally bestow rather more praise upon us than the noble Lord.' While Labour peers were straightforward in their opposition to such a proposal, because of the way it would extend private health care, the Minister responding to the debate based his case largely on the complexities that would be involved in administering any such arrangements.

Debates are usually arranged without much difficulty on all reports from select committees which are recommended for debate by the committee concerned (Table 7.4). The Chairman of the committee (or sub-committee) customarily introduces the debate, and several other members of the committee usually take part. The holding of such debates gives an opportunity for other peers who are knowledgeable on the subject to add their weight to – or make their criticism of – the report concerned; and, of course, the Government must provide a reply in the form of a front-bench speech.

Other motions debated in the same session are listed in Table 7.5. The Lords always debates the defence estimates, and most major government reports will be debated on take-note motions – for example the Hetherington-Chalmers Report on War Crimes (see below, p. 251). In April 1989 no fewer than fifty-four peers took part in a twelve-and-three-quarter-hour debate on the Green Papers on reform of the legal profession – held, incidentally, on a Friday. In the 1989–90 session the crisis in the Gulf following the Iraqi invasion of Kuwait was debated three times on 'take-note' motions. Amendments to such motions have been moved and voted on, though this is unusual and probably contrary to practice (for example on 5 February 1973, when the House rejected by 92 votes to 52 a Labour amendment to a government motion on 'The Programme for Controlling Inflation'). Included also in Table 7.5 are motions on delegated legislation, one of which was a motion for resolution pressed to a division, one of which sought the withdrawal of a Statutory Instrument, and two of which were 'prayers' (see below, p. 216).

The thirty-one unstarred questions debated in 1989–90 are listed in Table 7.6. Generally such questions are framed so as to emphasise some particular point – for example, Lord Rees-Mogg's question on 20 April which asked the Government 'What are their plans for the future of the Arts Council, and in particular whether they intend that it should continue to enjoy independence under its charter?' This resulted in the longest debate on an unstarred question of the session: over two-and-a-half hours, with twelve speeches. In a newspaper article (*Independent*, 23 April 1990) Lord Rees-Mogg explained that he and two other former chairmen of the Arts Council in the House had written to the Leader of the House seeking time for

Table 7.4 Debates on Select Committee Reports, 1989–90

Date	Peer	Party	Subject of motion	Length of debate	No. of speakers
European Communities Committee					
11 Dec.	Shepherd	Lab	Transport infrastructure	3h 20m	11
18 Dec.	Kearton	Cross-B	Delors Committee Report	4h 30m	19
5 Feb.	Middleton	Cons	Irradiation of foodstuffs	1h 42m	10
19 Feb.	Allen of Abbeydale	Cross-B	Community Social Charter	2h 59m	12
5 Apl	Oliver of Aylmerton	Cross-B	1992: Border controls, Health controls	2h 43m	11
22 June	Aldington	Cons	Relations with EFTA	2h 08m	11
13 July	Lockwood	Lab	European languages learning	2h 40m	11
12 Oct.	Cranbrook	Cons	Tropical forests	3h 09m	15
29 Oct.	Shepherd	Lab	Air Traffic Control	2h 16m	7
Science and Technology Committee					
30 Jan.	Carver	Cross-B	Greenhouse effect	4h 05m	20
22 Mar.	Caldecote	Cons	Overseas aid	3h 03m	12

Table 7.5 Other Motions Debated, 1989–90

Date	Peer	Party	Subject of motion	Length of debate	No. of speakers
22 Nov.	Brabazon of Tara	Govt	Foreign affairs and defence	7h 42m	36
23 Nov.	Mackay of Clashfern	Govt	Home affairs, health & social policy } QSD	6h 22m	28
27 Nov.	Trumpington	Govt	Environment, agriculture & food	3h 49m	14
28 Nov.	Caithness	Govt	The economy	7h 18m	26
30 Nov.	Allen of Abbeydale	Cross-B	Charities: a framework for the future (Cd 694) [c]	4h 25m	19
4 Dec.	Ferrers	Govt	War crimes (Cd 744) [b]	5h 29m	27
4 Dec.	Ezra	Lib D	Electricity privatisation [c]	3h 17m	13
17 July	Arran	Govt	Defence estimates (Cd 1022) [b]	5h 03m	22
6 Sept.	Caithness	Govt	The Gulf [b]	7h 18m	38

Motions on Delegated legislation (excl. Affirmative Orders)

Date	Peer	Party	Subject of motion	Length of debate	No. of speakers
29 Jan.	Mottistone	Cons	Mental health: code of practice [a]	1h 18m	9
23 Mar.	Swansea	Cons	Firearms (Variation of Fees) Order [d]	0h 55m	5
13 July	Houghton of Sowerby	Lab	Slaughter of Animals, etc. [d]	0h 52m	4
24 July	Russell	Lib D	Education (Student Loans) Regulations [a]	1h 02m	7

[a] Motions for resolution.
[b] Motions to take note.
[c] Motions for papers.
[d] Prayer.

a debate on the proposed restructuring of the Council. Even though the space found for the debate was on a Friday afternoon, it had clearly been thought most worthwhile by its participants. The shortest debate – on a question asked by Lord Thurso on salmon conservation – lasted only twenty-three minutes, a brevity no doubt encouraged by the fact that the debate did not commence until 11.46 p.m. Unstarred questions always come last in the day's business. In 1989–90, on only four occasions did debate on an unstarred question commence after 9.00 p.m.

This procedure does allow debates to be arranged at short notice so that the Lords can respond quickly to some new event or controversy. As may be seen from a perusal of Table 7.6, it is a highly flexible procedure, with debate sometimes being no longer than the twenty or so minutes which can be devoted to a single starred question, and at other times extending, occasionally, to over three hours. Labour peers initiated twelve such debates, including four from front-bench spokesmen; Conservatives eight; Liberal Democrats four; Social Democrats one and cross-bench peers six. Compared with Commons daily adjournment debates, the obvious differences are the varied length and timing of such debates and the relative (though not complete) absence of constituency-type subjects.

The Character of Debate

Under all these procedures the word 'debate' is in some ways a misnomer. Typically a motion (or unstarred question) gives rise to a series of speeches, each carefully prepared and often read almost verbatim. Succeeding speeches may deal with wholly diverse aspects of a subject. References made to other speeches are as likely to be personal – congratulations, reminiscences, and so on – as to be substantive arguments. Peers seldom interrupt each other's speeches, much less often than MPs in the Commons. A quite irrelevant or highly provocative speech may pass without comment, though if criticism is made this can be all the more effective in the Lords for the scrupulously polite way in which it is put.

The House of Lords in general appreciates speeches that are brief, relevant and based on real knowledge of the subject under debate. Many active peers take a kind of professional pride in making

Table 7.6 Debates on Unstarred Questions, 1989–90

Date	Peer	Party	Subject of motion	Length of debate	No. of speakers
29 Nov.	Joseph	Cons	GCSE	0h 34m	4
5 Dec.	Molloy	Lab	Cambodia	1h 23m	7
11 Dec.	Cox	Cons	Poland: aid	1h 34m	7
13 Dec.	Mersey	Cons	Tibet	1h 26m	8
18 Dec.	Dean of Beswick	Lab	Prisons: visitors' centres	0h 55m	4
17 Jan.	Mountevans	Cons	Transport policy	1h 39m	7
22 Jan.	John-Mackie	Lab	Scottish agricultural colleges	0h 50m	4
24 Jan.	Longford	Lab	Probation service	1h 12m	5
31 Jan.	Simon of Glaisdale	Cross-B	Legislation	1h 51m	8
14 Feb.	Nugent of Guildford	Cons	Traffic obstruction & public utility works	1h 08m	4
15 Feb.	Stallard	Lab	Ambulance service dispute	1h 29m	7
19 Feb.	Allen of Abbeydale	Cross-B	Disabled transport	1h 36m	7
28 Feb.	Raglan	Soc D	Planning protection for conservation areas	1h 17m	6
5 Mar.	Harris of Greenwich	Lib D	Mr Salman Rushdie: death threats	1h 47m	8
13 Mar.	Northfield	Lab	Development plans	1h 03m	6
22 Mar.	St John of Bletso	Cross-B	South Africa	1h 46m	8
23 Mar.	Cocks of Hartcliffe	Lab	Sullivan/*Bristol Evening Post* Inquiry	0h 27m	4

Table 7.6 (*continued*)

Date	Peer	Party	Subject of motion	Length of debate	No. of speakers
28 Mar.	Dean of Beswick	Lab	Council house rents	0h 40m	3
4 Apl	Renwick	Cons	International Literacy Year	1h 27m	7
18 Apl	Gardner of Parkes	Cons	Ticket touts	0h 53m	6
20 Apl	Rees-Mogg	Cross-B	Arts Council	2h 37m	12
23 Apl	Harris of Greenwich	Lib D	Money-laundering convictions	1h 07m	4
25 Apl	Hacking	Cross-B	Pharmaceutical innovation	1h 30m	7
2 May	Ennals	Lab	Westminster and Chelsea Hospital	1h 09m	5
9 May	Moran	Cross-B	Peat reserves	1h 37m	8
23 May	Longford	Lab	Sentencing levels	2h 01m	7
6 June	Thurso	Lib D	Salmon conservation	0h 23m	3
13 June	Kimball	Cons	Humber county boundaries	1h 11m	11
20 June	Dean of Beswick	Lab	Channel Tunnel workforce	0h 48m	4
13 July	Harris of Greenwich	Lib D	Birmingham Prison	1h 16m	5
29 Oct.	Kirkhill	Lab	A wider Europe: Council of Europe	1h 13m	7

original and pithy speeches, but by no means all are so disciplined. Much is made of the expertise the House possesses, and on many subjects the Lords can boast several 'authorities' among its membership. Most debates contain speeches from two or three peers recognised as experts, and perhaps from several more with some kind of direct personal experience of the subject. There is a presumption in the House, widely shared by peers, that one speaks only on a subject one really does know something about. One peer recently explained that his father had sat in the House for twenty-four years without ever speaking: 'if there had been a debate on large-leafed Himalayan rhododendrons, he might have made his maiden speech because he was an expert on that subject. In the event there was no such debate so he never spoke' (HL Debs, 25 April 1990, col. 625). However, not all peers follow this advice; most debates do attract one or two speeches from some peers who are recognised in the House as bores with nothing significant to say. Sometimes, too, it is noticeable that those peers best informed about a certain subject do not speak on that topic in a debate.

It is the initiator of a debate whose contribution is generally of greatest significance regarding the quality of that debate. He will usually contact a number of other peers from all political groups in the House who are recognised as particularly knowledgeable in the area concerned. He may discuss with such peers particular points which might be raised in the debate, and include in his opening speech some kind of lead for peers who are to speak later. He will very probably contact the government spokesman concerned, giving some advance warning of questions he will be posing, as indeed may other participants. Extensive contacts with outside groups may all be part of his preparation too.

Compared with the Commons, the significantly less party political character of the Upper House gives its debates a very different flavour. Even where subjects have been chosen by parties anxious to use a debate to advance a party cause, contributions will usually be made from cross-benchers, many of whom are genuinely apolitical. Speeches are always made from the party front benches, but party spokesmen often give themselves more latitude than their Commons counterparts, and back-benchers may blatantly contra-dict party policy. The House of Lords contains peers recognised as spokesmen for various groups, who will receive detailed briefing prior to a debate, and perusal of specialised media suggests increased attention being given to the reporting of Lords debates. Peers do attend debates in which they are not participants in greater numbers than MPs attend Commons debates. The relatively junior ministerial status of most government spokesmen who reply to debates may in part be counterbalanced by the presence of ex-cabinet ministers, permanent secretaries, judges, eminent scholars or captains of industry, a feature which contrasts sharply with the Commons' chamber. The presence of television cameras since 1985 has added a new dimension to Lords debates, with the possibility that extracts from speeches will be seen by a large television audience.

Assessment of Debates

But how influential are such debates? The major target of influence must be the Government. To this end the fact of government answerability in the Lords is important. Peers are different from other citizens in that they have unique opportunities to engage the Government in public debate. By no means all choose to do this, and by no means all have the skill or knowledge to do this effectively. But some do. A former service peer explained in interview that he values his membership of the Lords because 'If I were not a peer, they [the Government] could fob me off'. A former Permanent Under-Secretary (Lord Allen of Abbeydale) has campaigned in the Lords on a number of issues which fall in the ambit of his previous department, the Home Office. His questions and speeches on some topics have undoubtedly had repercussions within the Government. Other individual peers use Lords procedures to worry away at the Government over the years on particular subjects with some measure of success. Examples would include: Baroness Burton of Coventry on civil aviation and consumer matters generally; Lord Houghton of Sowerby on animal welfare; and Baroness Masham of Ilton on the disabled.

Success may depend, to a considerable extent, on how a peer follows up a debate. The mover of a motion may be asked to go and see the senior minister concerned. One peer, after what he felt was a rotten response from a Foreign Office Minister of State to a debate on World Hunger, went to see the Minister for Overseas Development and felt he got much further. Another peer, feeling that he had a similar poor response, wrote to the Lords Minister concerned and asked for a more considered reply. After interminable delay he got what he described as a 'hopeless' letter back, so he wrote again sharply, saying that his points had obviously not been understood but that rather than prolonging the correspondence he would put down further questions in the House. He then received a much more satisfactory letter from the Secretary of State.

If a motion specifying some action is carried against the Government, ministers are not thereby obliged to carry out that action. On the other hand, to fail to do so may expose the Government to further unwelcome public criticism. Some examples may help. The Government's decision to establish a trading fund basis for the Ordnance Survey was criticised in the House, and on 9 February 1983 a motion moved by Lord Shackleton 'urging HMG to refer this proposal to the new advisory board for the Ordnance Survey before laying the relevant order' was carried by 104 votes to 74. The following month the Government announced that it would do this, and in due course a report was received which recommended against the Government's proposals, following which the Government announced, in January 1984, that it would not proceed with them.

Another example concerns cuts in the BBC external services. Proposals for such cuts were (again) announced on 25 June 1981; a debate on an adjournment motion took place in the Commons on 23 July, but without a division. On 30 July, after a five-hour debate in the Lords (during which only five out of over thirty speakers supported the Government) the House voted by 82 to 45 'calling upon HMG to reconsider its instruction to the BBC to impose cuts'. Back in the Commons, on 26 October, a further debate took place on an opposition motion during which the Government announced a compromise, and in so doing gained the support of some wavering Conservative MPs, and won the division by 278 to 224. In the Lords on 26 November, Lord Byers initiated a further debate on an unstarred question, asking HMG 'why in view of the opinion expressed in this House on 30 July they decided to proceed with damaging cuts . . . ?' He claimed that the Government's compromise was 'horse trading or window dressing', but the extent of the cuts had been halved (from £3m to £1m) and the government compromise had clearly gone some way to satisfy peers.

On some subjects the House of Lords may be said to have a particular authority because of the expertise of some of its members. The judicial system is one such example, a point exemplified in the debate on the Fraud Trials Committee report which took place one month after the report was published on 10 February 1986 (see above, p. 59), or the debate on the Government's proposed legal reforms in April 1989 (cited above). A debate in the Lords on the Central Policy Review Staff proposals for a run-down of the foreign service 'killed these proposals stone dead', according to Lord Boyd-Carpenter (1980, p. 256). There are always a few peers whose political seniority ensures that they can command attention through speeches if they so wish. Examples would include Lord Home of the Hirsel's speeches on international affairs, the first Earl of Stockton's speeches on the policies of the Thatcher Government and the first Earl of Avon's speech on the Middle East at the time of the Six-Day War in 1967. Viscount Radcliffe's speech, also in 1967, on Mr Wilson's rejection of his report (the Radcliffe Report) on D-notices was described by Richard Crossman as 'the most effective quiet rebuke of a prime minister by a public servant of modern time', though Wilson himself made no mention of the speech in his memoirs (Crossman, 1976, p. 414; Wilson, 1971, pp. 417–18).

In some cases the object of a debate is to influence other bodies besides the Government. For example, a debate was held on the Press Council report on the 'Yorkshire Ripper' case in July 1983. Among peers who spoke were former journalists, ex-members of the Press Council and Royal Commissions on the Press (though none of the three former Chairmen of the Press Council in the House). In replying to the debate, the Home Office Junior Minister, Lord Elton, made it clear that he felt the real purpose of the debate was to concentrate the minds of those with responsibility in the press on the issues of concern. After a debate on Internal Drainage Boards in November 1981, the Minister who replied was surprised over the following months at how much notice had been taken by Drainage Board members of what was said in the debate. In 1982, Lord Nugent of Guildford emphasised in a speech the failure of the BBC and IBA to publish in their annual handbooks details of action taken on complaints received; the Minister replying said no doubt the relevant authorities would take note of this, and in 1983, when Lord Nugent again initiated a debate on the subject, he was able to express satisfaction that the handbooks did contain details of complaints.

Quite apart from any question of influence or power, debate in the Lords may serve a quite different purpose because of its cathartic value. Some peers make very pompous and boring speeches; others give vent to real anger and bitterness at times. Replying to a sour debate on the National Health Service in 1975, a Labour minister said he felt as if he was a passive bucket into which people were being emotionally sick, and added that 'no doubt the debate had provided an opportunity for people to discharge a reasonable amount of emotion and the cathartic effect must have been of immeasurable value' (HL Debs, 3 December 1975, col. 735). Ten years later the same peer, during another debate on the NHS, referred to the fact that he had been involved with a fair number of such debates over the years, but had come to the conclusion that this was 'a most depressive, useless and pointless exercise' (HL Debs, 20 November 1985, col. 582).

An analysis of Lords debates on foreign affairs produced examples where the House had arguably had some influence, and cases where it demonstrably had not (Shell, 1991). Almost everyone involved with the House acknowledges that a great deal of what is said there is worthless. 'Ninety per cent is puff', said one former minister in interview, but he then added: 'ninety per cent of Commons debate is puff too – only a different kind of puff.' The title of a book by a former *Hansard* assistant editor in the Lords, *A Hard Core of Wind* (Braham, 1986), exemplifies the sceptical attitude some close observers take to the value of Lords debates. But others offer markedly different views. Some two years after entering the Lords, Viscount Tonypandy, former Speaker of the Commons, wrote: 'My short experience of the House of Lords has convinced me that there is not the slightest doubt that the debating level . . . is much higher than in the Commons . . . there is not the same vested party interest. . . . There is an independence of mind and scholarship that serves the nation well' (Thomas, 1986, p. 226).

Oral Questions

The device of the parliamentary question has often been cited as a distinctive British contribution to the art of parliamentary government. In the Lords as in the Commons, Question Time assumes a prominent part in each day's proceedings. It was apparently in the Lords that the first 'question' was asked, irregularly, in 1721 (Chester and Bowring, 1962, p. 12). Subsequently the Commons took up the practice and formalised it, with the Lords following suit. In essence the procedure is the same in both Houses, with ministers providing government answers to questions put down by members. But within this simple framework the way the procedures for questions have developed in the two Houses has been very different.

In the first place, while the Commons decided to apply a time limit for oral questions, with the Minister answering as many as possible in the time allocated, the Lords decided to limit the number of questions to which oral answers could be given on any single day. Since 1959 this limit has been fixed at four. Typically the Commons may get through around twenty questions in the 45–55 minutes available, while in the Lords four questions usually take about 25 minutes. Thus the Lords spends less time on oral questions but considerably longer on each question.

A second major contrast with the Commons lies in the fact that in the Lords there is no ministerial rota for answering questions, and no equivalent to the twice-weekly contests between party leaders which occur at 'Prime Minister's Question Time'. Furthermore, given the fact that not all departments have ministerial representation in the Lords, replies to questions must frequently be given either by ministers in departments dealing with quite different policy areas or by Lords in Waiting.

A third contrast between the two Houses derives from the absence of a Commons-type Speaker in the Lords. This is seen in the character of proceedings on the floor of the House at Question Time, and with regard to responsibility for the actual admissibility of questions. With no time limit and no Speaker, and with many peers frequently endeavouring to participate in exchanges on a question, proceedings can become somewhat chaotic, though perhaps the degree of orderliness which does prevail is the more remarkable. It is the Leader of the House to whom peers look to guide them through this period of daily turbulence.

As to the admissibility of questions, peers are urged to take advice from the Clerks (*Companion*, p. 51) but, unlike MPs, they cannot be obliged to do so. A question may thus occasionally appear on the Order Paper which is primarily a statement of fact or an expression of opinion, or in some other way breaches guidance which has been given by successive procedure committees. Ultimately the Lords can refuse leave to a peer actually to ask a question put down in his name on the Order Paper, but this is very unusual (for example, HL

Debs, 19 January 1983, cols 1407–11). A minister may, of course, decline to answer an inadmissible question, and in the opinion of Lord Henderson of Brompton, formerly Clerk of the Parliaments, ministers should more readily exercise this right (HL Debs, 18 April 1985, col. 809).

The whole character of Question Time is therefore very different in the two Houses (Shell, forthcoming, 1992). The fact that ministers answering questions in the Commons invariably have direct responsibility for the subject involved, together with the more intense party political character of the House, has made Question Time primarily a set-piece activity for party politicians. At the same time the brevity of exchanges and the speed with which questions are taken serve to protect ministers from any kind of searching examination. While most ministers do find Question Time in the Commons a considerable ordeal, it is primarily the intensity of the party struggle which brings this about.

In the Lords party politics is much more muted, a fact illustrated by the character of Question Time. But it is by no means entirely absent. Opposition spokesmen listen carefully from their front bench when a question within their own area of responsibility is being answered, and have in recent sessions noticeably developed the practice of their Commons counterparts of 'riding in' with supplementary questions aimed at exposing some weakness in the government position. The fact that much longer is spent on each question in the Lords than in the Commons may also add to the demands made of a minister, because there is more time for peers to find any weak points in the answers given. Furthermore, a minister never quite knows who may pop up (from behind or in front of him), nor how the considerable experience and expertise potentially available in the House may suddenly be brought to bear on the subject matter of the question concerned. For these reasons some ministers believe that answering questions in the Upper House is a considerably greater ordeal than doing so in the Commons.

All government spokesmen dealing with questions do, of course, have civil service briefs available. But again, contrasts between the two Houses should be noted. Because of the rota system in the Commons, ministers know that only on certain days – for most only once in every three weeks or so – will they have to answer questions. In preparation for dealing with questions a Commons minister may therefore set aside several hours earlier that day to 'mug up' relevant facts, quotations, and so on. Furthermore, senior civil servants in the department know that, if necessary, they must put aside other tasks to help prepare their minister for his Question Time ordeal in the House. If he fails to perform well, the repercussions are likely to be damaging for the department as well as for the Minister. A Lords minister, however, has no set question days, and can expect to have to answer questions a good deal more frequently than his Commons colleagues. Furthermore, he is unlikely to find civil servants as aware of or as sensitive to his needs as they are to those of a Commons minister. He will receive a file with a draft answer (together with answers to possible supplementaries) and have the opportunity to discuss this with civil servants beforehand. But if he is not a minister in the department concerned, this can well mean a hurried few minutes being spent shortly before Question Time with a group of civil servants he has never met before. One former civil servant, later a peer, recounted in an interview how abruptly he had dealt with a Lords minister who once interrupted him during a lunch appointment to seek advice about answering a question in the House later that afternoon – an incident he looked back on with some regret after he himself had some experience as a member of the House of Lords!

Sometimes the inadequacies of hurried preparation become all too apparent at the Dispatch Box. Occasionally the wrong answer will be read out (e.g. 17 June 1985, col. 1) or basic ignorance on some fundamental point become evident (e.g. 8 February 1984, col. 1140). However, in general the Upper House is very understanding about such things; most peers privately praise government spokesmen for doing their difficult job as well as they do, and direct any anger they feel at civil servants for inadequate briefing. According to a report in the *Sunday Telegraph* (19 May 1991) Lord Colnbrook, Chairman of the back-bench Association of Conservative Peers, had recently been to see the Prime Minister in an effort to ensure that whips in the Lords were given better briefing to cope with oral questions, having himself observed the difficulties they were under when trying to cope with acknowledged experts in the House.

Where a senior minister is available in the Lords, the above points do require qualification. For example, Labour peers made a particular point of pressing questions to Lord Young of Graffham after his appointment as Secretary of State for Employment in October 1985. In two successive weeks he was absent from the

House, and employment questions were dealt with by another minister (the Minister of State for Defence Support). This brought protests from the Leader of the Opposition, and a promise from Viscount Whitelaw that Lord Young would be present in the House of Lords for the next question on employment. When this was taken, two days later, exchanges on a single starred question lasted twenty minutes, with the Leader of the House doubtless reluctant to curtail the questioning lest he be thought to be shielding the newly appointed Secretary of State (see HL Debs, 15 October; 22 October; 24 October 1985). In the following months a stream of questions on employment were tabled by Labour peers, driving Lord Young at one point to contrast his position as a minister in the Lords unfavourably with that of a Commons minister (HL Debs, 4 March 1986, col. 87).

For many years the *Companion to the Standing Orders* has emphasised that 'Question Time should normally be concluded in twenty minutes'. Such brevity had, however, become the exception rather than the rule by the early 1980s. In the 1984–5 session, questions were contained within the twenty-minute limit on fewer than a quarter of the sittings, and by 1988–9 fewer than one in six; sometimes questions in the Lords took forty minutes. In 1991 the Procedure Committee realistically recommended that the *Companion* should in future state: 'It is undesirable that Question Time should exceed half an hour' (HL 17, 1990–1). If the main reason for such longevity is the greater number of supplementary questions which are tolerated in the Lords (as compared with the Commons), a contributory factor has also been the lengthier ministerial replies considered appropriate to the Upper House, where conventions of courtesy and politeness demand that government spokesmen appear as helpful as possible to questioners. In recent sessions, however, replies have tended to be shorter, with the one-word reply – previously unknown – making a fairly regular appearance.

Among MPs there are wide variations in the use made of Question Time, with a relatively small group asking a highly disproportionate number of questions. In the Lords, disproportionality is even more noticeable. In both 1984–5 and 1988–9 fewer than twenty peers asked over half of all the starred questions, with six being responsible for a quarter of the questions in both these sessions. At the same time, in 1984–5 only 127 peers and in 1988–9 only 150 peers asked any starred questions at all (see Table 7.7, and

Table 7.7 Starred and Written Questions, 1984–5

	Starred (oral) questions		Questions for written answers	
	No. of peers who tabled questions	Total no. of questions	No. of peers with tabled questions	Total no. of questions
Conservative	57	203	77	331
Labour	30	231	51	430
Lib/SDP	23	107	24	239
Cross-bench	17	35	25	132
Total	127	576	177	1,132

Source: Derived from House of Lords' *Hansard*.

for 1988–9 session see Borthwick, forthcoming, 1992). Unlike the Commons, the opposition front bench in the Lords do ask oral questions (though individual practice varies a good deal). The proportion even of 'active' peers who ask oral questions is therefore under half, and of the total eligible to do so, only about 15 per cent in fact do.

Since 1989 no peer may have more than two starred questions on the Order Paper at any one time; before that the limit was three. But a really determined peer can still ask a large number of questions. Lord Hatch of Lusby asked more oral questions than any other peer in 1983–4 (thirty-seven) and 1984–5 (forty). Such proclivity provokes resentment elsewhere in the House; on 29 January 1985, when Lord Hatch's eleventh question of the session was being dealt with, a Conservative back-bench peer moved that 'the noble lord be no longer heard', and this motion was carried handsomely on division by 103 votes to 59.

Former MPs predominate among the most frequent questioners; of the thirteen who asked more than ten questions in 1984–5 nine had been MPs, while six of the nine most frequent questioners in 1988–9 were former MPs. While some degree of specialisation is evident in this group, the very regular questioners tend to ask about varied topics. If there is a common theme it is the advancement of the party political struggle. Lord Hatch of Lusby's forty questions in 1984–5 were mainly concentrated on foreign affairs or defence matters (though never an MP, he was for twenty years Commonwealth correspondent of the *New Statesman*). Lord Molloy (thirty-four questions) asked about the National Health Service, foreign affairs matters, and other miscellaneous topics. Both these peers were back-benchers, but Lord Dean of Beswick (twenty questions) spoke from the Labour front bench on Treasury matters, and most of his questions fell in this area. Three Conservative peers asked fifteen questions each in 1984–5: Lord Boyd-Carpenter, Orr-Ewing and Gainford – the former two, but not the latter, being ex-MPs. Their questions covered a miscellany of subjects.

A peer among this group of frequent questioners who clearly did specialise was Baroness Burton of Coventry; she asked twenty-nine questions, all dealing with consumer affairs. Ever since her entry into the Lords in 1962 she has been one of the most frequent questioners, persistently pressing ministers of all governments on consumer issues. Her sustained, shrewd questioning has earned the admiration of many peers, and several of her campaigns, spear-headed through Question Time in the Lords, have had an impact on government or nationalised industries.

Among less frequent questioners were Lord Hunter of Newington, an eminent doctor and cross-bench peer, whose six questions all dealt with medical matters; Lord Rugby, an optician, also a cross-bencher, who asked three questions on spectacles; Baroness Lockwood, a Labour supporter and former Chairman of the Equal Opportunities Commission, who asked several questions about the role of women in education, employment, and so on; Lord Nugent of Guildford, a Conservative back-bench peer, who asked mainly about road safety matters; and Lord Ezra, a Liberal peer and former National Coal Board Chairman, who asked several questions on energy policy. (A study conducted by Borthwick (forthcoming, 1992) on the 1988–9 session indicated a very similar position in respect not only of the distribution of questions but also with many of the same individuals continuing to ask questions in similar subject areas.) These are all examples of peers who know a great deal about a particular subject and use Question Time in the Lords as one means among others to advance arguments or ideas which they wish to press upon the Government. Party politics may not be absent from their thinking, but it is unlikely to be their primary consideration. They are unlikely to be out 'to get' a particular government minister. If they have a clear target in mind when asking their questions, it is more likely to be civil servants who deal with the subject in the relevant government departments.

When the Conservatives were in Opposition in 1975–6, Conservatives asked almost twice as many questions as did Labour back-
benchers. There were many more Conservatives available, even if
some Labour peers tried to make up for their lack of numbers by
their assiduity. As Table 7.7 shows, slightly more questions came
from the Labour Opposition than from the government back-bench
peers in 1984–5. However, Borthwick found that by 1988–9
Conservatives were asking more questions than Labour peers, a fact
which reflects in a small way the gradual depletion of active Labour
peers during the 1980s (see above, p. 66). Clearly many party-
minded peers would be reluctant to see a situation in which few
questions were forthcoming from 'their' side. On the other hand,
given the readiness with which mini-debates develop at Question
Time, it is possible for a partisan questioner to emerge bruised
rather than victorious when his question has had an obvious party
political intent. Within the Lords a group of Conservative peers who
sought to help their front bench by asking friendly questions was
established in 1982, but rapidly acquired the epithet 'own-goals
group' for exactly this reason.

Some questions are very broad in scope and can therefore become
pegs on which to hang mini-debates on some aspect of government
policy. For example: 'To ask HMG whether they consider they
have made effective use of the surplus earnings of North Sea oil'
(23 January 1985); or 'What is their attitude towards the creation of
a European central bank?' (20 April 1990). Compared with the
Commons, a significant contrast is the relative absence of constituency questions, but this absence is relative rather than absolute.
Some peers do ask about local issues. For example: Lord Jenkins of
Putney asked about Putney Bridge Station on 14 July 1982, and
Lord Dean of Beswick asked about a statement made by Lord
Young of Graffham on Radio York about unemployment in that city
(16 February 1987); he did this at the prompting of Labour's
prospective parliamentary candidate for the constituency of York,
and his answer was given publicity in the local press. On 4 April
1990 a Labour peer who worked as a general medical practitioner in
Kentish Town asked a question about the Bloomsbury Health
Authority. Occasionally peers with territorial titles ask questions
relating to their 'territory'; for example, Viscount Mersey on 8 July
1985 asked 'Whether the Mersey is still the dirtiest river in the
country?' and in the ensuing exchanges the Bishop of Liverpool

joined in, illustrating the concern bishops display for diocesan problems. The same Bishop asked a question on the Liverpool Philharmonic Orchestra, and in the 1981–2 session the Bishop of Rochester asked about Chatham Dockyard and the Bishop of Carlisle about training facilities in West Cumbria.

How worthwhile are starred questions in the Lords? As in the Commons, it is at Question Time that the chamber is most likely to be crowded, and the House at its liveliest, even unruliest. But much of what takes place seems like shadow-boxing between political opponents whose significance in the national party context is really very marginal. That is probably the least valuable aspect of Question Time. But peers use starred questions to keep some unpopular subjects or half-forgotten reports on departmental agendas. A Baroness Burton of Coventry, by sheer dogged persistence, may force reconsideration to be given to some decision convenient to bureaucrats but disadvantageous to the public. Another peer may, through a question, effectively serve warning on the Government that he is likely to pursue a subject through a full-scale debate unless some appropriate action is taken. Overall, given the extent to which Commons Question Time has become dominated by the scoring of party points, the Lords procedure may be regarded as a mildly useful complement.

Questions for Written Answer

Peers, like MPs, may put down Questions for Written Answer (QWAs). Such questions, together with the Government's answers, appear in *Hansard* at the end of each day's record of proceedings in the House of Lords. No limit exists on the number of questions which may be asked, and in recent years, in both Houses, their number has greatly increased, though the 1,200 or so per year in the Lords remains small by comparison with the 40,000 or so such questions in the Commons. Table 7.7 shows that, as with starred questions, a relatively small proportion of peers actually do ask QWAs – a total of 177 in 1984–5, though 508 peers took part in debates in the Lords in that year; in 1988–9 191 peers asked QWAs, while 534 took part in debates. Again, among peers who ask such questions, a very small number do so to a disproportionate extent: in 1984–5 seven peers together asked one-third of all written questions, and a total of seventeen asked over half.

Looking for a moment at the very frequent questioners, it is possible to derive some idea of the purpose to which this procedure is put. The peer who asked the most written questions in 1984–5 was Lord Melchett, the young Labour hereditary peer (born in 1948) whose concern for environmental matters is well known (he was president of the Ramblers' Association in the early 1980s). His eighty-eight questions dealt with many aspects of wildlife protection, areas of special scientific interest, use of pesticides, road-building schemes, and so on. Some were very specific, for example concerning the condition of a particular piece of footpath (25 June 1985); others highly technical, for example a question about the A34 at Whitway in Hampshire (31 March 1982) which was complemented by a starred question, and then an unstarred question with accompanying debate, all on the same subject, urging the Government to reconsider its decisions. By the late 1980s he had become a very rare attender at the House, though he still asked the occasional QWA.

In the 1984–5 session, the peer who followed Lord Melchett in the frequency of use of Questions for Written Answer was Lord Kennet, a leading figure in the Social Democratic Party, also a hereditary peer and a former Labour minister of the 1960s. His seventy-seven Questions for Written Answer concentrated on defence and maritime issues. In 1988–9 he asked 173 QWAs, far more than any other peer (Borthwick, forthcoming, 1992). Other peers who frequently used this device in 1984–5 were: Lord Jenkins of Putney, forty-two questions, mainly on nuclear-related topics; Lord Harris of Greenwich, SDP, thirty-three questions, many on wildlife; Lord Graham of Edmonton, a Labour whip in the Lords, thirty-two questions on various topics, mainly environmental; Lord Brockway, a veteran Labour peer who has for many years, in both Houses, sought to expose possible inconsistency or hypocrisy in the Foreign Office, which department answered most of his thirty-two questions.

In addition to regular questioners, the device of the written question does permit any of the 900 or so peers who, from time to time, sit in the House of Lords to raise particular issues which interest them. No fewer than 59 of the 177 peers putting down Questions for Written Answer in 1984–5 asked a single such question in the entire session. The eminent scientist Lord Flowers asked a single question about the Sizewell Nuclear Power Station; Lord Bancroft, former Head of the Civil Service, asked about the membership of the Museums and Galleries Commission; the Bishop of Rochester asked about grants for stadium safety precautions; Lord O'Brien of Lothbury (former Governor of the Bank of England) asked about the reserves banks were required to hold; Lord Aldington (formerly Toby Low, Conservative Minister in the 1950s) asked about first-class travel; and Lord Home of the Hirsel (formerly Conservative Prime Minister) asked about a particular training barracks.

Such examples illustrate the variety of questions put down for written answer. Most appear to be straightforward requests for information. Some seek a general statement from the Government concerning its policy or attitudes to a specified matter. The information so gained may be used in debates or other proceedings in the Lords. As in the Commons, some questions are 'inspired'. In such cases government sources suggest to a friendly back-bencher the wording of a question which can then be used to make public some government announcement or statement of information. A comparison of Lords and Commons *Hansard* for July 1985 indicates that approximately one-quarter of Lords' Questions for Written Answer have identical simultaneous parallels in the Commons; these questions were clearly 'inspired', though undoubtedly there were many more 'inspired' questions in the Commons in the same period, but probably only a very few others in the Lords.

Written questions can be used in an effort to expose inconsistencies or apparent stupidities in government administration, and this can assume a definite party political character, especially where very large numbers of questions are asked. Some MPs use written questions in this way in the Commons, but such use among peers is rare. Certainly in the Lords the most frequent use of this device is to enable peers to probe departments and to permit governments to publish information quickly and in an easily accessible form. Questions for Written Answer is a procedure which has a clear rationale and usefulness to all parliamentarians.

Conclusion

Non-legislative debate has a rather ephemeral character. It is difficult to be precise about the influence of such proceedings, just as it is difficult to be precise about how informed opinion or many policy ideas have been developed within society. Both within the

Lords as well as outside it, opinions diverge sharply as to the value of its debates. Disagreements arise in part because of the different criteria applied in making an assessment. Some emphasise the qualifications of those who take part in such debates, and not infrequently the *curriculum vitae* of speakers is highly impressive. Their listeners and readers may admire the quality of speeches made.

But that does not necessarily mean that the House is having much effect on Government, nor indeed on any of the other centres of power in society. The mere fact that peers taking part in a debate have an impressive list of qualifications is not in itself evidence for the political importance of those debates. The Lords contained some peers with considerable knowledge of the Falkland Islands, who took part in debates before the 1982 invasion, but without succeeding in impressing their concerns adequately on Government or public (see Shell, 1991). A debate may be no more than a kind of elite academic seminar on a subject, engaging with the forces that direct government activity in only the most superficial way. Lucid, original and sparkling speeches may have no more influence than boring and repetitive ones. As far as influence on the executive is concerned both alike may be merely the release of wind.

That would certainly be too harsh a conclusion. Indications have been given in this chapter of occasions when proceedings in the Lords – on questions or in debates on motions – do appear to have had an influence on Government. Most peers can quite readily give examples of where they believe this to have been the case: and most also nurture the belief that the proceedings of the House have a wider influence within society, even if this is usually both small and indirect.

8

Select Committees and Secondary Legislation

The role of Parliament in passing public bills and in debating government activity is comparatively well known. Less public attention is generally given to other aspects of Parliament's work, which are nevertheless of considerable importance. Some of these may be thought of as a kind of second tier of legislative activity. In this may be included private bills, Statutory Instruments and European Community legislation. Work on private bills has declined throughout this century, just as work on Statutory Instruments has grown and, particularly in recent years, work on European instruments. For much of this activity considerable use is made of select committees, which are also used by the Lords to examine particular subjects and sometimes particular bills, especially private members' bills. This chapter surveys the work of the House of Lords in all these areas.

In some respects this may seem a field of miscellaneous activities, and in part this is true. But there are common themes which can be mentioned now, and discussed later. Among these is the obscure nature of much of this work, especially that which deals with private legislation, and here the work of the Lords is much more nearly co-equal with the work of the Commons than is generally the case with public legislation.

Another theme which links much of this discussion is an institutional one, namely the use of select committees. Such committees have become more prominent in both Houses in recent years, particularly with the establishment of the departmentally focused select committees in the Commons in 1979. This prompts the question: to what extent has the Upper House been rivalling or duplicating the Lower House, or has it primarily been seeking to complement the work of the Commons – filling in the gaps, as it were? Discussion of developments which have taken place should offer us some help in answering this question, which will be taken up again in the Conclusion. Finally, we may once again take note of the degree of flexibility which has been shown by the Lords in adapting itself both to its own changing membership and to the new tasks being imposed upon parliament.

Private Bills

Private bills enable individuals, groups or bodies to do something which the law of the land – as enacted in past public legislation – does not otherwise allow. In the nineteenth century, private bills were both numerous and important. Throughout the twentieth century the trend has been to provide, by means of public legislation, procedures which enable bodies who hitherto achieved their ends through private bills to obtain the legal powers they need by other means. Thus the building of reservoirs, the digging up of churchyards, the construction of highways can usually be achieved today without resort to a private bill. Nevertheless, there are typically some thirty or so new private bills introduced every session, and in respect of these the House of Lords has co-equal powers to the House of Commons and in practice does a similar amount of work to the Lower House.

Parliamentary procedure on private bills is superficially similar to that for public bills. A first and second reading are followed by a committee stage, then a third reading takes place. But in fact the use made of these stages is quite different. The 'promoters' of a bill petition for the right to introduce it, and this is granted only after 'Examiners' (who are parliamentary clerks) have satisfied themselves that the elaborate Standing Orders concerned with the presentation of such bills have been observed. The purpose of these is chiefly to ensure that all interested parties have due notice of the bill. Bills are allocated for introduction evenly between the two Houses; bills which major on financial matters are taken first in the Commons, while a tradition favours the Lords taking most local-authority legislation first. After passing one House, bills must go through the other, though private bills, unlike public bills, may be carried over from one session to the next. In the Lords the second reading is usually moved formally by the Lord Chairman, but if opposition to a bill is likely the promoters must find some other peer to introduce it, so that the Lord Chairman preserves his neutrality. Unlike a public bill, the granting of second reading does not imply approval of the principle of a bill, only that the House feels that it may properly proceed to a committee.

Opponents of a bill may lodge petitions against it, in which case the bill is referred to a select committee, usually consisting of five peers, specifically appointed to deal with that particular bill. The proceedings in such committees are quasi-judicial, with promoters and petitioners arguing their case through counsel, sometimes for days on end. But only about half-a-dozen bills per session have, in recent years, been opposed in this way. Quite frequently petitions are lodged against a bill, but then withdrawn, in many cases because the two sides have reached agreement before incurring the considerable legal expenses of a full select committee hearing. Bills which are not formally opposed (by petitions) are referred to an Unopposed Bill Committee which consists only of the Lord Chairman (assisted by his counsel), though he may ask one of the Deputy Chairmen to attend.

The activity of the Lords on such bills has been at least as important as that of the Commons. In particular the House has done much work on bills promoted by local authorities. The 1972 Local Government Act stipulated that existing local legislation would lapse unless re-enacted by 1984. This was considered desirable in order to ensure that newly established local authorities were equipped with all the necessary powers to apply by-laws and carry out other functions, and that the Statute Book was not cluttered with outdated legislation. The first such bill presented was the County of South Glamorgan Bill, which took twenty-six mornings and fourteen full days before a Lords select committee in 1975–6. Fears that parliamentary machinery would be choked trying to cope with all such bills within the ten-year deadline were expressed. A Local Government (Miscellaneous Provisions) Bill introduced by the Government in 1976 obviated the need for some clauses in local authority bills by giving similar powers to all local authorities, and ultimately the ten-year deadline had to be extended only slightly.

Even though the time spent on the floor of the House dealing with private bills is short (usually less than 1 per cent of the total time in a session), private bills, if opposed, can be very time-consuming in committee. The Lloyd's Bill of 1982 involved a select committee in nineteen days of hearings. The Hampshire (Lyndhurst By-pass) Bill occupied a select committee of peers for fourteen days in 1987. This was a controversial bill, inherently so because it involved road-building in part of the New Forest, but additionally because the promoters, Hampshire County Council, used private-bill procedure to obviate the need to seek approval from the New Forest Verderer's Court. This does illustrate the point that on some matters promoters may have a choice between proceeding by means of a private bill or by some other route. In the case of the Lyndhurst By-pass Bill, two of its most vigorous opponents, the official verderer of the New Forest and his predecessor, were both members of the House of Lords. Despite their objections the bill was approved by the select committee and the House, though it was later rejected by the House of Commons.

This bill provided an example of the relatively few occasions when the two Houses have disagreed over their treatment of private bills. The most notable example was when the Lords threw out at third reading the bill to nationalise Felixstowe Dock in 1976 (discussed above, pp. 25–6). In 1980 a bill to give certain powers to the Dartmoor Commoners was rejected in the House of Commons after it had passed the Lords.

The possibility of using joint select committees for private bills has frequently been mooted. Such committees, it is said, could cut down expense to promoters in cases where bills are formally opposed, but against this it is argued that opponents of a bill are in a stronger position once they have heard the promoter's case fully deployed. Savings in parliamentary man-hours are another consideration. In the 1986–7 session it proved impossible to find MPs willing to serve on a select committee dealing with a particularly contentious private bill. The modern MP typically does not rate highly among his duties the spending of many days listening to barristers presenting arguments, often on very technical matters, which may be planning issues in a part of the country far removed from his own constituency. A joint select committee reported on the whole subject in October 1988 (HL 97, 1987–8), making numerous recommendations, though mainly for minor changes. Having weighed the arguments about joint committees, it recommended that for an experimental period promoters of private bills should be offered the option of taking their bill to a joint select committee. The report was debated in both Houses (HL Debs, 17 May 1989, cols 1180–1212) before the Government issued a consultative document in 1990 (Cd. 1110), with a view to introducing primary legislation to reform this whole area. The consequence of this may be to reduce the burden imposed on Parliament, but it is unlikely to diminish the relative importance of the House of Lords. In evidence to the joint select committee the Lord Chairman commented that the Lords, unlike the Commons, had not experienced 'the difficulty of finding members to serve on long-running select committees and of maintaining the attendance of members serving on such committees'. Indeed, in the Lords private-bill procedure 'works smoothly and expeditiously' (HL 97, 1987–8, p. 185).

It may be argued that all such activity should be remitted to planning inspectors or to the courts. But against this it is suggested that that section of the public who become involved in such matters appreciate direct contact with legislators, not simply officials or lawyers (HL 146, 1986–7, esp. pp. 17 ff.). The joint select committee concluded that 'private legislation continues to form a vital part of the work of Parliament'. A second chamber may have a particular value in making available legislators who have both the time to give to such work and the quality of being to some extent detached from party politics and electoral considerations.

A particular kind of private bill is one that deals with the affairs of a specific individual; these are known as personal bills and are always introduced into the House of Lords, from which, if approved, they proceed to the Commons. In the Lords they are referred to the Personal Bills Committee, which consists of the Lord Chairman and six other peers, two of whom must be law lords. No personal bill may be given a first reading until this committee has reported to the Lords. Its basic task is to ensure that such a bill is necessary to achieve the objective of the person involved, and that this objective is not inconsistent with public policy. Hence bills to relieve individuals of penalties for traffic offences imposed by the courts, or to confer academic awards where these have been withheld, have been excluded! If the bill is approved for introduction, it then proceeds in a way very similar to any other private bill. Such bills are few; typically they deal with estates, naturalisation claims or, most notable in recent years, marriage enabling bills, occasioned by the desire of particular individuals to become legally married in circumstances in which existing UK law forbids this. Because debate at second reading on marriage bills has sometimes brought the discussion of personal details to the floor of the House, a new procedure was agreed in 1986 whereby after a formal second reading such bills are dealt with in a small committee (the initial composition of which was the Lord Chairman, a bishop, a Labour baroness and a Conservative life peer). Several attempts have been made to relax the law on affinity by public bills (introduced by private members), but these all failed until a change – relating to step-relatives – was made in a successful bill introduced by Lord Meston in 1986. The House of Lords has a creditable record in dealing with matters in this sensitive area.

Some bills, while altering the general law of the land as public bills do, also have some of the characteristics of a private bill because they affect specific private interests in a way different from other interests of the same kind. These are known as hybrid bills and may, in respect of the clauses which affect private interests, be referred to a select committee (which deals with the bill in the same way as an opposed private bill), after which the bill is recommitted to a committee of the whole House (in the Lords) and goes through the usual public-bill procedure. The most obvious recent example of a hybrid bill was the Channel Tunnel Bill enacted in 1987 which, after going through the Commons, was referred to a select committee in the Lords which sat for thirty days dealing with petitions, eventually recommending over 100 amendments (alleviating particular concerns). In this case some uncertainties were expressed about the *locus standi* of petitioners, because several bodies representing interests in the north of England – such as local councils – wished to petition against a bill which they believed would intensify regional division. The committee decided that it would hear petitioners whose interests in the bill were indirect in this sense, as well as those directly affected by proposed construction works.

Secondary Legislation

The long-term diminution of private legislation, to which reference has already been made, has been accompanied by an upsurge in secondary legislation, also described as subordinate or delegated legislation. In Chapter 6 we considered the primary legislative process by which bills become Acts of Parliament. Many primary (or parent) Acts themselves confer legislative powers, which can be exercised by ministers subject to varying forms of parliamentary control. Most delegated legislation is carried out by means of Statutory Instruments, and before discussing the role of the House of Lords in relation to these, some general explanation is desirable.

Statutory Instruments (SIs) are basically of three kinds. First are affirmative Instruments, so called because they require the positive approval of both Houses of Parliament. In both Houses a motion must be moved and accepted, or carried on division, otherwise the Instrument concerned falls. Generally speaking, the most important Instruments are in this category. A much larger number are known as negative Instruments because these, once laid before Parliament, come into force automatically unless within a specified time limit (usually forty days) one or other House carries a motion (technically known as a 'prayer') calling for their annulment. Finally there are general Instruments, which are not necessarily laid before Parliament at all, though on comparatively rare occasions they may become the subject of parliamentary proceedings, for example through debate on a motion. The neatness of this categorisation is spoilt somewhat by the fact that primary legislation sometimes stipulates varied and unusual forms for SIs. Some Instruments – concerned with financial matters – require to be laid only before the House of Commons.

This categorisation by no means exhausts the rule-making mechanism which exists. In particular in recent years, increasing use has been made of codes of practice which have proliferated without any systematic forms for such codes being adopted, a development which has been criticised in a number of Lords debates on the subject (for example, 15 January 1986 and 14 February 1990). In addition to codes, which may or may not be statutory and may or may not be enforceable through the courts, other forms of 'quasi-legislation' can be identified – such as government circulars – all helpfully discussed by Ganz (1987, 1989). Such forms of 'legislation' have become more important as successive governments have assumed more far-reaching responsibilities in the life of society, or at least have attempted to influence behaviour in such areas as industrial relations, health and safety, race relations, the treatment of livestock, and so on.

Although the number of Statutory Instruments has not grown

particularly in recent years (from around 1,000 per year), their length and complexity appear to have expanded inexorably. Furthermore, as the Chairman of the Joint Select Committee on Statutory Instruments commented in 1986, 'a lot of SIs today no longer deal with means but with principles' (HC 350, 1986–7, Q4). Matters which, a few years earlier, would have been included in the parent Act, because they really deal with policy, are now being dealt with by SIs. In so far as this reduces the complexity of primary legislation it enhances the importance of secondary legislation, and the consequent need for Parliament to provide a satisfactory means for scrutiny of the latter. Emphasis is lent to this point by the increasing use of the so-called 'Henry VIII' clause in primary legislation, whereby power is conferred on ministers by means of delegated legislation to amend (or even to repeal) primary legislation (Lord Rippon of Hexham, 1989).

However, parliamentary procedures can be criticised because these allow for only a relatively perfunctory scrutiny of Statutory Instruments. Even the most important SIs are effectively subject to only a single stage in parliamentary proceedings. Furthermore, no SI can be amended; it can only be accepted or rejected. And the pressure on parliamentary time is such that in the House of Commons at least, the opportunities to debate SIs are now seriously curtailed.

Prior to 1973 both Houses had their own select committees to scrutinise Instruments (in the Lords this was known as the Special Orders Committee), but since that date a joint select committee has existed for this task. This consists of seven members of each House; it is an apolitical committee because its concern is not with the merits or policy implications of Instruments, but rather with their technical propriety. In other words, it considers such questions as: whether the Instrument is drafted properly; whether the power under which it is laid actually exists in the parent Act; and whether the Instrument represents an unexpected use of that power. This committee reports on all Instruments, but obviously it can issue substantive reports on only a tiny fraction of the six or so tabled every sitting day. Only occasionally does it take evidence from government departments. However, the joint committee does have legal advisers who scrutinise all Instruments carefully.

There are some differences in the detailed way in which the two Houses handle Statutory Instruments. A minor point is that affirmative Instruments cannot be approved by the House of Lords until they have been the subject of a report from the joint select committee, whereas in the Commons such Instruments may be debated and passed even before the Committee's report has been made. Occasionally, this has resulted in the Upper House alone being able to debate some aspect of a Statutory Instrument adversely commented on by the Committee. A more significant contrast lies in the circumstances in which debate takes place in the two Houses. In the Commons many affirmative Instruments – as well as prayers – are now debated in Standing Committee, and where this is not the case, debate on the floor of the House is almost always limited to one-and-a-half hours, and usually very late at night. In the Lords all affirmative Instruments (and those few prayers which are tabled) are taken in the chamber. In 1989–90 a total of 116 affirmative Instruments were debated in the Lords, some of them *en bloc* with other instruments.

Most debates in the Lords on affirmative Instruments are relatively brief, but the fact that they take place in the chamber does mean that a short explanation of the Instrument concerned is given by the Minister, and can easily be referred to in *Hansard*. Furthermore, such debates do afford opposition spokesmen, and other peers, the opportunity to engage in a certain amount of probing – sometimes friendly, sometimes unfriendly – which can help to elucidate the Instrument. Quite often the House spends only ten minutes or so on an Instrument; most such debates last less than an hour; a very few extend to two or three hours, or even longer.

Because the House of Lords retains a formal power of veto on orders, peers in general are reluctant to press opposition to an order to a division in which it might be rejected. Never has a prayer against a negative Instrument been carried, and only once has the House rejected an affirmative Instrument. This latter solitary example was the celebrated Southern Rhodesia Sanctions Order of 1968 which, however, was approved when relaid a short while later (Morgan, 1975, ch. 5). The inhibition the House feels about using its power in this area means that the Opposition Party in the House traditionally refrains from forcing votes directly against orders. Apart from the 1968 example, the Conservatives did not do so in the 1960s or 1970s. Between 1979 and 1981 Labour did divide the House on nine occasions against affirmative orders, but all these the Government comfortably won. Since 1981 Labour has reverted to the practice of not forcing such divisions. To do so could create precedents very unwelcome to any future Labour Government.

It might have been thought that, given this inhibition on the use of power, the House of Lords would have allowed proceedings on Statutory Instruments to become purely formal, or at least, if that were not the case (which manifestly it is not), the House might have ceased to have any real influence in this area. But this does not appear to be the case either. The House does sometimes force (or perhaps shame) the Government into withdrawing an Instrument (or maybe not laying it in the first place). To this end peers do use procedural means, other than direct votes against an Instrument, to record the view of the House. Motions, in the form of reasoned amendments, are sometimes moved at the same time as a motion to approve an Instrument, or at the same time as a prayer. In such cases the prayer can be withdrawn after debate (or the motion to approve the Instrument not formally opposed), while the motion expressing regret, or calling for the withdrawal of the Instrument on some stated ground, can be voted on, and may even be carried against the Government. Some illustration of such activity will help to clarify what is involved.

In 1984 the Opposition considered the possibility of voting directly against the order for the cancellation of the GLC elections. This was laid under the Local Government (Interim Provisions) Bill, which had stipulated that cancellation could take place only after the principle of abolition of the authorities concerned had been approved by Parliament. An answer to a parliamentary question in May indicated that the Government would see the rejection of this order as a breach of convention (HL Debs, 14 May 1984, col. 1268). Eventually the Opposition in the Lords tabled a motion stating that the House viewed cancellation of the elections as prejudicial to peers' consideration of the substantive Local Government Bill (which was then still before the Commons), but this motion was handsomely defeated (by 145 votes to 72, 18 December 1984). Had this motion been passed it would not itself have prevented cancellation of the elections, though it would have added to government embarrassment on the issue. If such a motion is carried, it simply records the view of the House.

In December 1983 a motion, stating that in the opinion of the Lords the Equal Pay (Amendment) Regulation did not comply fully with European Community stipulations, was carried by 108 votes to

104, but at the same time the regulations themselves were formally approved. This was part of a lengthy campaign within Parliament to intensify pressure for equal treatment of the sexes. Another example occurred in July 1985 when a motion expressing regret at top public-sector pay awards was approved by 140 votes to 135, at the same time as the Lord Chancellor's Salary Order was approved (the Lord Chancellor being the only Minister whose increase then required parliamentary approval). On this occasion Viscount Whitelaw, Leader of the House, explained that he would convey the views of the House to his cabinet colleagues. No doubt he did so (in case they didn't read the newspapers!) but the Government had won a vote on the same subject in the Commons, and the Lords' vote had no practical effect other than possibly adding a little to public embarrassment on this whole subject.

The Conservatives in Opposition in the 1970s sometimes used a motion for resolution to similar effect. For example, in 1975 a motion condemning the Government for laying an order providing for the withdrawal of funds from direct grant schools was handsomely carried (by 131 votes to 44), while the order concerned was not contested, despite the fact that in the Commons the Conservative Opposition had sought to defeat the order in a division. Sometimes, however, an adverse vote on such a motion does cause the Government to withdraw an order, even though the order itself has not been defeated. This happened in 1977 when Lord Duncan-Sandys moved a motion calling for the withdrawal of a Town and Country Planning Order, which was subsequently relaid in an amended form. This example was cited by the Liberal Democrat peer Lord Russell when in July 1990 he moved a motion calling for the amendment of the Education (Student Loans) Regulations (see Table 7.5). On this occasion a senior Conservative back-bench peer protested at the impropriety of such a procedure, but Lord Russell pressed his motion to a division, which the Government won by 94 votes to 62 – though it is worth noting that the Labour front bench declined to support Lord Russell in the division, thus illustrating their concern to avoid creating any precedent for the use of power by the House, even though the motion, if carried, would not have directly negatived the regulations (see HL Debs, 24 July 1990, cols 1403–48).

In 1968 the Government White Paper on Lords Reform stated that some Instruments had not been laid because of known opposition in the Lords. The most prominent example was probably the cabinet decision not to proceed with the decision to build a third London airport at Stansted, which was made shortly after a Lords debate on the subject in December 1967 revealed strong opposition in the House.

On other occasions hostile motions have been tabled and debated, but withdrawn in the light of government assurances. In May 1986 the Labour Opposition tabled a motion on the Hong Kong (British Nationality) Order which directly called for its withdrawal, and replacement by one which would give greater consideration to ethnic minorities. This was debated for three-and-a-half hours on a Friday, at the end of which the opposition leader, Lord Cledwyn, stated that the government Minister had gone substantially further than any Minister had done on any previous occasion in providing reassurance about minority groups, and the hostile motion was therefore withdrawn. The order was approved without a division on the promise of concessions from the Government (16 May 1986).

A hostile motion may be withdrawn even though no concessions have been promised. On 19 March 1985, the Labour Opposition tabled both a 'prayer' against an order restricting doctors' freedom to prescribe certain drugs and a motion deploring the decision; on this occasion a Liberal peer tabled an amendment to the opposition motion, which was also hostile to the Government. After debate a vote on the amendment took place, then the main motion was negatived without a division, and the prayer withdrawn. The debate had lasted almost four hours, and was part of a campaign in the Lords on this subject (debates had taken place under other procedures on 15 January, 6 and 20 February). On 18 June 1986, a prayer opposing government plans to test four sites for possible disposal of radioactive waste was moved by a Conservative back-bench peer. The debate did not begin until after midnight, but within an hour seven peers spoke, all critical of the Government's position. The following year the Government abandoned its plans, which had also been severely criticised in the Commons.

Occasionally, the motion to approve an order may be withdrawn after being heavily criticised in debate. The Funds for Trade Union Ballots Order was withdrawn in July 1982 because the government spokesman – a newly appointed Lord in Waiting – was unable to clarify ambiguities highlighted in two somewhat formidable opposition speeches – from Lord Wedderburn of Charlton and Lord

McCarthy. The motion for approval was moved the next day when the government spokesman concerned had been better briefed. In the previous session the Building Societies (Authorisation) Regulations had been withdrawn in somewhat similar circumstances, to be relaid when a difficult point raised by an opposition peer could be clarified.

Some Statutory Instruments may be classed as hybrid, and while the House of Commons has no procedure for distinguishing such Instruments, in the Lords these (if opposed) may be referred to the Hybrid Instruments Committee, which in turn may recommend a full select committee hearing. Successive governments have at times sought to eliminate or curtail this procedure, but it has been jealously guarded by peers (see Jones, 1966; also HL Debs on the Offshore Petroleum Development Bill, 10 February 1975, cols 1109–36; 25 February 1975, cols 648–64). It is rarely used; only three times since 1973 have full select committee hearings taken place on such Instruments, but one of these – a London Docklands Development Order in 1980 – involved a select committee sitting on forty-six days to hear petitioners.

Finally, mention can be made of special procedure orders upon which, under a procedure established in 1945, joint committees may sit; since then there has been, on average, one such committee per session. If the Government wishes to override a joint committee report, then a Confirmation of Orders Bill is required. The best-known example in recent years concerned the Okehampton by-pass. This was a particularly complex twenty-year-long saga, which eventually culminated in such a bill to set aside the verdict of a joint select committee, which had in turn found by a four-to-two majority against the outcome of a ninety-six-day public inquiry. Such bills proceed straight to third reading; in the Lords an eight-hour debate on 5 December 1985 represented the last opportunity for the Government's decision to be frustrated. The 'Okehampton Crisis Committee' published a large newspaper advertisement that day appealing for 'fair play' from the Lords. The bill's leading opponent was Lord Molson, an MP from 1935 to 1961 (when he became a peer), and the man largely responsible for parliamentary pressure which led to the 1945 procedure being established. His speech was a *tour de force*, revealing still some of the qualities which won him a First in jurisprudence at Oxford in the 1920s, but despite his pleas, his motion to reject the bill was lost by 27 votes to 112. A more circumspect motion (regretting the bill) was moved from the opposition front bench – and lost by 32 votes to 108. As a result, in the late 1980s, Okehampton gained its by-pass, running south of the town and infringing the Dartmoor National Park.

Returning in conclusion to secondary legislation generally, it is worth re-emphasising the growing importance of this area and the increasing difficulty evident in securing adequate debate in the Commons. Because the House of Lords contains many peers who have considerable experience of Statutory Instruments – notably as ministers or senior civil servants – it is well equipped to play a part in the parliamentary function of scrutiny. It probably does this most effectively on those Instruments which are not of foremost political importance. The power it retains has required peers to adopt some slightly circuitous procedural routes on those occasions when they want, formally, to register the opinion of the House in opposition to an order. It would seem, too, that during the 1980s Labour accepted a convention precluding the Party from attempting to exercise the formal power the House retains in relation to Instruments. None the less, a hidden but useful aspect of debates in the House on Instruments is the knowledge departmental lawyers have (Statutory Instruments are drafted within departments, not by parliamentary counsel) that their handiwork may be examined in this public and partially expert forum.

European Communities Committee

Membership of the European Community potentially imposed upon Parliament a new responsibility for scrutinising Community legislation, but the Community's legislative procedure focuses on the Council of Ministers, composed of representatives of the governments of the member countries. This has the task of approving or otherwise proposals put to it by the Commission, the 'civil service' of the Community. Hence national parliaments had (and still have) no automatic input into the legislative process. If they were to be involved at all, the most obvious way was through the scrutiny of draft legislation before this was put to the Council of Ministers for decision. As the date of British accession – 1 January 1973 – drew near, both Houses of Parliament set up select committees to consider how this might be done. In the Lords this committee became known as the Maybray-King Committee, after its Chairman, Lord Maybray-King, formerly Speaker of the House of Commons.

There were several reasons why the House of Lords was well placed to take a prominent role in this new parliamentary function. A much greater degree of consensus about UK membership of the Community existed in the Lords than in the Commons (peers had voted 451 to 58 in support of the principle of entry; MPs by 356 to 244), which meant that scrutiny of EC matters was less likely to be dogged by continued controversy over the principle of membership in the Lords. Arguably a chamber of influence, rather than of power, was better adapted to the actual scrutiny of draft legislation, given that the EC legislative process did not admit a formal role for national parliaments. Finally, and perhaps of greatest significance, was the simple fact that by the early 1970s the arrival of many life peers had swollen active membership of the House of Lords to the point at which it had surplus capacity to take on significant new work, which could hardly be said of the House of Commons.

Though the Maybray-King Committee initially recommended a joint select committee, this was not favoured by MPs, so the two Houses went their separate ways, though eventually fashioning scrutiny procedures which complemented one another rather well. The Government of the day was very tardy in its whole approach, with ministers showing all their usual suspicion of a new parliament- ary investigatory function. When the House of Lords debated the Maybray-King Committee report in December 1973, Labour peers in Opposition criticised the Government's reluctance to act quickly on the recommendations made; Lord Crowther-Hunt, in a maiden speech, drew attention to the fact that over 250 regulations had been approved since Britain joined the Community, but no parliamentary means for scrutiny had yet been established. After further discus- sions between the procedure committee, and first the Conservative and then the Labour Government, a select comittee was set up in April 1974, largely in the form the Maybray-King Committee had recommended the previous July (Kolinsky, 1975).

The terms of reference of the House of Lords committee enjoin it to report on proposals which 'raise important questions of policy or principle' and on 'other questions to which the committee considers the special attention of the House should be drawn'. This allows the committee to be selective about what it does, choosing certain proposals for investigation as well as making reports on aspects of

Community policy. Some of its reports are on items of draft legislation, others on Commission discussion documents or reviews of policy in some areas. By contrast, the Commons select committee reports briefly on every item of draft legislation, indicating whether or not it believes important questions of principle or policy are raised, but without entering into any discussion of the merits of such proposals. By avoiding such discussion it has no doubt been easier for the Commons committee to preserve its unanimity when making reports. While the Lords committee tends to produce lengthy reports with relatively large quantities of accompanying evidence, the Commons committee, by contrast, produces brief reports which simply alert the House as to whether or not debate on the proposal is considered desirable. Only rarely does the Commons committee now take evidence.

The Lords committee evolved a method of working which suited the conditions of the House. A main committee – initially of seventeen peers, later expanded to twenty-five – was established, with the actual work of investigation being carried on through sub-committees – initially five, but soon increased to seven (though reduced to six in 1987). These sub-committees have been subject-orientated, like the European Parliament committees, rather than based on Whitehall departments. Each sub-committee, as well as containing a few members of the main committee, co-opts other peers, and peers not co-opted may attend and participate in evidence-taking sessions. Peers retire in a five-year rotation from the main committee and chairmen of sub-committees move on after three years. In this way around eighty peers have, in recent sessions, had some part in the work of the EC committee (during the 1989–90 session eighty-two peers took part in EC committee inquiries). Thus the large part-time membership of the House, with its varied expertise, has been well utilised. For example, according to the House of Lords Information Office, in 1978, among the ninety peers then involved, seventeen were former ministers, nine former civil servants or diplomats, eighteen had held university posts, eleven were scientists, and eight farmers. Particular reports have some-times been signed by a galaxy of peers, experienced and authoritat-ive in the subject concerned. An inquiry into the European Monetary System was undertaken in 1983 by a sub-committee chaired by a former Governor of the Bank of England. On the committee were: another former Governor; a former head of the

Treasury; a former chief economic adviser to HMG; as well as several former ministers. The committee unanimously recommended that the UK should join the EMS at an early date, though not necessarily immediately (HL 39, 1983–4), a recommendation reiterated in further reports later in the decade.

The chairmanship of the main committee was, from the start, a full-time salaried post, held successively by Lord Diamond, Baroness Tweedsmuir of Belhelvie, Lord Greenwood of Rossendale, Baroness White, and then Baroness Llewelyn-Davies of Hastoe, who was succeeded by Baroness Serota in 1986. All these had held ministerial office in one or other House before becoming chairman. A professional legal adviser with special knowledge of EC law was appointed, followed later by an assistant legal adviser, several clerks seconded full-time to the work of this committee, and others who helped part-time. Sub-committees can also appoint specialist advisers for particular inquiries, and this has become general practice.

A major task for the chairman of the main committee has been to decide which proposals merit scrutiny and which do not. About 800 proposals are made annually, for each of which the government department most immediately concerned produces an explanatory memorandum. With the assistance of this document the chairman lists proposals initially in two categories: List A are proposals not requiring special attention (approximately 75 per cent); and List B contains those thought to require consideration (approximately 25 per cent). Reports from the main committee indicating the apportionment are usually published fortnightly while the House is sitting; these reports also show to which sub-committee proposals in the second list (List B) have been sent, and give information about the stage of scrutiny reached on each proposal. Some, having been remitted for scrutiny, are simply noted and given no further consideration. Others are investigated (sometimes by a special joint committee established between two sub-committees): a report is drawn up for approval by the main committee, sent to the House and published. Each such report states whether it is for information only, or whether it is also recommended for debate. An innovation in 1987 was the publication of exchanges of correspondence between the committee and ministers on draft proposals upon which time prevented a full inquiry taking place, a procedure used increasingly since.

Occasionally the main committee itself draws up a report. It did this in 1986 on the implications of the Single European Act which it believed would, in the long run, weaken the position of the UK Parliament, though it saw no difficulty for the committee in adapting its procedures to the proposed alterations (HL 264, 1985–6). In May 1990 an *ad hoc* sub-committee was established to examine proposals for economic and monetary union and political union. This took evidence from many expert witnesses and produced a lengthy and lucid report, which was the subject of a seven-and-a-half-hour debate in the House – a debate which passed unnoticed because it was held on 22 November, the day of Mrs Thatcher's resignation (HL 88, 1989–90).

Where debate is recommended, this invariably takes place, and without any undue delay – a further contrast to Commons practice. During the 1983–7 Parliament, of the seventy-six reports made, forty-eight were recommended for debate, and by June 1987 all but one had been debated, the exception being a report made only a month before dissolution. Sometimes more than one report is debated on a single occasion, and debates on reports occasionally take place alongside some other item of business – for example, the second reading of a relevant bill.

The total output of the EC committee is considerable. Each sub-committee produces roughly as many major reports as each of the departmental select committees in the Commons. The total number of reports in the 1989–90 session was 28, with some 500 pages of report, a further 3,500 pages of appendices and published evidence (see Table 8.1).

In seeking evidence, European as well as domestic sources are tapped, with the sub-committees almost always inviting an MEP to give evidence for each inquiry, and often hearing from members of the EC Commission as well. Frequently sub-committee members travel to Europe and hold informal discussions on the topic of an inquiry. The committee has developed close links with both the Commission and the European Parliament. One has the impression that informal contacts keep committee members abreast of the direction of thinking within Community institutions and the likely, most worthwhile, area for inquiries. The contribution of clerks from the European Office of the House of Lords is not to be underestimated here; generally, for example, a clerk is present at plenary sessions of the European Parliament. The chairman of the

Table 8.1 European Communities Committee Reports, 1989–90

Title of report	Date of report	Information or debate	Date of debate	Length of report	Length of evidence and appendices (no. of pages)
Sub-committee A: Finance, Trade and Industry and External Relations, Chm. L. Aldington					
Delors Committee Report	22.11.89	D	18.12.89	20	145
Relations between the Community and EFTA	22.05.90	D	22.06.90	29	156
A Single Market for Consumers	27.07.90	D	—	10	68
Sub-Committee B: Energy, Transport and Technology, Chm. L. Shepherd					
Appliances Burning Gas	06.03.90	I	—	4	17
Air Traffic Control	20.03.90	D	29.10.90	8	45
Civil Aviation: A Free Market by 1992?	05.06.90	D	29.10.90	22	160
A Community Framework for R & D	26.06.90	D	28.01.91	22	121
Road Safety	10.07.90	I	—	7	12
Community Driving Licence	27.07.90	I	—	9	42
Sub-Committee C: Social and Consumer Affairs, Chm. B. Lockwood					
A Community Social Charter	05.12.89	D	19.02.90	10	74
Free Movement of People and Right of Residence	06.02.90	I	—	13	64
European Schools and Language Learning in UK Schools	24.04.90	D	13.07.90	22	120
Medicinal products	24.07.90	I	—	3	41
Vocational Training and Re-Training	24.07.90	D	11.12.90	22	236

Table 8.1 (continued)

Title of report	Date of report	Information or debate	Date of debate	Length of report	Length of evidence and appendices (no. of pages)
Sub-Committee D: Agriculture and Food, Chm. L. Middleton					
Irradiation of Foodstuffs	12.12.89	D	05.02.90	24	146
Hill Livestock Compensatory Allowances	23.01.90	I	—	6	82
Farm Price Proposals	06.03.90	I	—	7	45
The Future of Rural Society	24.07.90	D	15.11.90	52	549
Sub-Committee E: Law and Institutions, Chm. L. Oliver of Aylmeston					
Voting Rights in Local Elections	06.02.90	I	—	15	46
Product Safety	22.05.90	I	—	28	150
Community Shipping Measures	30.10.90	D	14.02.91	23	147
Sub-Committee F: Environment, Chm. L. Nathan					
Freedom of Access to Information on the Environment	22.11.89	I	—	31	51
Tropical Forest	20.03.90	D	12.10.90	22	189
Paying for Pollution – Civil Liability for Damage caused by Waste	16.10.90	D	—	13	160
Ad Hoc Committee: Chm. L. Aldington					
Economic and Monetary and Political Union	30.10.90	D	22.11.90	55	307
Ad Hoc Committee: Chm. L. Nathan					
European Company Statute	10.07.90	I	—	24	259
Main Committee					
Correspondence with Ministers	06.02.90	I	—	—	72
Correspondence with Ministers	16.10.90	I	—	—	46

main committee, along with the chairmen of the sub-committees, make what has become known colloquially as 'the State Visit' to Strasbourg every three years.

Committee reports usually receive publicity in the serious press. Within Whitehall departments and among interested MPs evidence suggests that reports are regarded as extremely useful sources. Elsewhere in Community institutions, reports from the committee appear to be highly thought of and widely distributed. Tribute has frequently been paid to the quality of the committee's work (see Bates, 1985; Grantham and Hodgson, 1985). When the House of Commons Procedure Committee considered the whole subject of the scrutiny of EC legislation in 1989 it took evidence from Baroness Serota, the Chairman of the House of Lords Select Committee. She stressed the importance of developing the right contacts, knowing whom to send reports to, and the need to get in early when a subject was being considered and, more generally, to get the timing of inquiries right. MPs were clearly impressed by the way the Lords committee had gone about its work, and acknowledged that it had achieved an influence which the Commons committee had lacked (HC 622-II, 1988–9, Qs 403–53).

The committee seeks to provide an informed and expert appraisal of Community proposals, as well as indicating their probable effect on UK interests. Very rarely do sub-committees, or the main committee, vote to settle conflicts of view; instead, reports are drafted so as to reflect differences which remain after the process of evidence-taking and deliberation has been completed. Some of the chairmen seem to revel in the intellectual challenge of producing a cogent and convincing report which is fair to the evidence received and the opinions held within the committee. Reports are usually apolitical – not naïvely ignoring politics, but rather approaching subjects with an independent-mindedness which treats the political aspects of a question as one factor along with others that demand attention.

Whether by accident or design (or a bit of both) the Lords committee has come to play a very different role to the Commons committee. To begin with the two committees were often investigating the same document, and in some cases civil servants gave evidence to one committee one day and the other the next. But steps were soon taken to avoid such duplication of effort – for example, through making evidence obtained by one committee immediately available to the other. Distinctiveness within a co-operative framework became a characteristic of these committees.

The Science and Technology Committee

The Prime Minister was apparently 'put out' when the House of Commons failed to reappoint its Science and Technology Committee at the time of the 1979 reforms (HL Debs, 10 February 1984, col. 1434). The House of Lords decided to fill the gap, which it did by appointing, in January 1980, a select committee simply 'to consider science and technology'. Like the EC committee, this select committee is reappointed each session; it works through sub-committees (usually two as well as a general-purposes sub-committee); in addition to its fifteen members, other peers may be co-opted for particular inquiries, and the sub-committees invariably appoint specialist advisers and frequently travel overseas in the course of their inquiries.

The membership of this committee brings together peers eminent in the world of science and technology – Fellows of the Royal Society and leading industrialists – with politician peers, not least former ministers. The first chairman of the committee was Lord Todd, a Cambridge University scientist and former chairman of the Advisory Council on Scientific Policy. In 1984 he was succeeded by Lord Sherfield, former Permanent Secretary at the Treasury and an ex-chairman of the Atomic Energy Authority, who gave way in 1989 to the physicist Lord Flowers who, in a distinguished career, had served as chairman of the Science Research Council, of the Royal Commission on Environmental Pollution, and of the Committee of University Vice-Chancellors and Principals. By 1991 the Committee had published twenty-one major reports (see Table 8.2 for a full list), several of which had been supplemented by further reports. Almost all these had been debated in the House of Lords, usually within three months of publication. Such debates provided an opportunity for a preliminary reply from the Government – given in a minister's speech – but further replies, published either as White Papers or as special reports from the Committee, have become the norm (see Hayter, 1991).

The Government was initially very tardy about its responses, and when these appeared it was sometimes reasonable to infer that

Table 8.2 Science and Technology Committee Reports

Title of report	No. of report	Debated in House	Government reply	Further reports
Electric Vehicles (July 1980)	First report HL 352 (1979–80)	11.11.80	—	Third report HL210 (1981–2) (July 1982)
Scientific Aspects of Forestry (November 1980)	Second report HL 381 (1979–80) 2 vols	23.2.81	Second report HL 83 (1981–2) (Feb 1982)	Fourth report HL 211 (1981–2) (July 1982)
Hazardous Waste Disposal (July 1981)	First report HL 273 (1980–1) 2 vols	17.11.81	Third report HL 126, 1984–5 (April 1985)	Sixth report HL 234 (1984–5) (July 1985)
Science and Government (November 1981)	First report HL 20 (1981–2)	15.2.82	Cmd 8591 (July 1982)	
Water Industry (December 1982)	First report HL 47 (1982–3) 2 vols	25.5.83	Memo placed in House of Lords' Library (Nov 1983)	
Engineering R & D (February 1983)	Second report HL 89 (1982–3) 3 vols	4.7.83	First report HL 27 (1984–5) (Nov 1984)	
Occupational Health and Hygiene (December 1983)	Second report HL 99 (1983–4) 3 vols	15.11.84	Fifth report HL 289 (1983–4) (July 1984)	

Table 8.2 *(continued)*

Title of report	No. of report	Debated in House	Government reply	Further reports
Remote Sensing and Digital Mapping (December 1983)	First report HL 98 (1983–4) 2 vols	25.5.84	—	
Agriculture and Environmental Research (July 1984)	Fourth report HL 272 (1983–4)	—	Fifth report HL 233 (1984–5) (July 1985)	
Education and Training (December 1984)	Second report HL 48 (1984–5) 3 vols	25.3.85	Cmd 9653 (Nov 1985)	
Science and Technology in Local Government (November 1985)	First report HL 11 (1985–6)	21.1.86	Third report HL 243 (1985–6) (July 1986)	Fourth report HL 127 (1984–5) (April 1985)
Marine Science and Technology (December 1985)	Second report HL 47 (1985–6) 3 vols	7.5.86	Cmd 9861 (July 1986)	
Innovation in Surface Transport (January 1987)	Second report HL 57 (1986–7)	7.7.87	First report HL 40 (1987–8) (December 1987)	
Civil Research and Development (January 1987)	First report HL 20 (1986–7)	19.2.87	Cmd 185 (July 1987)	Third report HL 24 (1988–9) (February 1989)
UK Space Policy (December 1987)	Second report HL 41 (1987–8)	30.3.88	Fifth report HL 105 (1987–8) (October 1988)	Seventh report HL 61 (1989–90) (May 1990)

Table 8.2 *(continued)*

Title of report	No. of report	Debated in House	Government reply	Further reports
Priorities in Medical Research (March 1988)	Third report HL 54 (1987–8)	14.4.89	Fourth report HL 51 (1989–90) (April 1990)	
Agricultural and Food Research (December 1988)	First report HL 13 (1988–9)	21.4.89	Cmd 1127 (July 1990)	
R & D in Nuclear Power (December 1988)	Second report HL 14 (1988–9)	14.4.89	Fifth report HL 41 (1988–9) (April 1989)	
Greenhouse Effect (October 1989)	Sixth report HL 88 (1988–9)	30.1.90	Cmd 997 (April 1990)	
Overseas Aid (January 1990)	First report HL 16 (1989–90)	22.3.90	Cmd 1061 (May 1990)	
Nature Conservancy Council (March 1990)	Second report HL 33 (1989–90)		Sixth report HL 60 (1989–90) (May 1990)	
Innovation in Manufacturing Industry (January 1991)	First report HL 24 (1990–1)			
International Scientific Programmes (February 1991)	Second report HL 24 (1990–1)			

rather casual consideration had been given to the report concerned. In February 1982, in its reply to a report on forestry, the Government referred to the report as having been published the previous December, when in fact it had been published fourteen months earlier. The committee's third major report, on hazardous waste disposal, was published in July 1981 and debated in the Lords the following November, but no government reply was forthcoming until April 1985, despite questions in the House by the committee chairman. When the reply eventually came, the committee was highly critical, not only of the four-year delay but also of the Government's failure 'even yet to reach conclusions on three important recommendations' – namely, for registration of hazardous waste producers, quarterly returns of their waste, and the licensing of handlers of such waste. The committee returned to the subject, having been invited to review arrangements for hazardous waste disposal by a Department of Environment minister, but it continued, in two further reports made in 1985 and 1989, to be highly critical of the Government (see Table 8.2). Its persistence was to some extent rewarded when some of the committee's recommendations were embodied in the Environmental Protection Act of 1990.

Some of the committee's reports have dealt quite specifically with matters of current policy or legislative decision. In 1983–4 an inquiry was held into remote sensing and digital mapping. During this the terms on which the Government was proposing to privatise the Ordnance Survey came in for considerable criticism, and were indeed eventually altered. These alterations were insisted on by a minister who, after he had appeared before the committee to give evidence, realised the difficulties the Ordnance Survey faced. In 1985 the committee undertook a major inquiry into science and technology in local government, and actually issued a special report in April urging amendments to the Local Government Bill then before Parliament. Earlier, in 1981 and 1983, amendments to the Forestry Bill and the Water Bill respectively had been based directly on recommendations included in committee reports (Bates, 1985, p. 52). In November 1989 the committee's decision to inquire into the Nature Conservancy Council just as the Government was launching its Environmental Protection Bill, which included provisions for a radical reorganisation of the Council, was reported as having caused 'consternation' in Whitehall (*Daily Telegraph*, 16 November 1989). In its report the committee noted that 'the Bill shows many signs of hasty drafting' (HL 33, 1989–90, para. 1.4). The bill was amended during its passage through the Lords to meet many of the committee's points, with Lord Carver, the chairman for this inquiry, taking an active part in the proceedings.

Witnesses, including ministers and civil servants, who appear before the committee know that among its members are some who, on any reckoning, are authorities on the subjects concerned. On the whole, too, committee members have the time and persistence to keep worrying away at the Government on recommendations the committee makes. It has proved itself much readier than Commons select committees to follow up earlier reports and to do so by specifically inquiring into the implementation of recommendations which have been accepted. On topics the committee chooses to investigate, it has raised the threshold of awareness within government and public bodies. For example, its examination of science and Government in 1981 and its report on civil research and development in 1986 recommended strengthened structures within Government for developing, co-ordinating and giving priority to scientific policy. According to the former clerk to the committee, 'the Government's response, then and after subsequent exchanges with the Committee running on into 1990, was largely positive' (Hayter, 1991). The committee returned to the whole area of science research funding, issuing a further critical report in March 1991. On the other hand, despite the authoritative character of its reports, the Government has at times virtually ignored these, and if it does so the committee can do little other than publish a further critical report.

Ad Hoc Select Committees

Since 1970 the House of Lords has made limited but regular use of select committees to examine public bills on particular subjects. Eight committees have been established to examine bills and five to examine subjects. These committees have consisted of from seven to twelve peers; they have been appointed only to deal with a particular subject or bill, and have ceased to exist when their report has been completed.

All but one of the select committees appointed to examine bills have dealt with private members' legislation. The exception was the Hare Coursing Bill which, though introduced by the Labour

Government in 1975, had been a private member's bill the previous session. This is the only time a government bill has been referred to a select committee in the Lords since 1917. In some respects this committee was the least satisfactory. Its report recommended that the bill should not proceed, but the committee was divided, and this central recommendation was agreed by 4 votes to 3. The bill made no further progress.

Of the private members' bills referred to select committees, the first three were all introduced by Liberal peers. Baroness Seear's Anti-Discrimination Bill in 1972 dealt with the difficult subject of sex discrimination. This was a matter upon which the Government was under some pressure in both Houses; a Commons bill had lapsed in 1971–2 and a parallel Commons committee was established in 1972–3. The Lords select committee first considered the extent of sex discrimination, then reported specifically on Baroness Seear's bill. Both Houses, through select committees and private members' bills, goaded the Government into introducing its own bill in the 1972–3 session.

In 1977 a select committee examined a Bill of Rights introduced by Lord Wade. Though almost evenly divided on whether or not such a bill would be worth while, the committee did marshal the arguments on the subject effectively. One of the peers involved later wrote that he commenced with a strong prejudice against such a bill, but realised he was wrong, and became a supporter (Redcliffe-Maud, 1981, p. 145). No doubt the committee's report had a wider educative effect, and a bill based on the European Convention on Human Rights subsequently passed the House, but made no headway in the Commons.

One select committee came down unequivocally against the bill it was set up to investigate; this was the 1978 committee on Lord Byers's Foreign Boycotts Bill, a proposal which, though cast in general terms, was clearly aimed against the Arab boycott of Israel. The object of the bill was to make compliance with the boycott illegal. It was clear that the Government had no intention of supporting such legislation, but at the same time it felt the whole subject could benefit from public ventilation.

A subject which successive governments baulked at tackling was the welfare of animals used in laboratory experiments, even though during the 1970s at least seven private members' bills on this topic were introduced. In 1979 the House of Lords sent Lord Halsbury's

Laboratory Animals Protection Bill to a select committee. Lord Halsbury, a cross-bench hereditary peer, an FRS and a former member of both the Medical and Science Research Councils, later explained how he had taken Lord Houghton of Sowerby – a veteran animal welfare campaigner – into his confidence, and that it was Lord Houghton who had suggested this procedure (HL Debs, 28 November 1985, col. 1025). The resulting committee received some 900 letters and memoranda and took oral evidence at six of its sixteen meetings, eventually producing a much-revised draft bill, which the House of Lords duly passed, but which made no progress in the Commons. The Government was plainly reluctant to legislate in this area, but five years later, with animal rights groups becoming ever more troublesome, the nettle was grasped, and the resulting 1986 Animals (Scientific Procedures) Bill owed much to the work of this select committee.

In 1984 two bills seeking to alter the law on charities were referred to a select committee, which decided that neither was satisfactory; but under the chairmanship of Lord Brightman (a Lord of Appeal), the committee formulated a third bill which it recommended to the Lords; this was passed in the 1984–5 session. The object of this legislation was to bring clarity and accountability to the bewildering world of small charities, tens of thousands of which had tiny annual incomes, produced no proper accounts, and in many cases had simply gone to sleep. The 1985 bill empowered tiny charities to spend their capital, and many other small charities to amalgamate. This was a subject on which the House of Commons Expenditure Committee had reported in 1975, as had a National Council for Social Services committee under the ubiquitous Lord Goodman. The Government had considered both these earlier reports, but announced in 1980 that it would not introduce legislation. It was an area in which it was generally agreed something ought to be done, but deciding exactly what should be done was a very difficult matter. The Lords select committee cleared the way for legislation.

In early 1987, the Infant Life (Preservation) Bill, introduced by the then Bishop of Birmingham, Dr Montefiore, was referred to a select committee, which issued an interim report based on the evidence it managed to take before the dissolution of Parliament. One of its early witnesses was Dr Montefiore, himself no longer a member of the House because he retired from his See soon after introducing the bill. The committee was reappointed in autumn

1987 at the instigation of Lord Houghton of Sowerby, an opponent of the Bishop's bill. It made its final report in February 1988, and this was cited frequently when the Human Fertilisation and Embryology Bill was proceeding through the House in 1990 (HL 50, 1987–8).

Since 1970 five *ad hoc* committees investigating particular subjects have been established, three of which have been in the broad area of economic policy. A committee on commodity prices under Lord Roberthall – a professional economist – met forty-eight times during 1976 and 1977, producing a well-documented report illustrating the intractable nature of the difficulties involved in trying to get greater stability into commodity markets. In 1981–2 the Lords appointed a committee to examine unemployment, and in 1984 a committee to consider the causes and implications of the deficit in the balance of trade in manufactured goods.

This latter committee was prompted by the fact that in 1983 Britain had become, for the first time ever, a net importer of manufactured goods. It was chaired by Lord Aldington, a businessman who had once been a Conservative minister, and among its members were two other former Conservative ministers, as well as Lord Ezra, former Chairman of the National Coal Board, Lord Beswick, a former Labour Minister and former Chairman of British Aerospace, and Lord Kearton, former Chairman of Courtaulds, of BNOC, and of the Industrial Reorganisation Corporation, 1966–70. The committee's report, published in October 1985, attracted much public attention because it sounded severe warnings about the economic, social and political crisis Britain would ultimately face unless the Government took urgent steps to alter the situation. Unprecedentedly, the Secretary of State for Trade and Industry, the barrister Leon Brittan, issued an immediate statement rejecting the main findings of the committee. The House of Lords debated the report in December 1985, and it was widely cited over the following eighteen months in both Houses of Parliament and elsewhere. The Government's displeasure with the report was as real as the report's lucid and authoritative commentary on Britain's shrinking industrial base.

The two other *ad hoc* committees were, first, one on Sport and Leisure, chaired by the tenth Viscount Cobham, a former first-class county cricketer, which reported in 1973; and second, the committee on the Sentence for Murder, which reported in 1989. This latter committee strongly recommended the abolition of the mandatory life sentence. The Government refused to accept this advice. In April 1991 Lord Nathan, Chairman of the committee, with the support of the Lord Chief Justice and other members of the judiciary, moved an amendment to the Criminal Justice Bill embodying this crucial recommendation, on which the Conservative Government suffered one of its worst ever defeats in the Lords, with peers voting 177 to 79 in support of allowing judges discretion in the length of sentence imposed on convicted murderers.

Conclusion

The reception given to the report on the balance of trade in 1985 and the report on the sentence for murder in 1988 may be taken as illustrative of the strengths – and weaknesses – of the House of Lords in regard to select committee work. The Lords can appoint highly talented and experienced members to a range of committees. Witnesses can be cross-examined in a more searching way than is usual in the Commons. Reports almost invariably score well for their rigour in analysis, the lucidity and forcefulness of their argument, and their generally well-researched and sure-footed flavour. The report on overseas trade apparently ran through five editions in two years (Silk, 1987, p. 231). It was probably more widely read by undergraduates than any other recent select committee report. Indirectly, it may well have had a considerable influence. But select committees in Britain in the late twentieth century which produce reports challenging fundamental government policies – on employment, overseas trade, entry to the EMS, or whatever – cannot be expected to have immediate impact. The Government may momentarily yelp in frustration or embarrassment, but no more. None the less, in the longer term they may contribute to a remoulding of informed public opinion.

On the other hand, select committees which produce reports on complex issues, such as the tangled and outdated condition of the law on small charities, or how best to update the law on animal experiments, or how to standardise EC measurements of cereals, receive less publicity, but almost certainly achieve more of tangible consequence within the executive in bringing about legislative change.

In conclusion to this whole chapter, it seems reasonable to argue that the House of Lords does a considerable amount of work of a relatively obscure kind for which MPs do not, in general, show great enthusiasm – for example, on private bills and in select committees on subjects which lack political kudos. The House of Lords has tended, in recent years, to develop activities in ways which enable it to play a complementary role to that of the Commons. This point is taken up again in the final chapter.

9

What Role for the Lords?

The main concern of this book has been to analyse the House of Lords, to show what it consisted of and how it functioned, particularly during the period of the Conservative Governments led by Mrs Thatcher. But it would be odd if such a study did not conclude by offering some consideration of the possible reform or abolition of the Lords. While such questions faded from public debate through most of the 1980s, towards the end of the decade they returned to visibility, though certainly not to prominence. This final chapter takes up these matters, and in so doing offers a brief analysis of the various suggestions which have been made for reform of the Lords, as well as indicating some of the consequences which could follow abolition.

It is helpful to approach this whole subject by considering successively the functions, powers and composition of the House of Lords. That these three are interrelated, and ought to remain so, is obvious. But the general argument of this chapter will be that the functions and powers of the present House are a good deal more satisfactory than its composition. The discussion of functions will involve briefly reviewing and drawing some conclusions from earlier chapters of this book, and then indicating possible lines along which present functions could be extended. The discussion of powers will require some comparison between the role of the House of Lords under a Labour Government and its role under the Conservatives. The discussion of composition will include reference to schemes for reform.

The Functions of the House

If functions specifically are being discussed, it is reasonable to speak of these as being threefold: the House of Lords has a legislative, a deliberative and a constitutional role. Any of these may involve power, but in practice the former two are discharged largely without the question of power arising, whereas the constitutional role clearly does involve the assertion of power.

The scrutiny and amendment of legislation remains the most important task of the Lords. This is primarily a revising role, but it is not simply a matter of affording opportunities for draftsmen to improve their handiwork. It is also a question of making minor adjustments to legislation in response to anxieties and concerns which have surfaced in various ways during a bill's earlier legislative stages. Usually it is the give-and-take of the legislative process which produces as its end product a bill recognisably the same as the one first submitted to Parliament, but (at least in the case of major bills) different in many detailed ways. Sometimes, however, major adjustments are also forced on governments.

The fundamental forces which shape legislation lie well beyond the House of Lords. Their focus is primarily on the Cabinet and on Whitehall departments; in so far as they have a parliamentary focus, it is on the House of Commons. But the House of Lords, like the Commons, does mull over the details of legislation, though each House does this in its own way. The Commons generally takes much more time than the Lords, a feature made possible by the former's widespread use of standing committees, though the effectiveness of these is often criticised (see Griffith, 1981). Debate in the Lords is usually less thorough; it must be kept concise because every stage of every bill (almost) is taken on the floor of the House. But since all major bills go through the Commons first, this does not necessarily matter. Debate in the Lords can afford to concentrate more sharply on issues left outstanding by the Lower House. Of course in practice this is not always the case. Debate at times is repetitious, though again this may not be undesirable. If the executive appears to be contemplating giving ground, then arguments may need to be reiterated to encourage this process. The extent to which outside groups have given increased attention to the Lords in their recent efforts to secure adjustments to the details of legislation is worth reiterating. The survey of such groups cited in Chapter 6 suggested that from the perspective of the groups themselves the Lords was almost as useful for this purpose as the Commons (see Rush, 1990). Perhaps one reason for this has been the diminished emphasis placed on consultation with such groups at the pre-legislative stage by the Thatcher Governments. Perhaps too it reflects the fact that groups often realise the implications of legislation only while bills are being debated in the Commons. The existence of a second House affords them the opportunity to try to alter details to which they have been alerted by debate in the first House.

The fact that debate in the Lords is less obviously partisan may well be a further advantage as far as groups are concerned. The overall party political context is clear enough in the Upper House, but debate generally is freed from the incessant demands of party rivalry which dominate the Commons. Partisanship is not absent, but it is muted, and it is expressed differently in the Upper House.

On private members' bills the House of Lords has a creditable record of edging along discussion, especially on some issues which give rise to inhibitions among MPs and which governments dare not touch. Sometimes, through this form of parliamentary private enterprise, the Lords has helpfully had a cockshy at getting a difficult idea distilled into a viable piece of legislation.

Then there is a kind of underworld of parliamentary legislative activity, discussed in Chapter 8, relatively obscure and yet by no means without importance. In these areas the Lords appears helpful in relieving the Commons of tasks which the Lower House has little time and probably little enthusiasm to sustain.

The deliberative work of the House of Lords is conducted partly in the chamber, and partly in committees. The work in the chamber is difficult to evaluate. What *is* the outcome of all those Wednesday debates with so many worthy speeches, conscientiously prepared (on the whole) and faithfully recorded in *Hansard* for a wider readership (but how wide?)? Sometimes they are fascinating, informed and highly persuasive; sometimes boring, irrelevant and even almost incoherent. But such qualities, like beauty itself, lie at least in part in the eye of the beholder. Significant perhaps is the simple fact that many very busy and accomplished people, presumably not on the whole short of things to do, participate in debates.

Select committee work, too, has attracted many peers. A tradition of public service encourages such activities – perhaps the continuing strength of this tradition is a rather special British phenomenon, just as the House of Lords is unique among parliamentary chambers. At virtually no public expense the services of many experienced and talented individuals are mobilised for select committee work. Even if such activities do not have much apparent influence (and that depends on bodies besides the House of Lords), they can hardly be thought to do any harm. And some undoubtedly do have an influence, if not on Government then on other bodies, not least European Community institutions.

In regard to both legislative and deliberative work, the House of Lords essentially plays a complementary role to that of the Commons. Such complementarity is most obvious in relation to the newer parliamentary functions, notably work on European Community matters. In relation to more traditional tasks – such as the scrutiny of domestic Statutory Instruments and private bills, even the primary legislative process – reforms aimed at reshaping procedures to enhance complementarity (rather than the continuing formal duplication of roles) could be considered.

Mention was made in Chapter 5 of the Lords select committee on practice and procedure which recommended select committees to consider government legislation (see also HL 141, 1976–7). This proposal received a hasty burial when it was first made, but is worthy of re-examination. The committee recommended the estab-lishment of a range of subject-based select committees, to which bills would be referred as soon as they had received second reading in the Commons. These committees would monitor the progress of a bill in the Lower House, publishing a report indicating time taken on different sections of the bill, ministerial undertakings given, and other such information. Additionally, such committees would take evidence from interested parties, civil servants and others, in the same sort of way as the European Communities Committee takes evidence on draft legislation. Once a bill had reached the House of Lords, it could be referred to the select committee which had already been monitoring it (with the minister in charge and possibly some other peers added) at its committee stage. For bills introduced into the Lords, both the above stages might be taken together in an extended committee stage.

Such committees would, in part, be doing the kind of work Special Standing Committees (SSCs) in the Commons have undertaken since 1979 – on those rare occasions when the Government has permitted their establishment (see HC 49–I–II, 1984–5). It seems primarily to be executive hostility to such attempts to raise a little more of the legislative process above the waterline of public visibility which has so severely restricted the use of SSCs. But whilst one objection to their use in the Commons has been the time they take (and possible consequent delay in dealing with a bill), select committees on bills in the Lords could be at work while a bill was still before the Commons, and in this case no slippage in the legislative timetable need occur. The proposals made by the Lords select committee on practice and procedure were designed both to improve the quality of legislative scrutiny by the Upper House and to alleviate the problems caused for the Upper House by the very uneven flow of legislative business. The experience of the Lords with select committees on private members' bills provides encouragement for such developments.

There may be further arguments for extending select committee work in the Lords. The departmental committees which have existed in the Commons since 1979 do not provide a very satisfactory means for the critical evaluation of a department's administrative performance. It is the very closeness of the linkage between the Government and the Commons which appears to handicap all-party groups of MPs in regard to such work. Select committees formed in the Upper House are able to work in a noticeably more detached manner, and this is a feature of which greater use could be made. The creation of the 'Next Steps' executive agencies, and the concerns expressed over the need for parliamentary review of such bodies, add emphasis to this point. The availability in the Lords of at least some peers with substantial relevant experience ought not to be overlooked by the Commons. There is an obvious possibility here for the greater use of joint select committees.

The third function of the House of Lords is a constitutional one. This has not been given much prominence in this book: it is a much less clear role than that of revising legislation or deliberation. It also brings us inevitably to the discussion of power, so is best considered under that heading.

The Powers of the House

The constitutional role is twofold. On the one hand the House of Lords has certain powers vested in it which, in theory at least, would enable it to prevent the subversion of some basic constitutional principles, notably any unilateral action by a majority party in the Commons to postpone a general election. In addition, the power the House of Lords retains to delay any item of government legislation may also be thought of as a more general constitutional function. Both need to be considered here.

Under the Parliament Acts, the House of Lords retains an absolute veto over any bill to extend the lifetime of a Parliament. In 1915 and again in 1940, when the House of Commons passed bills to defer general elections then due, the House of Lords agreed to them, as did opposition party leaders. The unsuitability of holding elections in wartime conditions was reason enough for their postponement. But if a government attempted so drastic a step without opposition support – would the House of Lords in practice be able to exercise its veto? (And if the Government was a Conservative Government, would the House wish to exercise a veto?) No sure answer can be given to such questions, mainly because they presuppose a degree of ill-health in the body politic far beyond any malady recently experienced.

Again, it is conceivable that a Government might wish to sack a judge, a procedure which at present would require a majority vote in both Houses. This, it can be argued, helps to sustain the independence of the judiciary (Crowther-Hunt, 1980). But without being drawn too deeply into this area, it seems reasonable to suggest that the formal independence of the judiciary rests on more solid foundations than the continued existence of the House of Lords, and that the threats to judicial independence operate in a far more subtle way than through an open frontal assault by Parliament (consider, for example, decisions about the promotion of judges).

The constitutional role of the House of Lords in these areas may have a theoretical clarity, but in practice the circumstances involved appear so hypothetical that the ability of the Lords to take any effective action must also be described as hypothetical. The present basis on which the membership of the House is composed does little to enhance its suitability as a body capable of mounting some last-ditch defence of the Constitution, a point we will return to later in this chapter.

However, the constitutional role of the House of Lords must not be too narrowly defined. There is a sense in which simply by being there, as part of a parliamentary process through which all legislation must pass, the Lords has a constitutional function. Bills cannot become the law of the land until the Upper House has given its approval, or until its disapproval has been overridden by a public, and very precise, procedure stipulated in the Parliament Acts.

The power to delay legislation may be used very sparingly, but it remains an important part of the context within which the House of Lords carries out its functions. The way the power is understood has, however, altered drastically since it was first defined in the 1911 Parliament Act. At that time there was no suggestion that the Lords ought to refrain from using this power. Indeed the contrary was implied: the House of Lords would be neglecting its constitutional duty if it failed to impose delay on some bills of a highly controversial kind; and this the Lords did up to the First World War. But thereafter, for sixty years, the power to delay bills was unused – save, ironically, the delay imposed on the 1947 Parliament Bill, the measure which cut the Lords' power of delay from two years to one.

By the 1960s the House of Lords had not used its power for so long that the common understanding about the circumstances in which it might reasonably do so had changed. No longer was the exercise of power seen as a proper part of the discharge of the functions of the House of Lords in relation to the revision of controversial bills. Rather, the use of delaying power by the Lords had come to be viewed as a kind of ultimate weapon to which the House might be driven in extreme circumstances. In 1967 Lord Carrington, Conservative leader in the Lords, argued that the House should not delay the London Government Bill (which postponed London borough elections) because it could expect to use its delaying power only once; and therefore the power should be reserved for a matter of great constitutional and national importance (HL Debs, 16 February 1967, cols 419–24). Bee-like the House could sting once, then die, either through abolition or through having its remaining powers removed. It seemed as if a new convention of the Constitution had been established reserving the Lords' power of delay to matters of fundamental constitutional importance.

But another aspect to the possession of this power was the simple fact that it enhanced the credibility and standing of the House of Lords as a revising body. Introducing the 1947 Parliament Bill, Herbert Morrison, speaking for the Labour Government, had emphasised this point, stating: 'If the position were that the House of Lords sent their amendments to the Commons, but the Commons could indifferently ignore them and pass a bill into law without further ado, then the Lords would be entitled to say that there was no guarantee that any serious consideration would be given to their amendments, and that we might as well resort to single chamber government' (HC Debs, 10 November 1947, col. 38). The continued possession of some formal power was seen as necessary for the Lords to discharge its revising function adequately.

The corollary to this was that if the House of Lords felt that its proposed changes to bills – any bills – were not being accorded sufficiently serious attention, it could threaten delay. In the highly confused and unprecedented parliamentary situation of the mid 1970s, this is what happened. The Lords did use its power to delay two bills – not because the particular legislation objected to contained matters of great constitutional and national importance, but rather because it was exasperated at its treatment by a highly tenuous Commons majority. It is worth, for a moment, trying to describe the contrasting perspectives which the two major parties had on the exercise of power at that time.

The Conservatives saw a Government with the most fragile possible Commons majority insisting on passing a mass of contentious legislation. In a formal sense the Labour Government had attained office quite legitimately, but unlike past governments with low majorities (such as 1950–51, 1964–6) it appeared in no way to moderate its legislative programme. In particular in 1976 five major bills were 'guillotined' in the Commons, and none of these reached the House of Lords until very late in the parliamentary session. The Lords scarcely had the time to revise these bills properly, but then such amendments as it did make were rapidly reversed in the Commons under a very tight allocation-of-time order. When the bill nationalising aerospace and shipbuilding was found to be hybrid in regard to ship-repairing, the Government responded by putting down a motion setting aside the hybridity procedure in the Commons. How much undivided power was it proper for a Cabinet in control of a bare Commons majority to be able to enjoy (Hailsham, 1976)? Should not the House of Lords check the Government in some way, and if it failed to do so, was it not acquiescing in the devaluation of its own role as a revising chamber?

To the Labour Government the matter had a very different appearance. The legislation it advanced had been included in its election manifesto; in particular ship-repairing was specifically referred to in both the 1974 manifestos. It may have had a low Commons majority, but it had nevertheless clearly won the October 1974 election, and that was what mattered. The hybridity issue was a procedural red herring, which had arisen only because the private firms involved had been so uncooperative in refusing to provide enough information about themselves. If the parliamentary wing of the Labour Party was to retain the co-operation of the trade-union wing of the Party, then this legislation had to be implemented – at least, that was how it looked to the parliamentary leadership. The Lords was an anachronistic body which Labour had attempted – unsuccessfully – to reform. It was now quite wrong and completely irresponsible for the Conservative Opposition to use its built-in strength in the Upper House to overturn aspects of the Government's programme.

In the final debate on the Nationalisation Bill in 1976, both party leaders agreed that the matter of ship-repairing was not a great issue of principle. But while on the Labour side this point was emphasised so as to illustrate how foolish it would be to jeopardise the relationship between the two Houses (over a 'fragment of an industry'), Lord Carrington argued that this was exactly the sort of issue where the powers left with the Lords under the Parliament Acts ought to be used, and he quoted Herbert Morrison's statement (cited above) in support of this view: if the Lords were to perform a revising function effectively, then it would also be necessary, from time to time at least, to make use of its power (HL Debs, 22 November 1976, cols 1657–88).

This illustrates the ambiguity which surrounds the retention of power by the House of Lords. In so far as power is necessary for the Lords to act as a constitutional watchdog, then such power may be viewed as rather like the nuclear deterrent: to be kept in reserve, but to be used only once in extreme circumstances. In so far as power is necessary simply to ensure that adequate notice is taken of the Lords as a revising body, then a short delaying power is all that is necessary, long enough only to impose some awkwardness on the Government and perhaps partially to alert a slumbering public. This exercise of power should not give rise to any kind of constitutional clash or crisis. But many years of non-use of such power had created an assumption (encouraged by such statements as Lord Carrington's in 1967) that *any* exercise of power by the House of Lords must be a matter of supreme constitutional importance.

This analysis could be taken as indicating the desirability of keeping separate these two aspects of power: namely, the power to ensure that the Lords remains an effective revising body, and the power to defend important constitutional principles. The 1911 Parliament Act, by making special provision for any bill to extend the lifetime of a Parliament, pointed the way to such a distinction. Defining precisely a category of subjects upon which the House of Lords retained a power of veto (or at least a strong power, appropriate to genuine constitutional issues) would be difficult, and may be tantamount to producing a written constitution. While the power to be a constitutional check needs to be a strong power, the power to ensure that legislative revision is taken seriously need be only a brief delaying power. The 1968 White Paper proposed a six-month delay from the date of disagreement between the two Houses, which would be quite long enough to be effective.

The power of delay was used when the Lords rejected the War Crimes Bill in 1990. Most of those involved on both sides of the argument about the merits of this particular bill were at pains to point out that no constitutional crisis arose as a result of the action taken by the House of Lords. This view seemed to be borne out by the sequence of events (see Chapter 5). But in the longer term the constitutional significance of the whole episode may lie more in what it revealed about the attitude of the contemporary Conservative Party to the unreformed House of Lords. From the very commencement of debate about the possibility of introducing legislation to enable prosecutions to be brought against alleged war criminals, the view of the House of Lords had been made clear – in particular, the debate held on 4 December 1989 contained many powerful speeches arguing against such legislation. But ministers appeared to take no notice of the views of the House. In the same month the Commons held a very unsatisfactory three-hour debate on the subject, at the end of which MPs voted 348 to 123 in favour of the principle of legislation. A bill was duly introduced and passed through the Commons, but when it reached the Lords there was little surprise when peers threw it out, though the majority by which they did so – 207 to 74 – did cause some raised eyebrows. The

Government could easily then have decided to let the bill drop, but instead it was reintroduced under Parliament Act procedures in 1991.

When the Lords again debated it in April 1991, some peers who had originally opposed the bill took the view that given the inevitability of its passage into law following its approval for a second time by the Commons, it would now be better to give it a second reading, with a view to trying to amend it in committee to remove its most objectionable features. In particular Lord Bridge of Harwich, a serving Lord of Appeal, argued this 'pragmatic' case in a powerful speech which plainly influenced several other peers; no fewer than twenty-two who had voted against the bill in 1990 voted for its second reading in 1991. But other peers argued that it would be impossible to amend the bill satisfactorily, and that the House would look ridiculous if it simply reversed a view it had so overwhelmingly expressed the previous year: 'We are a House of Peers, not a House of wimps', said Lord Shawcross. The bill was rejected – by 131 votes to 109 – and then, without further debate in the Commons, it went straight for Royal Assent.

On the face of it, no constitutional impropriety attended the passage of this bill. Yet it could well be argued that the readiness with which the Conservative Government and the House of Commons brushed aside the views of the House of Lords was indicative of so changed an attitude to the House that its longer-term future had certainly been made much less secure. This was a bill that had not been included in any manifesto. It had been introduced by the Government, but no whip had been applied to secure its passage. There was no widespread public demand for the bill. It involved ethical questions, issues of conscience and public morality to an unusual degree. Present and active in all the debates on this bill were the law lords, some bishops and many former political and some military leaders. The Government and the House of Commons had treated the House with little short of contempt on a subject upon which peers were entitled to expect that their opinions would be given serious weight.

Or were they? For whatever expertise and whatever distinction many peers might be thought to have, one thing they all lacked: not one of them owed their position in the Lords to election. The boldness, if not the arrogance, of elected persons characterised the Lower House. The House of Lords might speak with the authority of experience and expertise, but not with the authority of democratic persons. As a result, the legitimacy of the House has become threadbare and its effectiveness even as a revising chamber called into question (see, for example, Sheila Gunn, *The Times*, 23 April 1991).

The present House may share in what Lord Hailsham once described as the priceless advantage of immemorial antiquity which characterises the British Constitution. In the British context this confers upon the House of Lords an element of legitimacy. But institutions need to adapt to a changing environment. To some extent the Lords has done this – for example, through the Life Peerages Act. But has its adaptation been adequate? Discussion of this question takes us on to consider the composition of the House of Lords.

Composition

The argument thus far in this chapter has been that as regards both functions and powers, while present arrangements are not ideal, they are nevertheless satisfactory. The functions of the House of Lords could usefully be developed somewhat, and if a clearer understanding of the distinction between power to defend basic constitutional principles and power to ensure an effective revising role could be developed, then this would be helpful. But composition is a problem.

From a practical point of view, the present mixture of hereditary and life peers may provide a body capable of performing most of the functions of the House adequately, at least under a Conservative Government. Though the membership favours the Conservative Party, there is no longer an overall party majority, and in any case there is enough independent-mindedness among peers for the House of Lords to be awkward enough, at times, to a Conservative Government. Legislation is revised, and at least some constitutional excesses are checked (as, for example, the proposal for an interim body to replace the GLC in 1984). But under a Labour Government this is not the case. Because a Labour Government is defeated as a matter of routine in the Lords' division lobbies, the Commons also, as a matter of routine, is asked to cancel Lords' amendments. The revising function is less well discharged, resulting possibly in the House becoming factious and digging in its heels even on matters for which the Government can claim an electoral mandate (as in 1976 over ship-repairing), or perhaps being intimidated into not using its power to check the Government when some constitutional impropriety is being perpetrated (as in 1967 over the postponement of elections in London).

This is the manifest consequence of the absurdity by which a parliamentary chamber contains a permanent built-in superiority for one party. But can the manner of composing the chamber be altered so as to avoid this?

There are three basic ways in which the House of Lords may be composed – inheritance, appointment and election. In effect the Lords has always been composed of a mixture of the first two methods, a combination of peers by succession and those themselves created hereditary or life peers, together with Lords Spiritual. The balance has recently moved in favour of appointed members, especially among the active element.

Little need be said about inheritance. It may so happen that individuals of great ability or unusual experience arise through succession, but many others with neither of these attributes also inherit peerages. The great disadvantage of a House composed in this way is that it reinforces the class division which remains one of the besetting weaknesses of British society. Abolishing hereditary membership of the Lords would on its own, of course, do precious little about this (one must keep a sense of proportion!), but the retention of this system of membership is indicative of an unwillingness seriously to tackle the legacy imposed by a class-based society and a class-based party system. But even those who repudiate the relevance of the above remarks must recognise that succession no longer establishes an acceptable claim to the legitimate exercise of power in a democratic society. Indeed, it is the very recognition of this fact which has made the Lords so reluctant to use its remaining powers and threatened it, at times, with extinction.

As to appointment, the drawback of the present method is the patronage power it allows a prime minister. The effectiveness of such patronage depends on the eagerness of recipients and potential recipients for the honour in question, but there seems little doubt that in recent years demand has been high. Any extension of the power of patronage would be unwelcome and ought to be resisted. The fact that the 1968 reform proposals, had they been implemented, would have resulted in a House composed entirely through the patronage of successive prime ministers was the greatest single reason for their demise – and that was before Mr Wilson's resignation honours list in 1976!

At present the only constraints upon a prime minister in regard to the exercise of this patronage are the honours scrutiny committee (with the right to veto obviously unsuitable candidates), possibly the Monarch (who might in some circumstances conceivably resist some awards), and the more general constraint of convention by which a certain number of nominations must be invited from the leaders of opposition parties. Assuming that any reform would leave the Upper House still, in part, composed through appointment, a more formalised machinery for initiating suggestions should be composed, maybe an expanded honours scrutiny committee which would be obliged to report on the balance of party membership and the range of expertise and experience represented in, and omitted from, the House of Lords. Perhaps a Speaker's conference should be called to define a formula which prime ministers would be required to observe in making nominations. Beyond that would lie the possibility of creating a system of appointment by committee, but this could too easily degenerate into producing even more of the safe, unimaginative, dull appointments that critics claim the present system already achieves.

Another form of appointment sometimes advocated is to extend the *ex officio* principle already embodied in the House through the bishops and the law lords. This sounds plausible, but at least two serious objections can be immediately mentioned. First, a considerable difficulty arises in defining precisely what office-holders would qualify, and how any list agreed upon at one time could later be altered. Second, it is doubtful whether a House composed in this way would be other than highly fragmented. In any case the present House of Lords does, to a considerable degree, represent the community in its functional aspects, informally and in a rather random way. So too does the House of Commons. Most groups have their spokesmen in Parliament already, and although these are merely spokesmen, this form of representation may be more suited to our parliamentary system than a formal incorporation into Parliament of office-holders within such groups. The argument that consent may be more readily mobilised for measures agreed to by a corporatist-style second chamber may have some validity. But the question does arise whether the leaders of such groups would actually take part in a second chamber which had no real power.

The remaining method which could be used to compose the House of Lords is some form of election. Most recent schemes of reform have advocated a House at least in part elected. Sometimes indirect election has been proposed, but there have been few advocates of such a change, unless it were carried through as part of a more sweeping reform – say one introducing regional assemblies throughout the UK (Crowther-Hunt and Peacock, 1973). Direct election has more frequently been suggested, usually on the basis of proportional representation, with only part of the House coming up for re-election at any one time. The Home Committee recommended such a scheme (1978), as did a Labour MP in a Fabian pamphlet (Bell, 1981). Election could, of course, be combined with appointment and even inheritance. The Home Committee would have had a House composed by all three methods for a transitional period, until existing peers by succession died.

The obvious objection to election is that the Lords would become a rival to the Commons. Election by some method quite different from that used for the Lower House might only intensify rivalry because the reformed second chamber could reasonably claim that its electoral legitimacy (derived through a proportional system) was greater than that of the Commons. Furthermore, any proposed reform would have to be accepted by the Commons, and it is extremely difficult to see a Lower House so jealous of its own position agreeing to such a change. The only likely basis for such a reform would be the introduction of an accountable regional tier of government. Perhaps the most one can say in 1991 is that if a devolution of power to the regions ever does take place, then second-chamber reform ought to be included as part of a general new settlement.

While it is difficult to see a reform which involved an elected House being introduced, other possible reforms are open to even greater objections. Should the House of Lords, then, be left alone or abolished? In 1978 the Home Committee stated that to keep the status quo was 'not a prudent policy. Indeed we are doubtful whether it is a policy at all.' That was said in the wake of the conflicts of 1975–6, at a time when 'at best the present House of Lords faces gradual but relentless atrophy' (*ibid.*, paras 66 and 68). Matters look at least a little different in 1991.

Sometimes when abolition is advocated, replacement is intended; such is the position of the Labour MP Stuart Bell in his somewhat misleadingly entitled pamphlet *How to Abolish the Lords* (Bell, 1981). In 1989 the Labour Party, in its Policy Review document, indicated that it would abolish the House and replace it with an elected second chamber. Against this, one has to say that radical discontinuity of the kind that totally sweeps away one institution and replaces it with an entirely new body has not been characteristic of British constitutional developments, and where it has taken place (for example, in local government) it has not, on the whole, been successful. (This may be regrettable or it may be laudable, but that is beside the point.) Change that adapted the present House of Lords, perhaps quite radically as the Home Committee proposed, is both more realistic and more likely to endure.

Labour's proposals were open to other objections. No ministers would sit in their proposed second House and no bills would be introduced there. As to power, for the great bulk of legislation the new House would only be able to ask the Commons to think again, to vote once more, no doubt sometimes at least under the pressure of a very tight guillotine. Such limitations at least prompt the question: What kind of people would compete for election to this new second chamber? It certainly seems unlikely that many of the present members would do so. Nor can folk with the kinds of experience generally thought desirable in a revising chamber be expected to clamour for membership of such a body! True, this proposed new chamber would have the power to delay for the lifetime of a Parliament measures affecting designated fundamental rights. But how would such a list would be drawn up, and who would have the responsibility of deciding when and how draft legislation infringed such rights? It does not appear that the Labour Party has given much consideration to these matters. At least, a debate in the Lords in 1990 (25 April) was singularly unrevealing.

Some who stress – and on the whole approve of – the gradual development and continuity of the Constitution have foreseen as part of this process the eventual abolition of the House of Lords through its own decay and collapse. Bagehot spoke of atrophy in the mid nineteenth century, just as the Home Committee did in the late 1970s. Nevil Johnson, himself a member of the Home Committee, saw the House of Lords as so marginal as to be almost irrelevant (Johnson, 1977, p. 43). But such decline to the point of possible collapse has – at least temporarily – been arrested.

If the House of Lords was abolished without replacement, the most obvious immediate effect would be the loss of opportunities to improve legislation. It may be argued that reforms in Commons procedure and increased numbers of parliamentary draftsmen could reduce the need for the extra legislative stages provided by the Lords. But the House of Commons has shown itself much more concerned to preserve legislative procedures, which serve the purposes of traditional two-party conflict, than to introduce reforms to these procedures so that they serve the purpose of effective legislative scrutiny. Special standing committees have been virtually unused, and proposals designed to ensure that every part of a bill receives at least some time in standing committee have been eschewed in favour of continued use of the 'guillotine'. To abolish the Lords or even to allow it to collapse quietly, without ensuring some *quid pro quo* changes in the Commons, would be foolish. If some legislation leaving the Commons now is unfit to be let loose on the public (Griffith, 1974, p. 231), this situation would only worsen.

Abolition may be advocated as part of a process involving the removal or diminution of every obstacle to the power wielded by a Commons majority. A concern for strong government may be seen as paramount over a concern to maintain parliamentary government; if so, the second chamber should be removed and the Commons subdued, and elective dictatorship allowed to flourish. The very lack of legitimacy of the present House of Lords is a convenience to those so minded. Any reform which enhanced its legitimacy could be a setback to their cause, and is accordingly resisted. But even the present House of Lords may prove much more difficult to abolish for all sorts of practical reasons (Crowther-Hunt, 1980) as well as more theoretical reasons (Mirfield, 1979). Awareness of this fact was no doubt responsible for the failure to include the Labour Party's 1977 Conference decision to abolish the House of Lords outright in its subsequent election manifestos.

Conclusion

The basis on which the House of Lords is composed remains unaltered because no sufficient agreement about an alternative basis has ever yet existed. This does not mean that the way in which the House of Lords is now composed commands any widespread support: it simply happens to be the status quo. The children of patronage mingle with the children of aristocrats, and neither group has a more obvious claim than the other to be afforded places in a modern Parliament.

Major obstacles lie in the way of replacing the existing House with an elected second chamber, but it is inconceivable that the House in its present form should continue indefinitely. And it would be quite wrong to expect a Labour Government to allow a House which remains dominated by hereditary and Conservative peers to continue. A simple measure excluding all hereditary peers from the House (or at least from the right to vote) would be the most straightforward way of reforming the Lords. Given the contempt shown for the House by recent Conservative Governments, it is doubtful whether such a change would meet with any very serious resistance. And once the hereditary peers had been excluded it might well be possible to sit down and discuss sensibly the introduction of an elected element to go alongside the nominated peers.

It has usually been crisis which has produced decisive constitutional change. It was a crisis which produced the 1911 Parliament Act, not the measured conclusions of the 'good and the great' at the Bryce Commission. But the Life Peerage Act did not arise out of crisis. And that simple measure, introduced without all-party agreement, is probably the kind of change which a Government of the future will introduce.

Meanwhile, the House has shown a remarkable resilience. It has adapted and expanded its activities. It has worked its way back from the margins of political life. It has, to a surprising extent, regained an importance within the whole business of government.

Appendix A

Expenses Payments for Peers and Remuneration for Office-Holders in the House of Lords

Before 1946 no allowances of any kind were payable to peers in respect of their attendance at the House of Lords. Earlier generations had assumed that peers were men of substance, unlikely to be concerned about such trifling matters as expenses payments. Ministers did receive salaries, but they were paid in respect of their ministerial office, on identical terms to the salaries paid to Commons ministers.

The post-war Attlee Government introduced a travel allowance in 1946, to which was added in 1957 an expenses allowance. Both of these were subsequently adjusted and extended in scope. During this period the salaries of ministers in the two Houses began to diverge as Commons ministers received an expenses allowance and then a parliamentary salary additional to their ministerial salary. Also a gradual increase took place in the number of office-holders in the House who became entitled to a salary. Each of these matters is briefly examined in this appendix.

A. Travel Allowances

In 1946 peers became entitled to claim for the cost of first-class rail travel between their nearest home station and London. An 'assiduity' rule allowed claims only from peers who attended over one-third of the sittings of the House (though in 1947 this was relaxed for peers who lived in Scotland). The object of this rule was to prevent casual attenders claiming for travel to London. However, the rule came in for increasing criticism on the grounds that many peers who attended less than a third of the time did contribute significantly to the work of the Lords. It was eventually abolished in 1972.

Meanwhile, in 1961, a car mileage allowance had been introduced as an alternative to rail fares, limited at first to the cost of equivalent rail travel. The car allowance was gradually increased and in the 1970s became linked to similar allowances payable to civil servants. After the latter had become graduated according to car engine size, MPs decided to accept a steeply tiered allowance, but peers voted (by 128 to 64) not to do so; instead they kept a uniform allowance based on medium-sized cars. Many peers believed that in so doing they were acting in a more responsible way than MPs (26 July 1984).

Gradually the basis of travel payments has altered from a system offering help only towards the rail fares of regular attenders to a system which basically pays the travel costs involved for any peer who attends the House of Lords.

B. The Attendance or Reimbursement of Expenses Allowance

The introduction of an expenses allowance in 1957 was open to criticism on three grounds. First, it was officially described as a 'daily attendance allowance', which implied that it could be claimed simply on the ground of attendance, whereas the intention was that only out-of-pocket expenses directly incurred in attendance should be payable. In 1981 it was officially renamed a 'reimbursement of expenses allowance'.

Second, the definition of expenses which could legitimately be claimed was left vague – deliberately so, it would seem – in 1957, but never properly clarified until 1975, in which year the Top Salaries Review Board found 'a great deal of confusion' among peers about the expenses to which they were entitled. A third, and related point, was that from the outset it was made clear that peers would not have to produce any evidence about their actual expenditures; the Leader of the Commons, R. A. Butler, thought such procedures would be 'undignified' for those he termed 'our distinguished brethren in another place' (HC Debs, 9 July 1957, cols 231–2).

The upper limit of the allowance was initially set at three guineas per day (£3.15), then raised to four and a half guineas (£4.72) in 1964 following the Lawrence Committee Report (Cmnd 2516). Thereafter, by resolution of the House the sum increased in 1970 to £6.50 and by stages to £13.50 in 1975.

The Top Salaries Review Body (TSRB) made the first thorough examination of the whole subject in 1975 (Cmnd 6749). A survey of peers found that 82 per cent of those eligible to claim expenses did so, and that 55 per cent thought the permitted maximum inadequate. In its report the TSRB recommended that four separate headings of permissible expenditure be identified: overnight accommodation, day subsistence, secretarial expenses, and finally – on the grounds that 'a revising chamber should be a well-briefed chamber' – the purchase of journals, subscriptions to bodies relevant to a peer's work in the House of Lords, and similar expenditure.

If implemented in full, the recommendation of this report would have taken the maximum daily allowance from £13.50 to £24.50. The Labour Government decided it could not do this because of its newly introduced pay policy; this was a curious decision given the emphasis that had always been placed on the fact that the peers' allowance was merely for expenses and not in any sense remuneration. The then prevailing £13.50 allowance did, however, cover all the expenses recommended by the TSRB except for overnight accommodation, so the effect of the Government's decision was to discriminate against peers living at a distance from London. For peers obliged to stay overnight in London a maximum of £16.50 was allowed from March 1977.

In 1979 the TSRB recommended that the fourth element in the allowance (as recommended in 1975) should be merged with the third, creating in effect a secretarial and research allowance; this was to meet objections to the four-element system which it had been suggested peers would find difficult to operate (Cmnd 7598). At the same time it recommended a maximum of £36 for peers requiring overnight accommodation, £17.50 for others, and this was accepted in full by the newly elected Conservative Government.

In 1982–3 the TSRB again made a full investigation of the expenses allowance system (Cmnd 8881). A survey showed highest dissatisfaction with the allowance system among the most regular-attending peers, but the Review Body felt unable to recommend remuneration as such for any group of peers. However, substantial rises were agreed, taking the daily allowance to £33 for those not requiring overnight accommodation and to £73 for those in need of such accommodation (HL Debs, 25 July 1983, cols 1370–4). Since 1984 these allowances have been linked to changes in civil servants' pay and expenses, which has obviated the need for any public announcement about increases being made in the Lords (HL Debs, 26 July 1984, cols 401–6). However, annual adjustments have been made: from 1 August 1990 peers could claim up to £68 for overnight accommodation; up to £26 for day subsistence and incidental travel; and up to £27 for secretarial expenses, a total of £121.

In 1987 the TSRB made a full inquiry into MPs' and peers' secretarial costs. This followed a Commons vote in which, to the anger of the Government, MPs awarded themselves a 52 per cent increase in their secretarial expenses allowance, at the same time as peers accepted a much more modest increase. A survey showed once again that it was the active peers who felt most keenly the inadequacy of the allowance. As stated in Chapter 4, the report of the Review Body (Cmd 131) particularly singled out the more or less full-time back-bench peers and the opposition front-bench spokesmen as most in need of additional help. Nothing, however, was done to meet the needs of these groups.

C. Salaries Payable to Ministers in the Lords

Ministers in both Houses received identical salaries until 1946 (and by modern standards these were generous salaries – that for a senior minister was fixed at £5,000 in 1830, and remained at this level until 1964). In 1946 ministers in the Commons became entitled to receive £500 of an MP's salary to cover the costs of constituency representation; subsequently this was increased, and in 1972 a parliamentary salary for Commons ministers was introduced. As a result the total salaries of junior ministers in the Lords (as well as of Lords in Waiting) fell considerably below those of Commons ministers, and lower even than the salaries of back-bench MPs. This state of affairs continued throughout the 1970s, because though the matter was regarded as anomalous by the TSRB in 1976, the Labour Government was unwilling to rectify it lest this appear to breach its incomes policy. (By 1979 MPs were paid £6,897, junior ministers in the Lords £6,622, and Lords in Waiting £5,522.)

The TSRB emphasised, in 1976 and again in 1979, that higher ministerial salaries for peers could be justified only if their ministerial responsibilities were greater than those of Commons ministers. This it had not found to be the case. However, Lords ministers did become entitled during the 1970s to a limited secretarial allowance for their parliamentary work, and also to a London salary supplement.

In the early 1980s the financial position of junior members of the Government front bench in the Lords attracted some attention, with questions being asked in the House (see 7 July 1980, col. 880; 12 March 1981, col. 379). In addition to increasing all salaries substantially in 1980, the Government decided, in 1981, to override the TSRB recommendation and pay ministers in the Lords higher ministerial salaries than their Commons counterparts. This decision received support in 1983 when management consultants commissioned by the TSRB examined the jobs concerned and recommended higher pay for Lords ministers on the grounds that they did have to do more work (though not necessarily more important work) than Commons ministers (see pp. 82–3). By 1991 Lords in Waiting received salaries £3,500 ahead of those paid to back-bench MPs, with junior ministers receiving £3,500 more again. While the relative pay of Lords ministers has improved greatly, their salaries remain modest by comparison with those payable elsewhere in the public sector (let alone at senior levels in the private sector). Cabinet ministers in the Lords received £48,381 in 1991, ministers of state £43,010, and Lords in Waiting £32,519. For comparison's sake the standard rate for a permanent secretary was £76,320 and for a senior principal (or grade 6) just under £34,000. In 1991 the Ministerial and Other Pensions and Salaries Bill introduced an overnight allowance for ministers in the Lords fixed at a level of 220 times the overnight allowance for peers. At the same time the London supplement for ministers was withdrawn. The new allowance was taxable, giving it an initial value of some £7,700 per annum (see HC Debs, 31 January 1991, cols. 1137–63; HL Debs, 26 February 1991, cols. 871–80).

D. Office-Holders

If we exclude government ministers (including the Lord Chancellor), prior to 1965 only one peer received a salary because of the office he held in the House of Lords, namely the Lord Chairman of Committees, whose salary has been long-standing and was linked to that of his opposite number in the Commons, Chairman of Ways and Means. In 1974 the salaried post of Principal Deputy Chairman of Committees was created (see Chapter 4).

In 1965 remuneration for the Leader of the Opposition and the Opposition Chief Whip was introduced. At first the Opposition Leader was paid £2,000 (compared with £3,250 for MPs). By 1979 this was £4,403, still well behind the MPs' salary, but the TSRB stated in its report that year that the post had 'hitherto been seriously undervalued'. From 1980 the salaries payable to the Opposition Leader and Chief Whip moved ahead rapidly, until by the late 1980s the holders of these offices were paid middle-ranking ministerial salaries.

Conclusion

Since 1980 both the allowances which peers may claim and the salaries paid to those who hold offices have improved very markedly. None the less, the whole expenses allowance system remains unsatisfactory because it fails to differentiate between peers whose commitments to the House and contributions to the work of the House vary enormously. However, the introduction of salaries for peers – or even some narrowly defined category of peers, such as opposition front-bench members – remains problematical. A more satisfactory system of recompensing peers is unlikely to be achieved until some fundamental reform of the composition of the House of Lords is brought about.

Appendix B

Peerages Disclaimed, 1963–91

Tony Benn MP	Viscount Stansgate	1963
John Grigg	Lord Altrincham	1963
Sir Alec Douglas-Home	Earl of Home	1963
(Lord Home of the Hirsel since 1974)		
Quintin Hogg	Viscount Hailsham	1963
(Lord Hailsham of Saint Marylebone since 1970)		
Charles Fitzroy	Lord Southampton	1964
William Collier	Lord Monkswell	1964
Sir Max Aitken	Lord Beaverbrook	1964
Victor Montagu	Earl of Sandwich	1964
Sir Hugh Fraser	Lord Fraser of Allander	1966
Anthony Lambton MP	Earl of Durham	1970
(also known as Viscount Lambton, MP)		
Dr Alan Sanderson	Lord Sanderson of Ayot	1971
Charles Reith	Lord Reith	1972
Arthur Silkin	Lord Silkin	1972
George Archibald	Lord Archibald	1975
T.O. Lewis	Lord Merthyr	1977

Four of the above disclaimers had died by 1991. These were William Collier in 1984, Sir Max Aitken in 1985, Sir Hugh Fraser in 1987, and Charles Fitzroy in 1990. The heirs to the Monkswell, Beaverbrook, and Southampton peerages all decided to take up their peerages, the former two becoming active members of the House of Lords, Lord Monkswell on the Labour benches and Lord Beaverbrook on the Conservative side. Sir Hugh Fraser left no heirs, so the peerage he had disclaimed became extinct upon his death.

Principal Sources

A. The main official sources used in this work have been:

House of Lords Hansard, cited in text as HL Debs, followed by date and column number, e.g. HL Debs, 26 October 1984, col. 343.

House of Commons Hansard, cited as HC Debs, and then as above.

Journals of the House of Lords (published sessionally).

House of Lords Committee Reports, cited as HL followed by number and session in which published, e.g. HL 31 (1986–7).

House of Commons Committee Reports (references given in the same way as those for House of Lords Reports).

The Standing Orders of the House of Lords Relating to Public Business, 1989 edition (SOs).

The Companion to the Standing Orders, 1989 edition (Companion).

Command Papers, Cmnd, Cd, Cmd, followed by number and year of publication.

The following official sources should be particularly mentioned:

Cd 9038 (1918)	Report of the Conference on Reform of the Second Chamber, Chairman Lord Bryce (Bryce Commission).
Cmnd 7380 (1948)	Parliament Bill, 1947. Agreed Statement on Conclusion of Conference of Party Leaders.
Cmnd 3799 (1968)	House of Lords Reform.
HL 141 (1976–7)	First Report of the Select Committee of the House of Lords on Practice and Procedure.
HL 9 (1987–8)	Report by the Group on the Working of the House.

All the above are published by Her Majesty's Stationery Office.

B. The major reference works used have been:

Who's Who, Dod's Parliamentary Companion, Whitaker's Almanac and *Keesing's Contemporary Archives*. The edition of *Erskine May's Parliamentary Practice* used and cited has been the 21st, edited by C. J. Boulton, published in 1989 by Butterworth.

C. Information has been supplied by the House of Lords' Information Office, the office of the Leader of the House and Chief Whip, and by the whips' offices of the other parties.

D. Interviews were held with some 45 peers, especially in 1984, but also intermittently before and since.

E. Major works on the House of Lords. Particular mention should be made of the following:

Bromhead, P.A.	(1958) *The House of Lords and Contemporary Politics, 1911–57*, Routledge & Kegan Paul.
Morgan, Janet	(1975) *The House of Lords and the Labour Government 1964–70*, Oxford University Press.
Baldwin, Nicholas	(1985) *The House of Lords*, unpublished PhD Thesis, Exeter University.

Bibliography

Bagehot, W. (1867 1st edn and 1963 edn) *The English Constitution*, Fontana.

Baldwin, Nicholas (1985) *The House of Lords*, unpublished PhD thesis, Exeter University.

Bates, St John (1985) 'Select Committees in the House of Lords', in G. Drewry (ed.) *The New Select Committees*, Oxford University Press.

Beamish, D. R. and Shell, D. R. (eds) (forthcoming, 1992) *The House of Lords at Work: A Study of the 1988–89 Session*, Oxford University Press.

Beith, A. (1981) 'Prayers Unanswered: Parliamentary Scrutiny of Statutory Instruments', *Parliamentary Affairs*, Vol. XXXIV, No. 2, pp. 165–73.

Bell, S. (1981) *How to Abolish the Lords*, Fabian Tract No. 476.

Beloff, N. (1976) *Freedom under Foot*, Temple Smith.

Blewett, N. (1972) *The Peers, the Parties and the People*, Macmillan.

Blom-Cooper, L. and Drewry, G. (1972) *Final Appeal: A Study of the House of Lords in its Judicial Capacity*, Oxford University Press.

Borthwick, R. (1973) 'Public Bill Committees in the House of Lords', *Parliamentary Affairs*, Vol. XXVI, No. 4, pp. 440–53.

Borthwick, R. (forthcoming, 1992) 'Non-Legislative Debate and Questions' in Beamish and Shell, *op. cit.*.

Boyd-Carpenter, J. (Lord) (1980) *Way of Life*, Sidgwick & Jackson.

Braham, S. (1986) *A Hard Core of Wind; Inside the Lords*, Val Publishing.

Bromhead, P. A. (1958) *The House of Lords and Contemporary Politics, 1911–57*, Routledge & Kegan Paul.

Bromhead, P. A. and Shell, D. R. (1967) 'The Lords and their House', *Parliamentary Affairs*, Vol. XX, No. 4, pp. 337–49.

Bruce-Gardyne, J. (Lord) (1980) 'Late Nights on the Ermined Treadmill', *Sunday Telegraph*, 2 August 1980.

Butler, D. (1976) 'The Australian Crisis of 1975', *Parliamentary Affairs*, Vol. XXIX, No. 2, pp. 201–10.

Butt, R. (1978) 'The Case for a Stronger Second Chamber', in J. P. Mackintosh (ed.) *People and Parliament*, Saxon House (for Hansard Society).

Carrington, Lord (1988) *Reflect on Things Past*, Collins.

Chester, D. N. and Bowring, N. (1962) *Questions in Parliament*, Oxford University Press.

Crick, B. (1st edn 1964, 2nd edn 1968) *Reform of Parliament*, Weidenfeld & Nicolson.

Crossman, R. H. S. (1975 and 1976) *Diaries of a Cabinet Minister*, Vol. 1 and Vol. 2, Jonathan Cape.

Crowther-Hunt, Norman (Lord) (1980) 'Labour's Threat to the Lords', *The Listener*, 4 December.

Crowther-Hunt, Norman (Lord) and Peacock, Prof. A. (1973) *Royal Commission on the Constitution, Memorandum of Dissent*, Cmnd 5460–II.

Devlin, Lord (Patrick) (1956) *Trial by Jury*, Stevens.

Devlin, Lord (Patrick) (1965) *The Enforcement of Morals*, Oxford University Press.

Drewry, G. and Brock, J. (1971) 'Prelates in Parliament', *Parliamentary Affairs*, Vol. XXIV, No. 3, pp. 222–50.

Drewry, G. and Brock, J. (1983) *The Impact of Women on the House of Lords*, Centre for the Study of Public Policy, University of Strathclyde.

Drewry, G. and Brock, J. (forthcoming, 1992) 'The House of Lords and Government Legislation', in Beamish and Shell, *op. cit.*

Drewry, G. and Burton, I. (1980) *Legislation and Public Policy: Public Bills in the 1970–74 Parliament*, Macmillan.

Franklin, M. (1986) 'MPs' Objections to Televising Parliament', *Parliamentary Affairs*, Vol. 39, No. 3.

Gaitskell, H. (1983) *The Diary of Hugh Gaitskell 1945–56*, ed. Philip M. Williams, Jonathan Cape.

Ganz, G. (1987) *Quasi-Legislation*, Sweet & Maxwell.

Ganz, G. (1989) 'Quasi-Legislation', in *Third Commonwealth Conference on Delegated Legislation*, HMSO.

Grantham, C. and Hodgson, C. M. (1985) 'Structural Changes: The Use of Committees', in P. Norton (ed.) *Parliament in the 1980s*, Basil Blackwell.

Griffith, J. A. G. (1974) *The Parliamentary Scrutiny of Government Bills*, George Allen & Unwin.

Griffith, J. A. G. (1981) 'Standing Committees in the Commons', in M. Ryle and S. A. Walkland (eds) *The Commons Today*, Fontana.

Hailsham, Lord (1976) 'Elective Dictatorship', BBC.

Hayter, P. D. G. (1991) 'The Parliamentary Monitoring of Science and Technology in Britain', *Government and Opposition*, Vol. 26, No. 2, pp. 147–166.

Heffer, E. S. (1973) *The Class Struggle in Parliament*, Collins.

Hennessy, P. (1987) 'The Other Opposition', Transcript of Radio 4 'Analysis' programme.

Hindell, K. and Simms, M. (1971) *Abortion Law Reformed*, Owen.

Home, Lord (1978) *Report of the Review Committee on the Second Chamber*, Conservative Political Centre.

Johnson, N. (1977) *In Search of the Constitution*, Pergamon Press.

Jones, G. W. (1966) 'A Forgotten Right Discovered', *Parliamentary Affairs*, Vol. XIX, No. 3, pp. 363–72.

Judge, D. (ed.) (1983) *The Politics of Parliamentary Reform*, Heinemann.

Kolinsky, M. (1975) 'Parliamentary Scrutiny of European Legislation', *Government and Opposition*, Vol. 10, No. 1, pp. 46–69.

Laski, H. (1938) *Parliamentary Government in England*, George Allen & Unwin.

Le May, G. (1979) *The Victorian Constitution: Conventions, Usages and Contingencies*, Duckworth.

Leopold, P. (1985) 'The Compulsory Detention of Peers', *Public Law*, pp. 9–14.

Leopold, P. (1989) 'The Freedom of Peers from Arrest', *Public Law*, pp. 398–406.

Livingstone, K. (1987) *If Voting Changed Anything, They'd Abolish It*, Collins.

Longford, Lord (F. Pakenham) (1974) *The Grain of Wheat*, Collins.

Miers, D. and Brock, J. (forthcoming, 1992) 'Government Bills in the House of Lords: Case Studies', in Beamish and Shell, *op. cit.*

Mirfield, P. (1979) 'Can the House of Lords be Lawfully Abolished?', *Law Quarterly Review*.

Moran, M. (1977) *Politics of Industrial Relations*, Macmillan.

Morgan, J. (1975) *The House of Lords and the Labour Government*, Oxford University Press.

Northfield, Lord (Donald Chapman) (1978) 'Reforming Procedure in the House of Lords', in D. Butler and A. Halsey (eds) *Policy and Politics*, Macmillan.

Norton, P. (ed.) (1985) *Parliament in the 1980s*, Basil Blackwell.

Powell, J. Enoch and Wallis, K. (1968) *The House of Lords in the Middle Ages*, Weidenfeld & Nicolson.

Punnett, R. M. (1973), *Front Bench Opposition*, Heinemann.

Redcliffe-Maud, John (Lord) (1981) *Experiences of an Optimist*, Hamish Hamilton.

Rhodes-James, R. (1986) *Anthony Eden*, Weidenfeld & Nicolson.

Richards, P. (1963) *Patronage and British Government*, George Allen & Unwin.

Richards, P. (1970) *Parliament and Conscience*, George Allen & Unwin.

Rippon of Hexham, Lord (1989) 'Henry VIII Clauses', in *Third Commonwealth Conference on Delegated Legislation*, HMSO.

Roth, A. (1972) *Lord on the Board*, Parliamentary Profile Services.

Roth, A. (1977) *Sir Harold Wilson*, Macdonald & Jane's.

Roth, A. (1986) 'Mrs. Thatcher's other Chamber', *New Statesman*, 11 July.

Rush, M. (ed.) (1990) *Parliament and Pressure Politics*, Clarendon Press.

Rutherford, M. (1984) 'The Rise of the House of Lords', *Financial Times*, 23 March.

Shell, D. R. (1983) 'The House of Lords', in D. Judge (ed.) *The Politics of Parliamentary Reform*, Heinemann.

Shell, D. R. (1985) 'The House of Lords and the Thatcher Government', *Parliamentary Affairs*, Vol. 38, No. 1, pp. 16–32.

Shell, D. R. (1991) 'The House of Lords and Foreign Affairs', in C. Carstairs and R. Ware (eds) *Parliament and International Relations*, Open University Press.

Shell, D. R. (forthcoming, 1992) 'Questions in the Lords' in M. Franklin and P. Norton (eds) *Parliamentary Questions*, Oxford University Press.

Silk, P. (1987) *How Parliament Works*, Longman.

Sochart, E. A. (1988) 'Agenda Setting, The Role of Groups and the Legislative Process: The Prohibition of Female Circumcision in Britain', *Parliamentary Affairs*, Vol. 41, No. 4, pp. 508–526.

Stewart, M. (1980) *Life and Labour*, Sidgwick & Jackson.

Strang, William (Lord) (1956) *Home and Abroad*, Deutsch.

Theakston, K. (1987) *Junior Ministers in British Government*, Basil Blackwell.

Thomas, G. (Viscount Tonypandy) (1985) *George Thomas, Mr Speaker*, Arrow.

Vincent, J. (1966) 'The House of Lords', *Parliamentary Affairs*, Vol. XIX, No. 4, pp. 475–85.

Walker, J. (1987) *The Queen Has Been Pleased*, Sphere Books.

Weston, C. C. (1965) *English Constitutional Theory and the House of Lords, 1556–1822*, Routledge & Kegan Paul.

Weston, C. C. (1986) 'Salisbury and the Lords, 1868-1895', in C. Jones and D. L. Jones (eds) *Peers, Politics and Power, 1603–1911*, Hambledon Press.

Whale, John (1985) 'Bishops in the Lords', *The Listener*, 8 August.

Wheeler-Booth, M. A. J. (1989) 'The Lords', Part IV of J. A. G. Griffith and M. Ryle, *Parliament: Functions, Practice and Procedure*, Sweet & Maxwell.

Wilson, H. (1971) *The Labour Government, 1964–70: A Personal Record*, Weidenfeld & Nicolson.

Windlesham, Lord (1975) 'The House of Lords: A Study of Influence Replacing Power', in *Politics in Practice*, Cape.

Index